Listening

to

His
Heartbeat

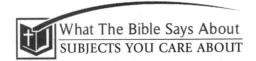

What The Bible Says About
SUBJECTS YOU CARE ABOUT

His Story — Our Response: What the Bible Says about Worship
Dinelle Frankland

The Life to Come: What the Bible Says about the Afterlife
Kenny Boles

Listening to His Heartbeat: What the Bible Says about the Heart of God
Harold Shank

Power from On High: What the Bible Says about the Holy Spirit
Jack Cottrell

Set Free: What the Bible Says about Grace
Jack Cottrell

Where Is God When We Suffer? What the Bible Says about Suffering
Lynn Gardner

Other Topics in the Planning:
The Church, The Doctrine of God, Prayer

What The Bible Says About
THE HEART OF GOD

Listening *to* His Heartbeat

Harold Shank

COLLEGE PRESS PUBLISHING COMPANY · JOPLIN, MISSOURI

International Standard Book Number: 978-0-89900-973-5

Abbreviations Used in this Book and Others in the Series

AD.....................*Anno Domini*
ASV ....American Standard Version
BC.....................Before Christ
KJV...................King James Version
LXX ....*Septuagint* (Greek Translation of OT)
MT ....Masoretic Text (Standard Hebrew OT)
NASB ....New American Standard Bible
NIV ....New International Version
NRSV ....New Revised Standard Version
NT....................New Testament
OT....................Old Testament
RSV ....Revised Standard Version

ABOUT THE SERIES

"What does the Bible say about that?" This is a question that should concern every Bible-believing Christian, whatever the particular subject being discussed. Granted, we know there are situations and activities that are not directly addressed by the Bible, because of changes in society, culture, and technology. However, if we truly believe that the Bible is to be our guide for living and especially for developing our relationship with God, then we need to look to it for information that will impact our everyday decisions. Even what may seem like abstract doctrinal matters will affect our religious practices, and if the Bible is indeterminate on a particular issue, then we need to know that too, so that we don't waste time on the kinds of controversies Paul warns about in 1 Timothy 1:4.

College Press Publishing Company is fully committed to equipping our customers as Bible students. In addition to commentary series and small study books on individual books of the Bible, this is not the first time we have done a series of books specifically dedicated to this question: "What DOES the Bible say?" Part of this stems from the background of CPPC as a publishing house of what has generally been known as the "Restoration Movement,"[1] a movement that gave rise to Churches of Christ and Christian Churches. The "restoration" of the movement's name refers to the desire to restore biblical teaching and emphases to our religious beliefs and activities.

It is important to understand what this series can and cannot do.

---

[1] In order to be more specific and recognize that these churches are not necessarily unique in the plea to restore the church of the apostles, it is also known as the "Stone-Campbell Movement," after the names of some of the 19th-century leaders of the movement.

Every author in the series will be filtering the exact words of the biblical text through a filter of his or her own best understanding of the implications of those words. Nor will the Bible be the only source to be quoted. Various human authors will inevitably be referenced either in support of the conclusions reached or to contradict their teachings. Keeping this in mind, you should use them as tools to direct your own study of the Bible, and use the "Berean principle" of studying carefully every part of the Bible to see "whether these things [are] so" (Acts 17:11, ASV). We would not be true to our own purpose if we encouraged you to take any book that we publish as the "last word" on any subject. Our plea, our desire, is to make "every Christian a Bible Student."

A WORD ABOUT FORMAT

In order to emphasize the theme of "What the Bible Says," we have chosen to place Scripture quotations and Scripture references in distinct typestyles to make them stand out. Use of these typestyles within quotations of other works should not be taken as an indication that the original author similarly emphasized the highlighted text.

FOREWORD

Futurists claim that the world's knowledge has doubled in the past 20 years and that it will again double in the next few years. More is known today about medicine, science, technology, and every other field than ever before, and the information explosion continues.

But what have we learned about the God who created us, planned for our eternal salvation, and one day will judge us?

In this present climate of learning no subject should compel us more than delving deeper into the heart of God. Who is God? What is He like? And what can we reliably know about His inner heart and nature?

This book is grounded in the conviction that God not only exists but that He has revealed Himself to us. This is a study that looks for ways to see into the divine heart through the many great stories in Scripture. In each one of them something of God's heart is revealed.

Some years ago I was blessed to study under John Macquarrie at Oxford University. His insightful lectures on the nature of God led to numerous questions from the class. This man seemed to see God from a depth of understanding well beyond many of us. The class was stirred to ask countless questions of this brilliant, yet unassuming man. One afternoon these queries prompted him to say, "You ask many questions about God as though I somehow might answer all of them. You see, any God that I might fully explain would be no greater than me." Macquarrie went on to encourage lifelong study of God with the reminder that while we can learn a great deal; we can never in this life fully understand the great God of this universe.

This Scripture-based study takes up the task to which Macquarrie called us. It skillfully searches the text for insight into God's mind, heart, and ultimately His very being. Because Scripture is the inspired revelation of God, its pages inherently contain much insight. Only because God is self-revealing do we know Him at all. The fact that a magnificent God shares His being with us is beyond comprehension, and yet from His self-revelation we catch a view of the loving God who wants us to know Him.

Harold Shank brings fresh understanding of the divine heart out of the experiences of his life. He planted a church in Milwaukee and later helped begin six inner-city churches in Memphis and three congregations in Ukraine. For 20 years he served one of the great churches of this country, the Highland Street Church of Christ. In 1996 Dr. Shank became the national spokesperson for the Christian Child and Family Services Association. Today in the university classroom he calls students to look beyond the mundane into the divine.

This work challenges readers to revisit familiar passages and seek nuanced revelations of the One who knows and loves us most. From this study will come newer understanding that is both deeper and more profound. *Listening to His Heartbeat* is important because it calls us to listen to God and to yearn for those deeper, more profound experiences with Him.

This book is a call to listen. Listen to God's word, and through that word to listen more carefully to the heartbeat of God. In listening, we find Him in new and fresh ways.

This book reminds me of Jeremiah's encouragement, *"Call to me and I will answer you and tell you great and unsearchable things you do not know."* (**Jer 33:3**).

Lynn A. McMillon, Ph.D.
Distinguished Professor of Bible
Dean, College of Biblical Studies
Oklahoma Christian University

ACKNOWLEDGEMENTS

What makes you smile? Chocolate? Coffee? Maybe for you it's the pounding of the waves on the beach or the banging of the ball on the backboard. We all have a list of items that make us smile.

What makes God smile? That's a more difficult question, but hardly less important. We all want to know what gives our God pleasure. That's what this book is about. In the first chapter we will explore what we hope to accomplish. As we seek to "listen to God's heartbeat" by asking "What does the Bible say?" we are, in effect, probing what makes Him smile.

What makes me smile? Sally, my wife, along with my sons, Daniel and Nathan, are at the top of the list. I get great pleasure from my work in ministry and teaching. A host of friends give me constant reason to smile. You would also find that woodworking, model railroading, genealogy, and travel are sources of pleasure.

But at this moment there are several others who put a smile on my face because they join me in working through this material. My earliest smile came when the people at College Press invited me to contribute to this series. I smile when I think of the Wednesday night class at Memorial Road Church of Christ in Oklahoma City where I piloted these thoughts and the people at Oklahoma Christian University who allowed me the time to put them on paper. I must mention the special help from Stefanie Anderson, John Harrison, Scott LaMascus, Bailey McBride, Lynn McMillon, Charles Kiser, David and Beverly North, Rick Trout, and Kathy Thompson. My wife, Sally, offered constant encouragement, feedback, and composed the questions at the end of each chapter. My son, Nathan Shank, a graduate student at the University of Oklahoma, and Peter Cariaga, one of my students at Oklahoma Christian University, read most every draft of this book and offered extremely helpful feedback. I owe them a great deal for how they stuck with me throughout the entire project. Right now, I have a smile on my face thinking of all these who had contributed to this volume.

Two people in my life have given me cause for multiple smiles. I have benefited in untold ways from the lives of Sally's parents, Wayne D. and Mary Jane Tague. This book is dedicated to their memory.

God bless us all as we explore what makes Him smile.

IN THIS BOOK

In This Book

WHAT'S NEXT?

Give your feedback to the thoughts in this book and read the reactions of others at www.haroldshank.com.

CHAPTER ONE

PREPARING TO LISTEN: A PAINTED HEARTBEAT

Begin your study of this chapter by reading *Luke 15:11-32*.

I looked at the painting for hours trying to figure it out. I was standing in front of a huge replica of Rembrandt's "The Return of the Prodigal Son." The original of the 1668 work hangs in the Hermitage in St. Petersburg, Russia, but there is a copy in an unusual museum in a small Ukrainian city called Bela Tserkva. That's where I studied this depiction of the moment in Jesus' parable in *Luke 15* when the prodigal son, representing all of the confused and hopeless people in the world, kneels before the welcoming father, who is a symbol of the living God.

For a long time I puzzled over the way the Dutch painter interpreted the scene.

Rembrandt could have chosen several different scenes for his canvas. He could have imagined the emotional instant when the younger son left home with his pockets stuffed with money, leaving the despondent father behind. I have always wondered how an artist would depict the riotous living in the far country where the younger son, surrounded by his temporary friends, enjoyed the nightlife. Or perhaps we expect a focus on the reunited family celebrating while the older brother pouts in the field. But Rembrandt did not choose to paint any of those scenes. He features a moment found in *Luke 15:20*: *"So he set off*

*and went to his father. But while he was still far off, his father saw him
and was filled with compassion; he ran and put his arms around him and
kissed him."*

Henri Nouwen's book, *The Return of the Prodigal Son*, helped
me understand the theological implications of this wonderful painting and informs my discussion here. Nouwen, author of several of
my favorite books on Christian spirituality, first saw a poster with a
detail of Rembrandt's *The Return of the Prodigal Son* on the back of
his friend's office door at L'arche, a French community that ministers
to people with mental handicaps. Later he traveled to Saint Petersburg, Russia, where the original hangs in the Hermitage. Acquired
by Catherine the Great in 1766, the painting now adorns one of
the many rooms in the giant museum along the banks of the Neva
River. Nouwen (3-15) reports sitting on one of the red velvet chairs
placed near the six-foot-wide by eight-foot-high painting for four
hours, pondering both the artist's interpretation and the original
story in *Luke 15*. Nouwen not only prompted my interest in the painting but also suggested the line "the heartbeat of God."

Timothy Keller (*The Prodigal God*) reflects another contemporary
attempt to focus on God through the parable in *Luke 15*.

The father stands before his mansion in Rembrandt's famous
painting. A silhouette of the unseen elder brother watches from the
shadows. The father's clothing reflects his affluence. The prodigal's
dirty, torn clothing recalls his degenerate journey. The boy kneels
before his upright father. With the father's hands on the boy's shoulders, the younger son turns his head to the right and places his left
ear on the father's chest. Only the right side of the boy's face is visible to the viewer.

Rembrandt's rendering puzzled me. Why did he paint the story
this way? Did the artist take a scene from his own life and project it
into the biblical story? If I had visually recreated the story on canvas,
I would have painted the father and son in full embrace with the
father kissing his son on the cheek. Rembrandt's portrayal seemed
stiff and formal to me. I could understand that the younger son on
his knees reflected his repentant spirit and his desire for reunifica-
tion. But the father seemed distant and almost uncaring. Rembrandt

ignored the *"put his arms around him"* and the *"kissed him"* and almost seems to miss the *"filled with compassion."*

What was Rembrandt's point?

Then I *saw* on Rembrandt's canvas what the boy *heard*: the prodigal son heard the father's heartbeat. His left ear was pinned against his father's chest. The boy listened to the beating of his father's heart. Rembrandt captured in a unique way how the son learned that his father was "filled with compassion." While the embrace and kisses surely followed, Rembrandt's painting depicted a crucial moment. What the younger son heard was the life of his father. He listened to the heartbeat.

The story in **Luke 15** reflects on the major doctrines and theology of the Bible. The two sons represent sinful humanity, one immersed in wild living the other in stubbornness and pride. The waiting father, who welcomes home the rebellious, but now repentant son, characterizes our divine Father who desires a relationship with humanity. He offers mercy instead of the punishment we deserve. He gives us the grace of the robe and ring that we have not earned. Motivated by a heart *"filled with compassion"* the father displays the love of God, love that reached its climax when God sent His Son to earth. The father points to the transformation called salvation: *"this son of mine was dead and is alive again; he was lost and is found!"* (**Lk 15:24**). In many ways the parable condenses into 22 verses the entire biblical story contained in Genesis through Revelation. The tale of the Prodigal Son is the gospel in story form.

Our task in this book is to listen to God's heartbeat. Let me explain what I mean by that goal. What the younger son heard with his ear pressed against his father's chest, we will hear with our ears open to the Word of God. I do not mean that we will listen to the literal heartbeat of God with questions about how fast it beats or what it implies about His physical health. Rather, our task is to probe the spiritual nature of God. By heartbeat, I mean the heart of God, the inner passions of the divine being, what we find when we really get to know Him. We seek to learn how God's heart beats throughout Scripture. *Our thesis is to listen to what the Bible says about the heart of*

> **Our task is to probe the spiritual nature of God. What makes God smile? What pleases Him?**

Preparing to Listen

God. What does Scripture say about God's inner being? What makes God smile? What pleases Him? In order to accomplish the goal, we first define more clearly what we hope to hear, second how we plan to listen, and third where in Scripture we will look.

WHAT WE HOPE TO LEARN ABOUT GOD

WHAT WE DO NOT PLAN TO DO

One might easily argue that the vast majority of the 845,000 or so words in the Bible are about God. Searching through Scripture's 30,442 verses **(Meredith, 217)** in order to "listen to the heartbeat" presents a daunting task. Before reading this or any other book claiming to be about God, one seeking to know the heart of God might most profitably engage Scripture itself. No study claiming to investigate God could approach the comprehensiveness of the Bible itself. So how do we find the heartbeat of God in the extensive material in the Bible about God? What do we hope to learn about God? We might begin by noting what we do not plan to do.

One of my college Bible professors was Hugo McCord, who listed these thirty-five names of God (his book is listed in the bibliography):

God	Jehovah Provides	The Redeemer
The Spirit of God	Fear	God with Us
Jehovah God	God the God of Israel	The Father
The True God	The God of Bethel	The Holy One
God Most High	The Mighty One of	Jehovah Our
My Lord Jehovah	Jacob	Righteousness
The Angel of Jehovah	Shepherd	The Branch
The God who Sees	The Stone of Israel	The Jealous One
Me	The King	The Servant
God Almighty	Jehovah My Banner	Husband
Judge	Jehovah Is Peace	The Savior
God Everlasting	Jehovah of Hosts	The God of Amen

---

1. **The Names of God.** Scripture abounds with names of the divine being. Entire books helpfully depict and investigate the appellations given to God (see Martin, McCord, Shelly, Spangler). Christian book stores often contain posters that attractively list the names of God or

of Jesus. Meredith (251-252) compiles thirty-nine different names for Jesus. Although listening to the heartbeat of God cannot ignore this area of study, and although we will do some exploration of the names of God, God's names are not the primary focus of this book.

2. **Proofs for God.** Apologetic works offer evidence that points to the existence of a divine being. C.S. Lewis may be the best known apologist of our time. In his *Mere Christianity* (17-39) he presents a compelling case based on the moral argument that there must be a God. I have learned much about God from Lewis and other apologists. Keller (**Reason for God**) is a well-known contemporary apologist for God. Our study assumes God's existence and encompasses a different area.

3. **Theodicy.** Any study of God faces what appear to be inconsistencies within His nature. Theodicy takes up the justice of God in light of evil and human suffering. For example, many make this argument: If God is good, He *should* stop all suffering.

> **Our study assumes God's existence and attempts not to defend God but to seek His heart.**

If He is powerful, He *could* stop all suffering. He has not stopped all suffering, so God must either not be good or not be powerful enough. Yet Scripture maintains He is both. The Bible takes up this question in *Job, Habakkuk,* and *Jeremiah.* Jesus himself spoke to the issue (*Lk 13:1-9; Jn 9:1-12*). Volumes such as *Creation and the Persistence of Evil* by Levenson address the problem. The focus of this book, though, is not to offer a defense of God but to seek His heart.

4. **A History of Views about God.** Reflecting on the nature of God has a long history. Along with the Bible, many documents from the ancient world speak about God and His nature. Early Jewish writings, the volumes by the church fathers, and a host of other books throughout history take up the question of God. Apologists seek to verify His existence, systematic theologians create an overarching system in which God plays a central role, historical theologians identify the trends in how believers and unbelievers view God, and preachers show the relevance of God to daily life. Each genre of literature contributes to an understanding of God. This study may draw on these contributions, but aims to probe God in another way.

5. **The Qualities of God.** Amy Ng Wong in her *Guide to God* lists 176 traits of God with at least one for every letter of the English alphabet (including 22 that begin with the letter "S"), filling 253 pages with nothing but citations from Scripture. J.I. Packer's long-lasting book, *Knowing God*, provides a penetrating guide to the nature of God. A substantial number of other volumes offer direction on the nature of God, describing God in human language. There are also books with devotional thoughts about God and texts that investigate the functions of God. Steve Brown (**1-23**) writes about how to know God. All of those areas touch on our goal, but this book narrows the focus in a different way.

THE PLAN

This study is clearly a subset of the books that investigate God's nature. Rather than offering a comprehensive view of all God's qualities, this study takes a more focused perspective on His heart. We seek not the traits one first encounters in thinking about God—His eternal nature, His immense power, or His deep wisdom. These are often the qualities that we assign in some degree to all divine beings. Rather, this study probes the deeper persona of our God, the attributes that make him distinctly the God we know from the Bible.

Central to the focus of this book is the idea that we can know *about* God and not *know* God, that we can name His qualities and not understand His heart, that we can define Him conceptually and not know Him personally. If the traits of God cover a wide spectrum from the external, cold, philosophical descriptions of divinity to the internal, warm, richly theological understandings of our heavenly Father, this study attends to the latter end.

Beyond a study of divine names and qualities, after determined reflection on the history of human investigation into God, and aside from attempts to prove His existence and resolve logical inconsistencies in our views about God, there remains a small area that emerges out of all these other disciplines that might be called the heart of God. There are no technical names for this area of study, although, as one of my associates suggests, it might be called theopathism (to coin a word meaning "the heart of God"). Clearly each of these other approaches touch on the heart of God, but this book proposes to center on God's passion, on His deep desires, on His heart.

Previous work on the divine names and qualities, along with the substantial contributions of all the historical studies about God, touch on His passion and heart. This book seeks to place a human ear to the chest of God, using the Dutch artist's visual metaphor, in order to hear what makes God's heart beat. Seeking the heart of God can be determined by a combination of the following criteria.

Our thesis is to listen to what the Bible says about the heart of God by following these lines of investigation:

1. We will focus on appropriate passages which speak of the "heart" of God.

There are 31 references in Scripture to the heart of God. In 15 of those occurrences, God speaks of His own heart while the other 16 are references by others to His heart. Our study will take up 28 of these passages: *Gen 6:6; 8:21; Deu 10:15; 1Sa 2:35; 13:14* (cited in *Acts 13:22); 2Sa 7:21* (paralleled in *1Chr 17:19); 1Kgs 9:3* (paralleled in *2Chr 7:16); 2Kgs 10:30; Job 7:17; 9:4; 10:13; 34:14; 36:5; Pss 33:11; 78:72; Isa 41:22; 63:4; Jer 3:15; 7:31; 19:5; 23:20; 30:24; 32:35,41; 44:21; Lam 3:33; Hos 11:8; Mt 11:29.* In the three unexamined texts (*Job 9:4; 36:5; Ps 33:11*), the word "heart" is used to refer to God as a thinking or wise being.

---

2. We will study passages which talk of God's intentions. This study makes no claim to even list all of the passages that refer to God's aims but simply traces several of the intentions of God that begin in *Genesis*.

3. We will concentrate on what delights and what hurts God. There are a large number of words for delight or desire in Scripture that are associated with God. This study does not explore all of these, but centers on one particular delight of God that is repeatedly used in both testaments.

4. We will examine the passages in which God reveals Himself and His nature. These texts of self-disclosure often move beyond the external attributes of God to His motives, values, and passions. God discloses Himself in any number of passages. No attempt is made here to list all such occurrences. This study will take up the self-disclosures of God that are repeatedly quoted in the Bible itself.

5. We will end up talking about Jesus. In Jesus, we see the fullness of God. Jesus most fully depicts God for us. As we gather up the most

> **We will find that the most explicit texts about God are all on the journey toward Jesus.**

explicit texts about God, we will find that they are all on the journey toward Jesus. With the complete biblical revelation in front of us, we will realize that the more we know about the Father, the more we also know about His Son.

WHAT WE WILL ENCOUNTER

Experiencing the heart of God takes us on a long journey. Humans face limitations in knowing the deeper qualities of other humans, so we should expect those same boundaries to restrict our understanding of God, if not more so. Suppose I introduce you to one of my friends, named David. After telling you his name, I might describe several of his qualities. As you get to know David, you would learn about his personal history and what others think about him. Soon you could list several of his outstanding qualities. For example, he might be 6'6", with wavy black hair, and a nice Southern accent. You might notice that he can draw well and that he has an extensive vocabulary. Beyond all that, we know there is a smaller area called passion or heart. You might know David for several months before you learn that he gives twenty percent of his income to fight AIDS in Africa. Even when you learn about his sacrifice, you still need to dissect what drives that passion.

If we experience limitations in getting to know other people, we should anticipate restrictions on coming to understand God. We can catch glimpses of God that reveal a wealth of depth to His character, but we can never fully comprehend the divine heart. We might know the external qualities of God, just as we know some of the more evident aspects of my friend David. Just as we get to know David more fully, we realize that there is even more about him that we do not know, so our study, while enlightening us about God's heart, may make us realize that there is more about God that we simply do not understand.

Another example might be drawn from *Luke 15*. The prodigal son grew up in his father's home. He knew his father's name. He could describe his father's physical, mental, and emotional qualities and recount the story of his father's life. In the far country, he sensed that there might be a spot for him again in his father's house. Despite being his father's son, even with the years of living in his father's shadow, he believed only that his father might be willing to let him live and work among the servants. But when he encountered his father's welcome home, or in Rembrandt's depiction only when he placed his ear against his father's beating chest, did the son know his father's deep compassion.

Jesus' parable about the Prodigal Son might be viewed as a mirror of our getting to know God. We watch as the son progressively understands his father more fully. Yet even as the story ends, we sense that the father's warm welcome, while revealing something new of his heart to his son, is not the full extent of the father. The son is just beginning a life-long journey of knowing his father.

We find ourselves in the roles of the sons in the story. We are often like the older son, not understanding the father at all. We also desire to be like the younger son, able to listen to his heartbeat. Although we seek the heart of God, this book is incomplete. Nobody can finish what we start. Listening to God's heartbeat is by its nature an impossible task to complete.

> **We find ourselves in the roles of the sons in the story.**

One of the stories about Samuel also reminds us of our limits to see inside the heart and contrasts our inability with God's willingness to be seen. When God sent His prophet Samuel to the house of Jesse to anoint a new king for Israel, the prophet thought only in externals while God saw beyond the externals to his heart. God told Samuel, *"Do not look on his appearance or on the height of his stature, because I have rejected him; for the LORD does not see as mortals see; they look on the outward appearance, but the LORD looks on the heart"* (*1Sa 16:7*). God's words make clear distinction between human and divine eyes.[1] Though we cannot see into each other's hearts, God can and does. Clearly we have ways of understanding the hearts of other people: we listen to what they tell us and we watch what they do. We try to deduce what their words and actions say about their heart. Yet we cannot look into the heart of another in the same way God does.

Chapter 1
Preparing to Listen

---

[1] The Bible uses many different names for God. In this passage He is called the LORD. This particular name of God will be explored more fully later. This study will simply identify the divine being as God.

In this verse God says nothing about whether we can see His heart. I would argue that we cannot any more see the heart of God than we can see the hearts of each other, but I would also hasten to suggest that when God reveals His heart, we then by His power see what we cannot see on our own. We can also see into God's heart through His words and actions. Even God's choice of David as king instead of the older and more experienced Eliab or Abinadab tells us about God.

Just before Samuel's journey to Bethlehem, God reveals something of His heart through Samuel. Samuel tells Saul, *"but now your kingdom will not continue; the LORD has sought out a man after his own heart; and the LORD has appointed him to be ruler over his people, because you have not kept what the LORD commanded you"* (*1Sa 13:14*). God finds a man who connects with His heart. Three chapters later, we learn David is that man. David is "better than" Saul according to *1 Samuel 15:28*. The full story comes in Stephen's speech in Jerusalem. Referring to God's disappointment with Saul, Stephen points out,

> *[22]When he had removed him, he made David their king. In his testimony about him he said, "I have found David, son of Jesse, to be a man after my heart, who will carry out all my wishes." [23]Of this man's posterity God has brought to Israel a Savior, Jesus, as he promised.* (*Acts 13:22-23*)

God states His preference for David. He calls David a man after His heart. He reveals His confidence in David's obedience and uses David to accomplish His work in Jesus. Yet those who read the many chapters about David and the *Psalms* by David must speculate about why God found David to be so much after His heart because God never explicitly reveals the reason. Anderson, McKenzie, and Swindoll explore the character of David and speculate about what God found so attractive about David.

We may not fully understand why David was a man after God's own heart because God is in many ways incomprehensible. Spurgeon (cited by **Packer, 13-14**) noted that the subject of God was so vast that our thinking gets lost in the immensity of the object being discussed.

We cannot complete the picture of our loving God.

Our plumb line cannot sound its depth and our eagle eye cannot see its height. Rembrandt finished the portrait of the loving father, but we cannot complete the picture of our loving God. We might study the systematic theologians' attempts to sketch the boundaries of what God may look like, but no theologian can depict every detail of an infinite being. Human language cannot describe God with any kind of comprehensive view. The son in Rembrandt's painting heard the father's heartbeat at that unique moment in time, but he did not fully comprehend the heart of his father and its significance.

The complexities of life often force us to reduce existence to its simplest terms. We regularly take difficult ideas and boil them down to a single word or phrase. For example, an artist may have some vague notion of the chemical makeup of a certain color, or the alphanumeric value assigned to a particular hue, or even a detailed knowledge of where the tint falls on the color spectrum, but generally the artist must settle for the description "red." Red is shorthand for a chemical formula, the raw materials, the numeric value, the manufacturing process and the exact pigment on the spectrum. Life is too complex to live in all the details. If we had to think about all the intricacies of the color red before we painted, we would never get to the canvas.

However, our tendency to reduce life to its simplest terms presents certain dangers when it comes to the divine being. We prefer to have a category in our mind, like a box which we label "God." We reduce the complex list of names, the long descriptions of His qualities, the hundreds of volumes discussing historical perspectives on His being, and what we know about His passion and heart into the simple word "God." The danger in that reduction comes when we assume that God remains completely in our category of "God" or in our box with "God" stenciled on the side. God defies such reduction. He defies classification. Because of God's immensity we cannot completely hold Him in our minds.

Those seeking the heart of God can only probe and investigate. The son, despite his years of living with his father, underestimated his father's compassionate heart. Like that son, we must recognize our limitations and His complexity. We must acknowledge our attempt to reduce all to simple terms and His resistance to any simple description. We must finally be content to listen to the heartbeat for a brief moment as a means of understanding His passion.

HOW WE CAN EXPERIENCE
GOD'S HEART

The series title "What the Bible says . . . " dictates the fundamental approach to listening to the heartbeat of God. Such an approach does not exclude or deny other attempts to understand God through a study of the created world (*Rom 1:20*), or through reflection and philosophy (*Ecclesiastes 1–12; Acts 17*). Yet even within the general guideline of "What the Bible says . . . " there are different approaches, so I will outline which methodological presuppositions guide this study.

INDIVIDUAL SCRIPTURES
MUST BE PONDERED

To ponder means to spend time in a text and to probe its depth and meaning. Eugene Peterson in *Eat This Book* explores this kind of study and the following material draws on his observations.

Scripture itself calls for such pondering. The Psalter begins:

> ¹ Happy are those
> who do not follow the advice of the wicked,
> or take the path that sinners tread,
> or sit in the seat of scoffers;
> ² but their delight is in the law of the LORD,
> and on his law they meditate day and night. (*Ps 1:1-2*)

This Psalm teaches us to ponder over the law. The writer tells the person thinking about Scripture to bracket out other sources of information and direction. Ignore the advice of the wicked, the sinner's path, and the decision-making process of scoffers. Instead delight and meditate on the law. Such pondering calls for a poetically *"day and night"* focus.

The Hebrew word behind the English "meditate" suggests a moaning, muttering, or growling over. *Isaiah 31:4* compares God to a lion. In the comparison, God's attentiveness to a task parallels the lion's nature. After capturing the prey, the beast gives attention to its feast. *"As a lion or a young lion growls over its prey"* (*Isa 31:4*) describes how the conqueror lingers over his meal. The word translated "meditate" in *Psalm 1* becomes "growl" in *Isaiah 31*. Those engaged in Bible study about the heartbeat of God should be as reluctant to leave their verse as the lion is to leave his dinner.

God speaks directly to Joshua with the same directive and using the same word: *"This book of the law shall not depart out of your mouth;*

you shall meditate on it day and night, so that you may be careful to act in accordance with all that is written in it" (*Josh 1:8*). God demands that Joshua concentrate on the *"book of the law,"* just as the lion remains at his banquet. Joshua is to spend as much time in pondering (*"day and night"*) as the Psalmist does in **Psalm 1**.

We, too, want to meditate on Scripture. As we search for the heart of God we will often dwell on only a few passages and search the depth of each one. While citing 178 different passages that speak about the qualities of God (**Wong**) may have its place, the methodology used here settles in with the meat of one text, growls over it, enjoys the banquet all day and into the night, rather than taste-testing one verse after another without any pondering or meditating at all.

Such a method means that at times this book takes up fewer texts than other studies. In many cases it does not seek to multiply Scripture references, but to think deeply about a few. Citing multiple references offers the advantage of a wider view of the passion of God, but prevents one from considering each Scripture for an extended period of time. Yet not all pondering considers just one text, for there is another helpful way to ponder.

> **We will settle in with the meat of one text, growl over it, and enjoy the banquet.**

FOLLOWING TRAJECTORIES

Different biblical authors often speak about the same divine passions, or to state it differently (and perhaps more accurately) God Himself reveals the same qualities of His heart multiple times. These thoughts run like threads throughout the Bible. Brueggemann (**"Trajectories,"** 162) calls them *trajectories*, concepts that wind their way through Scripture, surfacing repeatedly. For example, Brueggemann (**"Impossibility,"** 613-638) follows the thread of God doing "impossibilities" throughout the Bible. I borrow his term "trajectories" to describe the methodology of this study.[2]

Because Scripture uses trajectories, the early Christians effectively used the OT as the text of their preaching and teaching. Paul spoke of the usefulness of the OT when he said,

---

[2] Often called "canonical trajectories," this method of theological interpretation avoids isolating a particular text from the repeated use of it in the larger canonical context. See the discussion in Parry (**314-316**).

*[16]All scripture is inspired by God and is useful for teaching, for reproof, for correction, and for training in righteousness, [17]so that everyone who belongs to God may be proficient, equipped for every good work (**2Tm 3:16-17**).*

As a contributor to the NT, Paul, in the midst of writing his part of God's Word, cites his dependence on the Scripture available to him. The Bible itself testifies to the different roles that the two major divisions of Scripture play, but in texts such as this one, the Bible witnesses to the continuities. There are truths about God in both testaments. Early Christians used the first one to teach and preach about God and their faith.

I accept the teaching of Paul in *2 Timothy 3* that all Scripture is inspired by God and profitable in our study. Based on that teaching, this book seeks the trajectories that inform us about the heartbeat of God. Furthermore, this book proposes a link between pondering and trajectories. Meditation on a particular text permits the trajectories to emerge. It is clear that NT authors meditated on OT texts. They often cite trajectories between what they pondered in the OT and the material they penned in the NT. The abundant number of quotations and allusions to the OT by NT writers testifies to this connection.

STARTING POINTS

The Bible reveals just one God. The God described in the OT is the same God worshiped in the NT. The early Christians served the God of Abraham, Isaac, and Jacob. One divine being stands behind the biblical story of humanity from the days of creation to the preparation for heaven. There are several implications of our belief that the Bible speaks of just one God:

1. We should expect to find a consistent view of God in all parts of the Bible. The trajectories about God in Scripture are amazingly constant despite the diversity of authors and time periods. We know only what is revealed. He is so complex that we constantly see different sides of Him. Yet throughout the biblical journey there is an unfailing presentation of God.

2. Our study necessarily starts in the OT. The story of each testament depends on an understanding of the other.

Throughout the biblical journey there is an unfailing presentation of God.

Teachers who compare the Bible to a two-act play give us a helpful illustration. Anybody who comes for the first act of the play and leaves before the second act misses out on the whole message of the play. Likewise, anybody who comes late and catches only the second act will not be able to fully comprehend the message because they missed the first part. Jesus and the NT authors constantly quoted the OT because it was the first act of God's dramatic presentation to humankind.

> **Jesus and the NT authors constantly quoted the OT — the first act of God's presentation to humankind.**

3. We expect to find more about God in the OT. The OT covers more years (from Abraham to Malachi is about 1500 years compared to the 100 or so years covered in the NT), more pages (in my Bible the OT covers 1408 pages while the NT takes up only 466 pages), involves more people, and deals with a wider range of situations. Our study will dig deeply into the OT texts about the heart of God, but will not be content to stop there. Our journey will take us to the NT revelation about God.

4. The myth that the OT God is one of wrath and the NT God is one of grace is not found in the Bible. God shows grace to Noah (*Gen 6:8*) on the opening pages of the OT, and the NT closes with a clear description of the wrath of God (*Rev 19:15*). The myth of two Gods counters the Bible's own claim that there is just one God.

Marcion, a shipbuilder by trade, in his work *Antitheses* from early in the second century AD, expressed the view that the God of the OT (the creator God) and the God of the NT (the God revealed by Jesus Christ) are not the same. The God of Christ was a God of grace. The God of the OT was a God of feelings, violence, and anger. Marcion went so far as to totally discount the OT from biblical canon and advocated that Christians read only an edited portion of the NT. Marcion was pronounced a heretic for this belief in AD 144 by the church in Rome.

---

5. We focus on the theology of Scripture. The Bible is a complex book, but let me clarify that complexity by suggesting that the Bible confronts us fundamentally with three kinds of material. First, the

Bible is *historical*. The bulk of Scripture unfolds events in historical fashion. For example, **Joshua** tells the historical story of how the Israelites took the Promised Land while **Acts** reveals the historical story of how the early Christians took their world for Christ. Second, the Bible is a form of *literature*. Scripture includes prose and poetry, and uses different literary means to convey its message ranging from narrative, commands, proverbs, and sermons to a host of other literary tools. Third, the Bible is *theology*. The term "theology" basically is a word about God. Although theology has come to refer to the overall study of the many aspects of religion, it is rooted in teaching about God.

This book aims to read the Bible as a book of theology, that is, as a book about God.[3] That does not discount the Bible as a historical book with great literary value; indeed, the theology travels on the back of the historical and literary features of the Bible. In pondering over a text, this study asks, "What does this text say about God? What does it reveal about His passions?" Often those approaching the Bible raise historical issues such as "When did this happen?" or literary questions such as "What is a parable?" While those are important steps in Bible study, the goal of this study is to learn about God. In some cases, the question, "What does this text say about God?" never gets asked because the historical or literary questions dominate.

> As you read through this book, pay attention to the main texts cited in each chapter. When you read those texts, continually ask yourself, "What does this say about God?"

6. We will investigate the explicit theological statements in narrative. The bulk of Scripture takes the form of narrative. Most of **Genesis** tells a story that continues well into **Exodus** and dominates most of **Joshua, Judges, Ruth,** the books of **Samuel, Kings, and Chronicles** through **Ezra, Nehemiah, and Esther.** The story reappears in the Gospels and con-

---

[3] To avoid confusion, I am doing a biblical theology, which is different from that of systematic theologians or dogmatic theologians. Systematic theologians draw on Scripture, the writings of church leaders, and philosophers to create a logical and comprehensive system of how God works. Dogmatic theologians seek to provide the church with a comprehensive doctrinal position based on Scripture and church teaching. This study aims to state a biblical theology about God which may be less than comprehensive from a historical, doctrinal, or philosophical point of view, but seeks its comprehensive nature in the canon of Scripture. House (**11-57**) notes the dangers and limitations of this method.

tinues through *Acts*. Even books that are largely nonnarrative contain narrative (cf. *Leviticus 10; Amos 7; Galatians 2*). Yet frequently in the midst of the story, there are lines that tell us about God.

This study centers on the explicit theological statements embedded within the narrative. Identifying such statements involves some subjectivity, but explicit theological statements include the words of God and highly theological terms such as the names of God, sin, grace, love, and salvation. Generally such statements are easily identifiable. Consider this text:

> [15]*Realizing that their father was dead, Joseph's brothers said, "What if Joseph still bears a grudge against us and pays us back in full for all the wrong that we did to him?"* [16]*So they approached Joseph, saying, "Your father gave this instruction before he died,* [17]*'Say to Joseph: I beg you, forgive the crime of your brothers and the wrong they did in harming you.' Now therefore please forgive the crime of the servants of the God of your father." Joseph wept when they spoke to him.* [18]*Then his brothers also wept, fell down before him, and said, "We are here as your slaves."* [19]*But Joseph said to them, "Do not be afraid! Am I in the place of God?* [20]*Even though you intended to do harm to me, God intended it for good, in order to preserve a numerous people, as he is doing today."*
> *(Gen 50:15-20)*

This brief scene near the end of Genesis tells of the crises in the family after Jacob's death. The dialogue among the brothers reveals the situation, but Joseph's answer moves the narrative in a new direction. His comment contains words with ample theological content: fear, God, good, preserve. Joseph uses explicit theological language. Joseph asks a critical, theological question: "Am I in the place of God?" His question recalls the dreams where Joseph plays a dominant godlike role. Even the Egyptians had elevated Joseph to a high, almost

|| **Joseph is not God, but he knows the heart of God.**

godlike level. We understand Joseph to mean that he is not God, but he goes on to reveal to his brothers, and those readers peering over their shoulders, that he knows the heart of God. "God intended it for good." Joseph knows the intentions of God!

A historical approach concerns itself with the brothers in Egypt or the way in which these events were recorded and used by the community of faith. A literary approach takes up the nature of the dialogue, how this event caps the narrative of *Genesis 37–50*. Though both approaches are helpful, a theological look seeks the heart language of the text in order to ask the question, "What is this text saying about God?" The answer to that question will come in a later chapter. The Joseph text here serves to illustrate the means of identifying explicit theological statements embedded within the narrative.

7. Start at the beginning. *Genesis 1:1* immediately raises the issue of God. God dominates *Genesis 1–11*. Even in the closing lines of the Bible's first book, the question of God (*"God intended it for good" 50:20*) continues to surface. Although not a necessary starting point for all study about God, *Genesis* is the starting line for this investigation. By probing deeply into this text for the first several chapters, by seeking a theological reading of this ancient book, by looking at explicit theological passages, and by finding trajectories that begin in *Genesis*, this study of the heart of God will quickly move into all areas of Scripture. The methodology is not superimposed on the text in some organized pattern that guides the search, but rather each piece of the study leads to another piece. In fact, at each juncture there are multiple paths to pursue, many trajectories to trace. Starting with *Genesis*, this study follows the trajectories that offer the most exposure to the heart of God.

> **This study follows the trajectories that offer the most exposure to the heart of God.**

WHERE IN SCRIPTURE WE WILL LOOK

Genesis narrates the relationship between God and humanity by narrowing the focus on Abraham and his family ending with the remarkably theological conversation between Joseph and his brothers mentioned above. That conversation gives us entry into how God has come to regard humanity and His intent toward us. We turn to that material in Chapter 2, "Guidance: Directing Each Step."

The first occurrence of the word "heart" in reference to God comes at the flood. The Bible opens with a powerful, creative God who makes humankind in His image only to be disappointed with His relationship with the ones He has made. The flood story offers remarkable insight into God's heart and is explored in Chapter 3, "Loyalty: God's Heart for Change."

Three trajectories about the heart of God begin in *Genesis* and run throughout much of the Bible. A chapter is dedicated to each of these trajectories. Beginning with Abraham, God promises to be with us (Chapter 4, "Immanuel: God on Our Side of the Street") which He does by regularly visiting the earth (Chapter 5, "Mission: God in Our Neighborhood") and by giving us blessing (Chapter 6, "Blessing: God Doing People a World of Good.").

In the book of Exodus God makes two significant self-revelations, one about His uniqueness (Chapter 7 "Jealousy: There Can Only Be One") and a major disclosure about His inner qualities (Chapters 8–10 "God's Self Introduction: Up Close and Personal," "The Divine Response—Faithful to the Unfaithful," "Always Appropriate"). Following the parameters of the major disclosure in *Exodus 34*, the final chapters explore the implications expressed in related texts about how He seeks out the broken hearted (Chapter 10 "Broken-ness: The God Who Cares"), how He delights in justice and right-eousness (Chapter 12 "Delight: What Makes God Smile" and Chapter 13 "Righteousness and Justice: What Makes God Act"), how He uses violence (Chapter 14 "Violence: God and the Sword"), and how He protects the orphan (Chapter 15 "Care for the Fatherless: Running Home to God").

Our journey takes us through the passages that speak of His heart, intentions, and delights with a special focus on a set of passages in which God self-discloses His inner being. We follow the trajectories throughout the entire Bible, hoping to find clues and insights into the passions of God.

This book seeks to do in print what Rembrandt did on canvas. It seeks to turn us into listeners. It puts our ears next to the heart of God, so we can hear the beat of the divine heart.

| **This book seeks to turn us into listeners.**

WHAT DO YOU SAY?

1. What are some trajectories that you see in Scripture? How do you think they relate to God's heart?

2. At this point, what are some of the issues that you think are on God's heart?

3. Scripture calls David a man after God's heart (*1Sa 13:14*). What can be learned about David's heart from these *Psalms*?

   a. *Ps 5:10-11*

   b. *Ps 9:1-2*

   c. *Ps 15:1-3*

   d. *Ps 19:9-11*

   e. *Ps 37:4-5*

   f. *Ps 61:1-4*

   g. *Ps 131:1*

   h. *Ps 139:23-24*

4. Pondering the Scriptures is one way to begin discovering God's heart. How do you personally ponder or meditate on Scripture?

5. On page 18 is a list of 35 names for God. Pick three of those names, ponder them, and write what the name means to you.

CHAPTER TWO

GUIDANCE: DIRECTING EACH STEP

Begin your study of this chapter by reading *Genesis 50:15-21*.

M y first exposure to the Bible was with the book of *Genesis*. Reared in an unchurched family, I began attending Mildred Stutzman's Sunday school class in sixth grade. Her topic? *Genesis*. There I encountered for the first time people named Adam and Eve, Cain and Abel, Abraham and Sarah, and Joseph and Pharaoh.

Later I learned that people tend to think of *Genesis* as the early history of humankind or as the battleground between creation and evolution. I was struck by the questions people asked after they read Genesis: Where do the cavemen fit in? Where do we put the dinosaurs? Were the days in *Genesis 1* 24-hour days? Where did Cain get his wife? Did Noah's flood cover North America? I learned that people loved to argue over the answers to those issues.

I also asked those questions, but there were other issues about *Genesis* and about God that puzzled me, and I think troubled others: Who is God? What is He like? Where is He when I need Him? Is He really interested in helping me?

In some ways, *Genesis* presented a God that I did not know. I did not have conversations with God like the ones Adam and Eve had in the garden. God never confronted me about my sin in the same way He dealt with Cain. God never spoke to me in a vision in the way He repeatedly did with Abraham. In my dreams, I never saw a ladder to heaven or heard God preview my life. But that is the way Jacob knew this God.

Over the years I have repeatedly studied *Genesis*. Now I see the larger points of the book. *Genesis* reveals that God is in control of life, not just the lives of the people such as Adam and Noah who talk with Him up close and personal, but He is in control of the lives of people like

Genesis reveals that God is in control of life — the lives of people like me.

me. Even when the events of life turn negative and even when people do evil things, even behind those events, *Genesis* tells me God is working. He is directing each step.

Let me explain it this way. *Genesis* in a sense presents life as if it were played out on a stage in a theater. We are in the audience watching the drama of life unfold on the stage. In the first act God is one of the actors. He talks and interacts with the other actors and actresses. In the subsequent acts, God is not on the stage, but we can hear His voice talking to the actors who are still on stage. In a couple of scenes God occasionally appears at the edge of the stage for a brief moment and then disappears. Finally, in the last act of the play God never appears on stage at all, and only one actor hears His voice. The main actors and actresses occasionally speak about God, but they never talk to Him directly. In fact, at times, it appears God has been written out of the script. Then at the end of the play we learn that during that act when God never appeared, He was backstage controlling all the lights, determining who went on and off stage, changing the scenery. We did not see Him, but He was directing all the action on stage.

I do not mean that God is simply an actor, but rather I use the theater story to illustrate the point *Genesis* makes about God. *Genesis* tells us, that whether we see Him or not, even whether we believe in Him or not, God is directing all the time. *Genesis* presents God being in charge in different ways. Sometimes He is on stage. Sometimes He is backstage. Wherever He is, He is in control.

Newspapers often interview the actors and directors after a theatrical performance. In those interviews we often hear the actor say, "This is my whole life. I love the theater." The director of a certain performance may tell us, "I never feel more alive than when I am directing a play." We may not pick up on that passion from the play itself, we only learn it when the people involved tell us of their heart.

At the end of *Genesis*, God tells us how important the events of *Genesis* are to Him. He does not sit for an interview, but in a striking way we find out about His intentions. We learn that being in charge is close to His heart.

Using the theater illustration to map out this chapter, the first part of the chapter will compare *Genesis* to a play showing how God moves from being on stage to being backstage. The second part of the chapter will take up the "interview," look deeply into the closing dialogue in the book of *Genesis* which happens to be about the "intents" of God.

GOD AND THE
THEATER OF GENESIS

Genesis speaks volumes about God. In a book that mentions the names of God almost 450 times in 47 of its 50 chapters, it should be no surprise that the book delves deeply into the questions about the divine being.[1] From the opening verse with *"In the beginning God"* to the closing dialogue between Joseph and his brothers about the work of God, Genesis begins the biblical discussion about God. So, this study also begins the quest to know the heart of God by looking at *Genesis*.

> **Genesis mentions the names of God almost 450 times in 47 of its 50 chapters.**

This chapter asks, "What does *Genesis* as a whole say about God? How is God revealed in the Bible's opening book?" Pondering fifty chapters of theological narrative may seem beyond human comprehension, so a method for dividing up the book by the major characters lays the foundation for asking the critical questions about God. In a sense, *Genesis* works much like a four-act play.

Divisions of Genesis

There are many ways to divide *Genesis* into smaller sections. Let me outline two of the most common methods: see overleaf ➡

---

[1] The numbers here simply indicate how frequently God appears in the narrative. Throughout the book I'll supply this information to help us understand how often the words appear in the text.

First, students of *Genesis* often frame the story historically, pointing to the historical hinge between *Genesis 11* and *12*. The first 11 chapters chronicle events in primeval times while *Genesis 12–50* unfold the patriarchal history generally thought to take place around the turn of the second millennium BC. Such a framework offers a valid approach, but calls for further subdivisions of the long narration from *Genesis 12–50*.

Second, other students of *Genesis* offer a literary frame for the book by means of characterization. The use of the word "character" does not mean that the person is unhistorical, but rather that in terms of the literary development of the book, a person appears to be one of the major players. When viewed as literature and through the prism of its characters, four divisions emerge for the book: *Genesis 1–11; 12–25; 26–36; 37–50*. Cohn (**3-16**), whose work stands behind much of this chapter, offers an in-depth look at this kind of division-making that I summarize here.

1. *Genesis 1–11* presents a series of events with a constantly changing cast of characters. Adam and Eve give way to Cain and Abel who are eventually replaced by Noah and later by the tower builders at Babel. The only person present from beginning to end of *Genesis 1–11* is God. He dominates the events from creation to tower building.

2. *Genesis 12–25* introduces additional figures who play a prominent role, but the one who dominates the narrative is Abram, later called Abraham. Unlike *Genesis 1–11* where God plays a significant role in every narrative, in *Genesis 12–25* God is absent from several events.

3. *Genesis 26–36* features the life of Jacob. A few episodes at the beginning focus on Isaac, but Jacob is the towering figure in the material in three events: Jacob's conflict with Esau, Jacob's conflict with Laban and then Jacob's reconciliation with Esau. Like *Genesis 12–25*, there are substantial sections where the text makes little mention of God.

4. *Genesis 37–50* tells the story of Joseph, who dominates this tightly written, novel-like material. While God speaks and appears regularly in *Genesis 1–36*, He speaks only once in a dream in the final 14 chapters.

As *Genesis* unfolds, God plays a different role in each section. The effect is quite dramatic. God moves from the main character on the stage in the first act (or division), to brief appearances at the edge of the stage and a voice from offstage, to even rarer appearances, and finally to no appearances or presence onstage at all. Watch as God's role changes as we work our way through these four divisions of *Genesis*.

CENTER STAGE IN GENESIS 1–11

In *Genesis 1–11* God seems to be everywhere all the time. He starts off as the only character on the stage: *Genesis 1:1–2:4a* chronicles the creation. The word "God" appears 35 times in the 35 verses, and as a character He stands behind all the action that takes place. Alone at the beginning of the chapter, He creates and gives power to heavenly bodies, assigns the task of reproduction to plants and animals, creates humankind in His image, and grants them power to subdue and have dominion over the earth.

In *Genesis 2:4b–3:24*, the divine being now takes the name *"the LORD God,"* which occurs 20 times, while the serpent and the woman call Him "God" four times. Although in *Genesis 1* God stands at an unknown location, speaking, naming, and evaluating, in *Genesis 2–3* He comes to the earth and walks in the garden He has created. He appears in every part of the narrative about Adam and Eve except when the couple eat the fruit of the tree of the knowledge of good and evil (*Gen 2:23–3:8*).

While often called the Cain and Abel story, *Genesis 4:1–16* more accurately takes up the story of the LORD and Cain. God and Cain do all the talking. Abel *acts* in a faithful way, earning him a place in the *Hebrews 11* "hall of faith," but is ultimately a silent character. With the exception of the murder in the field, the LORD is present in each part of the narrative. In fact, God's name occurs ten times in this brief narrative. Unlike the docile couple Adam and Eve, Cain appears defiant and uncooperative. Despite Cain's assertiveness, God remains in control, deals with Cain at each stage of his rebellion, and finally protects him from harm.

God appears regularly in *Genesis 6–9*. Following the genealogies, God guides the events in the short discussion of the sons of God marrying the daughters of men (*Gen 6:1–4*). *Genesis 6:5–9:19* tells the flood story. Just as God controls creation, so God orchestrates these events with many echoes of *Genesis 1–2*. The creator uncreates creation. Chapter three of this book takes up the insight into the heart of God in the flood story.

After the sin at Noah's tent and the table of nations, God visits the construction site of the Babel tower (*Gen 11:1-9*) where He investigates the construction, speaks to Himself, and scatters the people.

One of the remarkable aspects of God's role in *Genesis 1–11* is His humanlike appearances. He forms the dirt into a human shape, and then He breathes into it the breath of life (*Gen 2:7*), performs surgery on the man (*Gen 2:21-22*), talks with the couple (*Gen 3:9-19*) and Cain (*Gen 4:1-16*), and plays other humanlike roles in *Genesis 1–11*. As the playlike book of Genesis unfolds, we will see God gradually leaving those roles behind. *Genesis* is making a point about the different ways in which God directs the world.

These humanlike appearances are often call anthropomorphisms and anthropopathisms. An anthropomorphism is when human characteristics are applied to something not human. In this case, God takes on human qualities. An anthropopathism is when human emotions are applied to something not human. In the flood story, God grieves in his heart. Human emotions are applied to God.

Some students of the Bible suggest that these humanlike descriptions of God are merely figures of speech. They argue God never walked in the Garden and talked to Adam and Eve, but that language is used to help us understand those events. Some suggest that God cannot be the sovereign God while taking on human form.

Other students of the Bible reject the idea that these humanlike appearances of God are mere figures of speech. They do not argue that God is simply reduced to a human body and ceases to be God, but that in some way God does enter our world. They point to the fact that the Bible repeatedly describes God as speaking and listening. He has eyes, a face, even a nose (more about that in a later chapter). In this book, I take these humanlike appearances of God seriously. I believe we can hold to a lofty view of God who also has the ability to visit the earth in human form.

This study centers not on the events of *Genesis 1–11*, sketched out in the previous paragraphs, but on God. God appears on the earth; He speaks frequently, dialoguing with the humans; He places limitations on creation, gives orders, destroys the earth, puts a rainbow in the sky, and confuses the languages of humankind. God is the only character present from

God is the only character present from beginning to end.

beginning to end. He takes up a wide variety of performances, all of a universal nature. In every one, God is firmly in charge.

OFF STAGE IN THE ABRAHAM STORIES IN GENESIS 12–25

As the second act of Genesis unfolds, we see a change in the role that God plays. In the first act, He was the main character in almost every action. Now, God's role becomes more complex. Abraham is the main character and God interacts with him and others in a variety of ways. Take a glance at the variety of God's appearances:

God speaks in dreams and visions to Abraham and Sarah—*Genesis 12, 13, 15, 17, 18, 22*

God talks to Hagar and Lot through an angel—*Genesis 16, 18–19, 21*

God appears once to Abimelech in a dream—*Genesis 20*

The narrator refers to the actions of God—*Genesis 12:17; 15:18; 19:24,29*

People in the story refer to God—*Genesis 13:4; 16:2; 21:22; 24*

In most of *Genesis 14* and *23–25*, God makes no appearance either in person, by dream, action, or reference. While in *Genesis 1–11* God appears in person frequently, in *Genesis 12–25* He does so only once, when He makes a brief appearance on earth in *Genesis 18*.

Aside from God's conversation with Abraham in *Genesis 18*, this section does not depict God in a humanlike way. In *Genesis 1–11*, God never appears in a dream or works through a mediator. In *Genesis 12–25*, God now regularly communicates through dreams and speaks through angels.

Using the theater illustration, in the first act God regularly appears on stage, visits with a changing cast of characters. He even changes the scenery from stage center, ordering new backdrops and directing new actors and actresses. God is persistently present, directing each step, and always in control.

In the second act, God only appears on stage for a brief moment. Mostly we hear His voice from offstage. His voice commands and directs the action. The actors and actresses on stage know God is in charge, but their encounters with Him are more indirect. They hear His voice, but seldom see His face. This

> **In the second act, God only appears on stage for a brief moment.**

second act prepares us for another change in God's role in the third section of *Genesis*.

OFF STAGE IN THE JACOB STORIES IN GENESIS 26–36

Just as God's role became more complex in the Abraham narrative, so God continues to interact with humanity in a multifaceted way. Look over this summary of God's interaction with people:

God briefly speaks to Rebekah in response to her question— *Genesis 25:22-23*

God makes brief comments to Isaac in visions—*Genesis 25:21; 26:2f.,23f.*

Laban claims God spoke to him through divination and dreams—*Genesis 30:27; 31:24,29*

God speaks to the main character Jacob on five significant occasions:

At Bethel in a dream—*Genesis 28:10f.*

At Paddan-aram in a dream—*Genesis 31:3-13.*

At Mahanaim through an angel—*Genesis 32:1*

At Penuel in a wrestling match—*Genesis 32:22f.*

Again at Bethel in covenant renewal—*Genesis 35:1-15*

God's communication with Jacob occurs only at strategic turning points in his life.

The narrator refers to God's actions—*Genesis 28:12; 29:22,31f.; 30:17,22; 35:5*

People also refer to God—*Genesis 26:28-29; 27:20,27-28; 28:3-4; 29:32-35; 30:2-30; 31:5f.,42f.; 32:9; 33:5f.,11*

God's interaction with Jacob seemingly parallels His discussions with Abraham, yet a reading of both narratives reveals that God speaks more frequently with Abraham about a wide variety of topics, while He speaks infrequently with the main character Jacob and only about major life events.

While God deals with universal concerns in *Genesis 1–11* (creation of the whole world, worldwide flood, etc), God addresses the issues in one family in *Genesis 12–36*. The humanlike appearances of God, so frequent in *chapters 1–11*, are reduced to the appearances in *Genesis 18, 28*, and *32*. After serving as the main character from a literary point of view in *Genesis 1–11*, God increasingly plays a more distant role, especially in *Genesis 26–36* where God is not part of the narrative for longer periods of time.

Drawing on the theater image, in act three God's voice offers guidance only at crucial moments. The drama takes a striking turn in the finale of *Genesis*.

BACK STAGE IN THE JOSEPH STORIES IN GENESIS 37–50.

> # The drama takes a striking turn in the finale of Genesis.

This last section of *Genesis* follows the life of Joseph from favorite son and disliked brother to the depths of false accusation and imprisonment to the seat of Egyptian power. God speaks only once in this section, when He appears in a vision to Jacob telling him to go to Egypt (*Gen 46:1*). The narrator refers to God's actions[2] while players in the story frequently refer to God.[3] The *Genesis* text never records God speaking or appearing to Joseph. The God who regularly appeared in dreams in *Genesis 12–36* now appears in none of the dreams (save the vision to Jacob in *Genesis 46*) recorded in *Genesis 37–50*.

God does not speak or appear in *Genesis 37–50* (except for the one vision), but His presence is acknowledged in significant ways in two clusters of texts. First, after Joseph's arrival in Egypt, he serves in the house of Potiphar where he rises to high position and then sinks to imprisonment. Events in Potiphar's house and in the Egyptian prison are not by chance. Four times the text (*Genesis 39*) reveals the real power behind the unfolding events:

> [2]*The LORD was with Joseph, and he became a successful man; he was in the house of his Egyptian master. [3]His master saw that the LORD was with him, and that the LORD caused all that he did to prosper in his hands. (vv. 2-3)*

> [5]*From the time that he made him overseer in his house and over all that he had, the LORD blessed the Egyptian's house for Joseph's sake; the blessing of the LORD was on all that he had, in house and field. (v. 5)*

> [21]*But the LORD was with Joseph and showed him steadfast love; he gave him favor in the sight of the chief jailer. (v. 21)*

---

[2] *Gen 38:7,10; 39:2-3,5,21,23.*
[3] *Gen 39:9; 40:8; 41:16,25,28,32,38-39,51-52; 42:18,28; 43:14,23,29; 44:16; 45:5ff; 48:3,9,11,15,20,21; 49:18,25; 50:17-25.*

> [23]*The chief jailer paid no heed to anything that was in Joseph's care, because the* LORD *was with him; and whatever he did, the* LORD *made it prosper.* (**v. 23**)

These passages reveal an attentive God who is in charge. Even Potiphar knows the reason for Joseph's success and his own prosperity. God even arranges events so that the prison warden treats Joseph kindly.

A second cluster of texts comes when Joseph reveals himself to the visiting brothers:

> [5]*And now do not be distressed, or angry with yourselves, because you sold me here; for God sent me before you to preserve life.* (**Gen 45:5**)

> [7]*"God sent me before you to preserve for you a remnant on earth, and to keep alive for you many survivors.* [8]*So it was not you who sent me here, but God; he has made me a father to Pharaoh, and lord of all his house and ruler over all the land of Egypt.* [9]*Hurry and go up to my father and say to him, Thus says your son Joseph, "God has made me lord of all Egypt; come down to me, do not delay"* (**Gen 45:7-9**).

In this second set of passages, Joseph, who interprets dreams, now offers an interpretation of his own life. Despite his misfortunes, Joseph states that God controlled his life, setting all these events into action. Joseph understands that while the brothers may have actually bartered his life into slavery with the passing caravan, that the whole passage from Canaan to Egypt was the work of God. Joseph also knows that despite his own leadership abilities and work experience, his role as lord over Egypt is the result of God's guiding hand.

To use the theater image one more time, the last act of the *Genesis* play is completely different from the previous three acts. In the last act, God never speaks to the main characters. We do not hear the voice from off stage giving directions except for the brief word to Jacob. In fact, for most of the dialogue on stage there is no mention of God at all. Only rarely do the actors mention Him, but when they do, they acknowledge that He directs the entire play. All the action and every character are under His guidance.

The actors acknowledge that He directs the entire play.

Pondering over the entire book of *Genesis* presents a demanding task. The chart offers a brief summary of the previous discussion.

	Gen 1–11	Gen 12–25	Gen 26–36	Gen 37–50
Main Character	God	Abraham	Jacob	Joseph
God's role	Direct	Direct/mediator	Directly to Jacob	Indirect
God appears	In person	Dreams/angels	Dreams/angels	Not at all
Focus	universal	family	family	family/universal

When I discovered this pattern of God's interaction with humanity, I was filled with joy and hope. God did not speak directly with me about my sin although he did with Cain, nor did He talk to me in visions like He did with Abraham and Jacob, but I can with confidence find a parallel to my own life in the experiences of Joseph. He never walked with God in a garden or heard God in a dream, but Joseph lived with the reality that God was directing every step of his life.

What we find in *Genesis* we find all through the Bible. At times God again works much like He does in *Genesis 1–11*. Other biblical narratives parallel the experiences of Abraham. Still others in the Scripture narrative find life like Joseph did.

For instance, God visits Mt. Sinai to talk with Moses, dwells in the inner sanctuary of the tabernacle, and is present on earth dealing with humanity in person through the incarnation of Jesus. These encounters are much like the appearances of God in *Genesis 1–11*. God is in charge during the early days of *Genesis* just as He controls events at Mt. Sinai or in the ministry of Jesus.

God continues to appear to humans in dreams and through mediators such as angels. Abraham's experience with God anticipates the kind of God-human relationship experienced by the likes of Solomon or Peter. We recall Solomon's dream in which God gave him wisdom and wealth. His experience parallels Abraham's. God directs the steps of both men through dreams. Many of the biblical authors such as Isaiah and Paul encounter God in visions or dreams only at strategic times much like Jacob.

God also works behind the scenes in Scripture just as He does in the Joseph narrative. In other biblical material such as *Esther*, God is seemingly absent. God never speaks or is referred to in Esther's story, but most agree that the book points to God's control of events in the Persian court.

Genesis illustrates the broad spectrum of how God shows His control and power to humanity. Not every human is confronted by God

> **Genesis tells us that no matter how we encounter God, He is there, directing each step.**

walking in the garden like Adam and Eve. Most people do not have God-filled dreams or visions. Nobody else seems to wrestle with God in the same way as Jacob. In fact, such divine-human encounters are rare. But *Genesis* tells us that no matter how we encounter God, He is there, directing each step.

GOD AND THE GENESIS INTERVIEW

In our theater image, we imagine ourselves in the audience watching a play. We compare the book of *Genesis* to a four-act play. I do not mean to imply that *Genesis* is fiction like a play, but only use the image as a way of understanding the complexities of the Bible's first book. We then continued the play image by showing how we learn about the people who produce the play. Often we read a magazine interview with one of the actresses or the director in which we learn about her or his passion for theater. In a similar way, *Genesis* presents us with an "interview." God never speaks, but in this dialogue we learn about the heart of the God who directs events from *Genesis 1* to *Genesis 50*.

Students of *Genesis* note that the book makes one of its clearest statements about God at the end. The entire book leads up to the discussion about God between Joseph and his brothers, and the revelation there about God serves as a lens through which much of the narrative of *Genesis* comes into focus. *Genesis* tells us that God wants to be known, and that despite what we sometimes conclude about Him, He is very much in control. After this initial look at God from the perspective of the whole of *Genesis* with a special focus on *50:20*, the next four chapters will probe *Genesis* further for insights about His heart (Chapter 3), His presence (Chapter 4), His mission (Chapter 5) and His methods (Chapter 6).

The Joseph story dominates *Genesis 37–50*. Joseph is the son of Jacob's favored wife, Rachel, and Jacob dotes over young Joseph, treating him in preferential ways. His older brothers, displeased with their lower status, sell Joseph to some traders bound for Egypt. In Egypt, Joseph eventually rises to a position of power. When famine strikes the land of Canaan, Jacob sends some of his sons to find food in Egypt. The brothers who sold Joseph into slavery now unknowingly bow before him to beg for food. Finally, Joseph reveals his true identity and moves the entire family to the security of Egypt.

After living in harmony for several years, the elderly Jacob dies. The brothers reason that, with their father gone, Joseph may now retaliate against them for selling him into slavery. They fear what their powerful brother might do to them. The family dialogue comes at the end of the *last chapter* in *Genesis*:

> [15]Realizing that their father was dead, Joseph's brothers said, "What if Joseph still bears a grudge against us and pays us back in full for all the wrong that we did to him?" [16]So they approached Joseph, saying, "Your father gave this instruction before he died, [17]'Say to Joseph: I beg you, forgive the crime of your brothers and the wrong they did in harming you.' Now therefore please forgive the crime of the servants of the God of your father." Joseph wept when they spoke to him. [18]Then his brothers also wept, fell down before him, and said, "We are here as your slaves." [19]But Joseph said to them, "Do not be afraid! Am I in the place of God? [20]Even though you intended to do harm to me, God intended it for good, in order to preserve a numerous people, as he is doing today. [21]So have no fear; I myself will provide for you and your little ones." In this way he reassured them, speaking kindly to them. [22]So Joseph remained in Egypt, he and his father's household; and Joseph lived one hundred ten years. (**Gen 50:15-22**)

The dialogue begins with thoughts of fear and revenge but ends with insight into God and His heart. The brothers believe that Joseph's respect for their elderly father keeps him from revenge. Jacob even shares those thoughts and urges his sons to seek the forgiveness of their younger, but now more powerful, brother. Jacob and his sons put Joseph in the position of dispensing forgiveness. Jacob raises the issue of God. He urges the sons to identify themselves as *"servants of the God of your father."* Joseph weeps in response to his brothers' plea which prompts the whole family to weep. In striking language the brothers who sold Joseph into slavery, now identify themselves not as *"servants of the God of your father"* but as *"slaves"* of Joseph. They place their brother on a pedestal. Joseph senses that the brothers elevate him in fear, and after telling them not to be afraid, Joseph asks a critical question: *"Am I in the place of God?"*

That question recalls several events earlier in the story. First, the inquiry recollects the events of *Genesis 37* where young Joseph dreams firstly of all the sheaves of the field bowing down to his sheaf and then of the sun, moon, and eleven stars bowing down to him. Joseph's dreams place him on a high pedestal.

Second, Joseph's question also reflects the sociopolitical reality of the family's situation. Egypt made Joseph second only to Pharaoh. Joseph is the family patron. They enjoy their situation in Egypt due to their younger brother's position of power. In terms of the social and political context, Joseph is on a pedestal.

Third, in Egyptian thinking, Joseph approaches divine status. Pharaohs are considered divine, and Joseph is close to the Pharaoh. There were likely people in Egypt who considered Joseph to be a god. Asking about Joseph's divine status may have been quite appropriate.

Fourth, when the brothers come to Egypt seeking food, Joseph plays a godlike role with them. He knows things they do not know, orchestrates events behind the scenes, and in effect is in control of their lives. At times Joseph seems to act in superior ways when he treats his brothers as lowly subjects.

Now, however, the response to the question is clear. Joseph expects a negative response. Joseph is not God. He never has been God. Despite his power, Joseph did not ultimately control events.

Joseph admits that his brothers did wrong. *"You intended to do harm to me."* This line recalls the events of **Genesis 37** when the brothers put him in a pit, sell him to the passing caravan, and deceive their father about his fate. The brothers want Joseph out of the way and waste no time getting it done. Their intent is evil.

After clarifying that he does not consider himself a god and affirming the evil intent of his brothers in selling him into slavery, Joseph takes on the role of a theologian. He speaks about God. He interprets all the events

God takes a malevolent deed and does something marvelous.

from **Genesis 37–50** and beyond in one sweeping statement: *"God intended it for good."* The brothers put Joseph in a pit, but God uses the evil action to accomplish good. The brothers sold Joseph into bondage, but God takes that malevolent deed and does something marvelous. The passage goes on to show how the proper understanding of God's role leads to a different kind of family circle.

Joseph knows the intent of God. Genesis does not explain how or when Joseph came to this understanding. God does not explain this reality to Joseph in a dream, or talk to him in a vision. Joseph simply articulates this understanding of God.

Joseph understands the work of God. Even when God is not literally present, even when there is no spoken word from God, even when events seem to have logical explanations, Joseph knows another reality. He knows the providential hand of God. God works backstage, pulling levers, raising curtains, arranging scenery, controlling the events onstage. The audience never sees God. The actors never hear God. But God is at work. God directs each step.

Joseph understands how God reforms evil human deeds into good things. The brothers sold their brother into slavery, but God used Joseph to provide the family with a place to go during the famine in Canaan. God promises Abraham many descendants. He repeats the promise to Isaac and Jacob. When the brothers sell one of those descendants into bondage, their deed seems to work against the promise. But God uses Joseph's Egyptian experience to provide a way to keep the promise to Abraham. The small group that migrated to Egypt under Joseph's patronage years later becomes a mighty nation.

> God's commitment to His promises shows His intention to do good. When God's promise to Abraham is threatened by Abraham's lies about his wife Sarah, God provides a way out of trouble. Later when the same promise is postponed by Israel's enslavement in Egypt, God frees the Israelites. When God's covenant with Israel is threatened by Israel's attraction to other gods, God not only remains faithful but provides ways for Israel to return to Him. When we today are not able to be faithful to God because of our sin, God is faithful on our behalf through Jesus Christ.

The insight about God that comes at the end of *Genesis* is the theme of much of the book. Humans act in evil ways. God uses their actions to bring about good. Adam and Eve disobey the commands of God. God responds to human sin with a plan for salvation. Abraham lies to Pharaoh about Sarah. God uses Abraham's visit to Egypt to make him a rich man. Jacob uses deceit to steal his brother's blessing and then becomes a fugitive. God uses the situation to give Jacob a large family. God recasts human evil into good.

God recasts human evil into good.

The theological insights from the Joseph story fit into the broader context of *Genesis*, and in the process the insight into God's intent deepens. Throughout *Genesis*, little is said about the evil intent of humans or God's ability to take human evil and do good. In the final chapters of *Genesis*, God never speaks to Joseph. God does not visit Egypt. Nobody sees Him in a vision. Yet God's unseen hand is at work, and the influence of what God does is evident to all.

CONCLUSION

Joseph's dialogue with his brothers at the end of *Genesis* provides a fitting climax to a book that presents in broad strokes the ways in which God chooses to make Himself known and to confirm that He is in charge. In the end, Joseph interprets the events, reveals that God, despite not speaking or appearing, maintains control of all events. Not only does God exert control, but He takes human actions with evil intentions and turns them into good. *Genesis* closes with events unfolding exactly as God intends.

Strikingly, the theologically weighted confession of Joseph appears to reflect a constant theological concern in the book. Eve submits to the serpent's temptation and shares her sin with Adam, but in the following curses God promises to use the woman's seed to crush the serpent. Evil human intentions turn to good in the hands of God. Jacob secures both the birthright and blessing through unscrupulous means, but God works in his life to bring about good.

Genesis presents a spectrum of ways God interacts with humanity. Sometimes it is direct and personal, other times indirect and impersonal. Sometimes God is visibly present, other times He is seemingly absent. Yet God is working in both cases. God is in control. God works directly and indirectly. God wants to be known. He wants to be known as one who transforms human evil into divine good.

God is working when visibly present, and when seemingly absent.

Joseph's experience with God is much like our encounters with God. At the end of the story, he looks back over the variety of life events and sees the effect of the hand of God. He never sees God. He never talks with God. He never hears God. He never dreams of seeing God. God works offstage arranging the events of Joseph's life, but never directly encounters Joseph.

Who is God? *Genesis* gives us generous insight into His nature and His concerns.

What is He like? *Genesis* tells us He wants to be known.

Where is He when I need Him? *Genesis* introduces us to the doctrine of God's control over the world. We may not see him, but He is always there.

Is He really interested in helping me? He intends good. Exactly how that good plays out is explored in the next four chapters.

Just as the prodigal son in Rembrandt's rendition of Jesus' story presses his ear to hear his father's heartbeat, so the goal of this study lies in pressing to hear the heart of God in Scripture. By pondering over the Bible's first book, by looking for what it says about God, by searching for the theologically explicit passages in the narrative, I hope we can hear isolated beats of the heart of the living God. I make no claim at being comprehensive about a being that by nature is incomprehensible, nor do I aim to exhaustively find every evidence of God's passion–especially in a book that defies any exhaustive study.

Isolated beats of God's heart surface in the Bible's first book, giving hope and direction to those whose ears are pressed against God's chest.

WHAT DO YOU SAY?

1 Did reading this chapter change any preconceived ideas you had about God? If so, what were they?

2 In your personal experience, has God ever used an evil intent for good? Explain.

3 What can Joseph's trials and difficulties teach us about God when troubles come into our lives?

4 Compare the ways God interacted with humanity in *Genesis* with the way God interacts with humanity today? What does this imply about God's heart?

5 If you are discussing this chapter with a group, share with the others what surprises you most about God in *Genesis*.

6 What roles do you think God has played in your life? How do they match up to those presented here?

CHAPTER THREE

LOYALTY: GOD'S HEART FOR CHANGE

Begin your study of this chapter by reading *Genesis 6–9*.

t was a night I'll never forget. From the late evening call to the yellow tape screaming "Police lines: Do not cross," from the blood-stained body to the weeping teenager in the backseat of the squad car, the details are engraved in my memory. She called at about 10:30 PM, shortly after I had gone to bed, sobbing about her husband's murder, pleading with me to come. For the next several hours, a friend and I sat with this distraught woman in the living room as the officials removed her husband's bloody body from the upper bedroom. Slowly we pieced together the events earlier that evening. Her husband and son had argued again, as they often did. Her son grabbed a kitchen knife and in a frenzy of anger plunged it deep into her husband's abdomen. She called 911, but the paramedics could do nothing. The police handcuffed her son and stuffed him in the backseat of a Memphis police car.

I'll never forget her anguish. She was grieved in her heart. She wept. She replayed the scene. At times she grieved over what had happened to her husband. Other times she mourned over what was about to happen to her son. She had lost her husband, the man she could never hold again. She was about to lose her son, a boy she possibly would seldom embrace again.

I felt so helpless. She was in deep pain and my efforts to comfort seemed so ineffective.

53

During the night I went to the squad car to visit with her son. I'll never forget his regret. His heart was torn apart over what he had done. Over and over he said, "I'm sorry. I'm sorry. I didn't mean for it to turn out this way." I watched him shake his head from side to side as if he could undo what he had done by the constant twitching.

I felt so helpless. He was in deep lament and my words seemed so futile.

Grief and regret. The grief of the wife and mother. The regret of the son. Two hearts torn by some of life's most universal emotions. Grief and regret are common responses to the events of life. All of us have experienced them. All of us will face them again. We expect life to bring a certain amount of grief and regret.

But there is something we do not expect. We do not expect to find grief and regret in God's heart. Yet we do.

Barely six chapters into the Bible, God tells us about His heart. We might conclude certain things about His heart based on His words and actions. In *Genesis 1–5* God's speeches and activity provide insight into His heart. But then in *Genesis 6*, God uses the word "heart." God tells us what is going on in His heart. He tells us His divine heart is filled with grief and regret.

> **We do not expect to find grief and regret in God's heart. Yet we do.**

This investigation into the heart of God focuses on the key players in the Flood story and on how the text describes these characters. The previous chapter divided *Genesis* by the characters that dominated each section showing that God is the main character in the narratives of *Genesis 1–11*. In the Flood story, two other characters join God: Humankind and Noah. As we ponder over this passage we will reflect on the qualities of each of these participants in the Flood story.

In much of *Genesis* God speaks to the other participants in the unfolding story. He talks to Adam and Eve, confronts Cain, gives boatbuilding instructions to Noah, and on it goes. But when God speaks about His heart, He is not talking to anybody in the narrative. In the language of the theater, it is a soliloquy. God speaks to Himself. We overhear the divine mind at work. He reveals His thoughts to us. We hear words that the people in the biblical text do not hear.

> **Despite His own grief and regret, He remains loyal to the human race.**

God's grief and regret come in the midst of the story of Noah and the Flood. It is the first mention of God's heart. In His grief and regret we understand how human actions affect the divine heart, we witness what He does out of His grief and regret, and we learn that despite human evil, and despite His own grief and regret, He remains loyal to the human race.

EAVESDROPPING ON GOD'S HEART

Von Rad (*Genesis*, 152-155) and Westermann (*Promises*, 44-56) note the increasing severity of sin in the opening chapters of the Bible: Adam and Eve eat from the forbidden tree, their son commits fratricide. Cain murders his brother, and Lamech kills a child.[1] Finally, all humankind sins in the most severe ways all of the time. The *"very good"* world of *Genesis 1:31* becomes the *"only evil continually"* world of *Genesis 6:5*.

Genesis 6:5-7 and *11-13* offer summaries of how bad the world has become. Both passages use explicit theological language.[2] Humans are wicked (*6:5*), evil (*6:5*), corrupt (*6:11,12*) and violent (*6:11,13*). The passage offers a clear analysis of humanity: *"The LORD saw that the wickedness of humankind was great in the earth, and that every inclination of the thoughts of their hearts was only evil continually"* (*Gen 6:5*). This verse announces that human evil was worldwide (*"great in the earth"*), deeply imbedded in the human thought (*"every inclination of the thoughts of their hearts"*), and constant (*"only evil continually"*), tracing sin across geographical, psychological, and temporal lines.

---

[1] Lamech says, "I have killed a man for wounding me, a young man for striking me" (*Gen 4:23*). The Hebrew for "young man" can be understood to refer to a young male child, in which case we have the first record of an adult harming a child.

[2] *Gen 6:5-7* speaks of humankind while *Gen 6:11-13* mentions the earth. For example, *Gen 6:5* speaks of the *"wickedness of humankind"* while *6:11* mentions *"the earth was corrupt."* While one might argue that the second set of references refers to the planet earth or to the dirt on the planet, I assume that earth refers to the population of the planet and those who walk on it.

The Flood story comes to us as a narrative. The storyline is a familiar one: God announces the flood and gives instructions to Noah about building an ark and loading his family and the animals. God then sends the flood waters, which destroy all living things except the passengers and cargo on the ark. After considerable time, God allows the waters to recede, and Noah sends out a series of birds. Finally, Noah exits the ark, offers sacrifice and begins life again.

Genesis does not list doctrinal truths in propositional form, but rather tells of a terrible flood. Yet embedded in the narrative are several passages with clusters of theologically significant words. At least two texts in the Flood story exhibit these qualities: *Genesis 6:5-13* and *8:20-22*. These texts also contain the references to the heart of God.

God watches as human wickedness soars to unprecedented heights. God had created the world to be good. He had made humanity in His image and likeness. He had given people dominion over the earth, had told them to subdue it. He had blessed the couple He had made. God had put the humans in a delightful garden and had asked them to take care of it. He had provided. He had directed. He had supplied. He had made the good world where they live.

Humanity responded with sin. Now the sin grows to titanic proportions. How will God respond? What will He do? I have learned a great deal about the answers to those questions from Brueggemann (*Genesis*, 73-87) and the following discussion depends on his observations about the Flood story.

As mentioned in the last chapter, the Bible's opening section presents God acting in humanlike ways. To borrow from Trible (**79, 89, 95**), God becomes creator, gardener, legislator, evaluator, potter, executive, anesthesiologist, surgeon, architect, builder, designer, divine matchmaker, interrogator, judge, executioner, and barricade builder.

Although the anthropomorphic descriptions of God appear abundantly in the Flood story, the entire Bible uses similar means to communicate its message. God's words appear in the Bible, but in the form of human words. The prophets repeatedly recite the messenger formula: *"Thus says the LORD."* God speaks just as humans speak. Jesus promises to provide rooms in God's heavenly mansion, suggesting that God has a dwelling place much like humans have houses. The heavenly scenes in *Revelation* picture God sitting on a throne just as humans use chairs for work and play. The Bible repeatedly and consistently uses human means to describe God.

Given the use of this kind of language throughout the Bible, the anthropomorphisms of *Genesis 6–9* cannot be easily dismissed as "figures of speech." Although God shutting the door of the ark or smelling Noah's sacrifice may depict God in unusual humanlike roles, how can they be regarded as "figures of speech" when *"Thus says the LORD"* is taken literally? Both use human images to help humans understand the divine world.

This study takes the anthropomorphisms seriously but not woodenly. The reference to God's heart is understood to reveal insight into the mind of God and to what concerns Him (taking it seriously), without pressing the heart of God into a literal organ with four chambers (taking it woodenly). The reference to God's heart is taken seriously as a means to help humans understand the deeper levels of God, without woodenly arguing that God looks like us, complete with a beating muscle on the left side of the chest.

Anthropomorphisms help the writer as well as the readers relate to God better. The *Genesis* materials have their origin with God mediated through a human writer. The presence of anthropomorphisms suggests a plan on God's part to communicate in human language and images in such a way that those pondering the material would come to a correct understanding of what God intended.

In the Flood story God takes on additional human features: He sees (*Gen 6:5,12*), speaks (*6:7,13; 7:1; 8:15,21; 9:1,8,12,17*), walks (*6:9*), shuts a door (*7:16*), remembers (*8:1*), and smells (*8:21*). Additionally, *Genesis 6* mentions God's eyes (*v. 8*), face (*v. 11*), and His heart (*v. 6*).

GOD REVEALS THAT HIS HEART HURTS

The appearance of God's heart so early in the biblical story provides opportunity to ponder and to explore what we might hear. What we hear are two more humanlike features: Grief and regret. Some of the most explicit theological language about God in *Genesis 1–11* appears in response to the descriptions of human sin:

*⁶And the LORD was sorry that he had made humankind on the earth, and it grieved him to his heart. ⁷So the LORD said, "I will blot out from the earth the human beings I have created—people together with animals and creeping things and birds of the air, for I am sorry that I have made them." (**Gen 6:6-7**)*

God creates humans in His image, commands them to properly fill and subdue the earth and to care for His garden. Humanity responds with wickedness, evil, corruption, and violence. God has two reactions: *Grief and sorrow.*

First, God was *grieved* in His heart. The Hebrew word *'atsab* refers to hurt, pain, or grief. The wickedness of humanity touches God's heart. Brueggemann (**Genesis, 77**) expresses surprise that God is filled with grief instead of anger. Human sin prompts pain and not wrath, hurt and not heat.

The Hebrew word *'atsab* appears here for the third time in the Genesis story. When God punishes Eve for eating of the tree, He promises she would experience *pain* in bearing children. Her pain becomes God's *grief*. God's heart fills with the same kind of pain a women experiences in labor. Noah's father had high hopes for his son, believing his boy would somehow *"bring us relief from our work and from the toil of our hands"* (**Gen 5:29**). The word for "toil" is the same word as the "grief" of God's heart. God's heart fills with the same kind of burden that a man feels in the unrelenting work of life.

Second, God was *sorry* that He had made humankind. The Hebrew word *nacham*, as in the case of many Hebrew words, often does double duty. It describes the sense of regret, loss, grief, and sorrow in response to events, and also expresses the offering of comfort and pity to those in that situation. The word translated "sorry" appears nine times in the OT when God regrets or changes His mind,[3] and occurs another 13 times in connection with the phrase *"repented of the evil"* or *"repented of good"* (KJV) or *"change your mind"* (NRSV) where God is the subject.[4]

God grieves and He is sorry. We do not expect these to be the first qualities we learn about His heart. But God Himself provides this insight. He does not speak to Noah, but He talks to the reader, to us. In His divine plan, He gives us an initial glimpse into His grief and regret.

---

[3] *Gen 6:6,7; Num 23:19; 1Sa 15:11,29[2×],35; Ps 110:4; Jer 4:28.*
[4] *Ex 32:12,14; 2Sa 24:16; 1Chr 21:15; Jer 18:8,10; 26:3,13,19; 42:10; Joel 2:13; Jonah 3:10; 4:2.*

> The question of whether God actually changes His mind or whether the language merely accommodates to human understanding sparks considerable debate about the nature of God. Many find any prospect of God changing His mind contrary to their conception of the divine being. Others argue that these texts point to God's ability to be God and still change His mind. Kaiser (209) offers insight into this ongoing debate.

The description of God's heart raises significant questions. Did God mean the same thing by the word "heart" that we mean today? Was His regret like our regret? Did He grieve like we grieve? What do these words mean? Why does He tell us these things about Himself?

Whenever I read these passages about God's heart in *Genesis 6*, I think back to that night when a son murdered his father and I sat with the grieving widow and talked with the regretful son. They responded in grief and regret to a terrible deed. As I walked with them in the following days, the widow continued to grieve, perhaps with less uncontrolled sobbing and hysterical cries, but she continued to mourn her loss. The son constantly regretted his action, especially as he worked his way through the criminal justice system.

When we read these words about God's heart, grief, and regret, we cannot help but bring our own experiences of these emotions to the passage. We know we cannot impose our experiences on God; I do not mean to imply that God grieved like that widow or that He had regret like that son. Those are just the most dominant pictures of grief and regret that I bring when I read. We only seek to understand and to probe what these words say about God and about His heart.

By sharing what He feels, God tells us human actions affect Him. In order to communicate that to us, He chooses our words "grief" and "regret." He decides to use the word "heart" to refer to the part of Him that is affected. Together these qualities describe a God with a heart for humanity, deeply touched by human failures, mistakes, brokenness, and rebellion.

Genesis covers considerable territory in its revelation about God. *Genesis* begins with a God who creates humanity and now tells about a God who regrets creating humanity. *Genesis 1* tells

These qualities describe a God with a heart for humanity.

of a God who evaluates all He has made with the divine stamp of *"it is good,"* but *Genesis 6* speaks of a God who evaluates His creation with the proclamation, "It is bad!" God is not a distant being untouched by His creation, but a God who watches over His new world and is deeply affected by what He sees.

After God reveals His heart, He takes action. God's response to His negative evaluation of humanity comes in a repeated set of responses. He will blot out what He has made (*6:7; 7:4,23*), make an end of all flesh (*6:13*), and destroy all living things (*6:13,17*), all by means of a flood (*6:17; 7:4*).

In *Genesis 1–11*, Von Rad (*Genesis,* 152-155) and Westermann (*Promises,* 44-56) note an increasing severity in punishments: Adam and Eve are told they will die. All humans live with the expectation of death. Additionally, Adam and Eve are cursed with pain and toil and expelled from the garden. Cain commits the first murder. Afterwards he is banished from the land, though given a mark to protect him from others. Life spans are shortened after the intermarriage of the sons of God and the daughters of men. Now the punishment reaches near total destruction of all human life.

But humanity is not completely destroyed. In the midst of the negative verdict on humanity is Noah. Noah is obedient, righteous, blameless, and he walks with God. Noah is the first person in the Bible to receive an explicit offer of grace.[5] God looks on Noah with favor, saves him from the flood, and through Noah provides a remnant of humanity to allow the race to continue. Noah's personal qualities separate him from the negative judgment passed on the rest of humanity. He is saved from the destructive flood waters because God gives him grace.

> Noah plays a central role in *Genesis 5–9*. He appears briefly in *Genesis 5:29-32* at the end of the Sethite genealogy. Despite his prominence in the telling of the Flood story, Noah never speaks in the passages about the Flood. He talks only in *Genesis 9:24-27*, after the Flood. Three times the text does some variation of *"he did all*

[5] God's actions toward Adam, Eve, and even Cain illustrate grace, but it is not stated explicitly. The *Genesis* text does not explore the basis on which Noah found favor in the eyes of God. He was a righteous man in a wicked generation. That pleased God. God responded by saving Noah from the impending flood.

*that God commanded him" (**Gen 6:22; 7:5,9**). **Genesis 6:5-13** notes
four key qualities about Noah:*

First, according to **Genesis 6:8** "Noah found favor in the sight of
the LORD." Favor is the same word for "grace," which appears in
adjectival form in God's list of His own qualities in **Exodus 34:6**.

Secondly, Noah was a righteous man (**Gen 6:9**). God and
Abraham would talk extensively about righteousness in **Genesis 18**.
Ten righteous people could not be found in Sodom. Noah was a
single righteous man in a sinful world.

Third, Noah was blameless (**Gen 6:9**). The word means to be
complete, whole, or sound. Most of the translations understand it to
mean free from the oppressive sinful activity that surrounded him. In
Genesis 17:1 God commands Abraham to be blameless, a state
Noah had already achieved.

Fourth, Noah walked with God (**Gen 6:9**). Joining Enoch before
him (he walked with God in **Gen 5:22**), the trait uses anthropomorphic
language. Walking often denotes ethical behavior in Hebrew (e.g.,
Mic 6:8), and the anthropomorphic image suggests that anybody permitted to walk alongside God would be one of moral character.

Jesus frequently told His followers: "follow me" and Peter later
beckoned Christians to "follow in his steps" (**1Pet 2:21**), both using
the walking image in the sense of modeling the character of the
walking partner. Charles Sheldon, in the nineteenth century, wrote
a novel entitled *In His Steps*, in which a group of people in a small
community decide to live by asking, "what would Jesus do?" of
every decision. Those who make decisions as Jesus might have are
contemporary examples of people seeking to "walk with God."

The same heart that grieved and regretted the rampant sin of
humankind finds room for a single good man. God's regret at making humanity is not a total regret. His grief over their actions is not
pain at every human action. If the language of heart, grief, and regret
reveal that sinful human actions touch the heart of God, then the
favor and salvation of Noah affirm that obedient human actions also
affect the heart of God. God does not give up on the human race even
though their wickedness affects Him deeply. Even in the midst of His
grief and regret, God remains loyal to the humans He created.

Human sin touched God at a deep level, prompting the drastic
response of a disastrous flood. Yet without a look at the post-Flood

Chapter 3
God's Heart for Change

scene, the investigation into His heart is incomplete. Noah and his family survive the flood. As Noah offers a post-Flood sacrifice, God smells the pleasing odor. Then God speaks to Himself again. He evaluates the destruction:

> *I will never again curse the ground because of humankind, for the inclination of the human heart is evil from youth; nor will I ever again destroy every living creature as I have done. (**Gen 8:21**)*[6]

One might expect that the Flood would curb human sin, encourage human faithfulness, cure the wicked human heart, but the human heart *after* the Flood mirrors the human heart *before* the Flood:

> *. . . the thoughts of their hearts was only evil continually (**Gen 6:5**).*

> *. . . the inclination of the human heart is evil from youth (**Gen 8:21**).*

Unlike the destruction of Sodom and Gomorrah (**Genesis 18–19**), there is no opportunity for Noah or another representative of the human race to barter with God over humankind's punishment. No righteous man will prevent this destruction. The punishment, save for Noah, is universal and complete.

Genesis does not speak about the effect of the destruction on the earth's population. Philosophers, artists, and movie makers often depict the plight of humanity's agonizing struggle against the unrelenting flood waters. As **Genesis 7** comes to an end, all life perishes, the earth is covered with water, and the passengers on the ark are left.

Despite Genesis' silence about the effect on the human race, subsequent biblical passages will display the destructive side of God. The destruction of Sodom and Gomorrah, the catastrophe in Egypt, the conquest of Canaan, the fall of Samaria, the destruction of Jerusalem, the end time destruction and the establishment of the eternal hell depend on the same quality of God and are taken up in a later chapter.

The Flood did not change the human heart or human evil. The massive destruction of humanity and all living things except those saved

[6] Some wonder who is intended by the term "humankind" in **Gen 8:21**. The suggestions include that "humankind" refer to: 1) those destroyed by the flood; 2) Noah and his family, the only living humans immediately after the flood; 3) the subsequent human generations, given that the text is not written down until years after the flood; or 4) humankind in general.

in the ark had no effect on human sinfulness. Those who sinned are punished. The wrongdoers are gone. But human sinfulness is not stopped by the Flood. In fact, following the flood, Noah, saved by God from the Flood because of His righteousness, gets drunk and sins in his tent (*Gen 9:20-28*).

> Genesis' description of human sin anticipates *Romans 1–4*. As Paul confronts ethnic tensions in the Roman congregation, each group seeking to advance its own cause, he echoes the conclusions of the Flood story by showing that since all people are caught up in sin, neither Jew nor Gentile can claim superiority. When he concludes that people in his own time *"exchanged the truth about God for a lie and worshiped and served the creature rather than the Creator"* (*Rom 1:25*), the apostle restates the same analysis as *Genesis 6*. He goes on to compile a list of stinging OT passages (*Rom 3:9-18*) which recite human wickedness with the same exhaustive language as *Genesis 6* before concluding *"all have sinned and fall short of the glory of God"* (*Rom 3:23*), which could be an apt summary of the pre-Flood world. This parallel shows that in the multiple centuries between Noah and Paul, humankind does not change.

Genesis 6–9 offers a negative verdict on human sin. Human wickedness and evil corrupt the world, leading to violence. God responds with a violent, destructive flood, but the human wickedness remains unaffected.

GOD REVEALS THAT HIS HEART REMAINS LOYAL TO HUMANITY

The post-Flood scene contains the second explicit biblical reference to God's heart. It comes immediately after Noah empties the ark, builds an altar, and sacrifices to the Lord. The text states that, pleased with the sacrifice, *"The LORD said in his heart, 'I will never again curse the ground because of humankind, for the inclination of the human heart is evil from youth'"* (*Gen 8:21*). The text tells the reader what God speaks in His own heart. The line is not directed to Noah, but to God Himself. The reader is permitted access to God's private thoughts. Although more explicit here than in *Genesis 6:5f.*, God speaks in both texts not to Noah, but to Himself, and for the benefit of the reader, about what He is thinking.

Before the flood, Noah's walk with God prompts favor. After the flood, Noah's sacrifice to God results in divine pleasure. After the sacrifice, God reveals His future plans.

God reveals a different agenda from the pre-Flood text. Before the flood God's negative evaluation of humanity prompts Him to destroy humanity. After the flood, God's evaluation of humanity is equally negative, but His response is to make a promise of *"never again."* In the coming verses He promises *never again* to

> curse the ground (**8:21**)
> destroy every living creature (**8:21**)
> cut off all flesh by a flood (**9:11**)
> destroy the earth with a flood (**9:11**)
> destroy all flesh with a flood (**9:15**).

After the flood, His response is to make a promise of "never again."

The post-Flood narrative repeats "never again" five times. The variations in the promise are not significant for our study, but the change in God's response to humanity is significant. Succinctly put, God has changed His response to human sin:

> I have determined to make an end of all flesh. (**Gen 6:13**)
>
> Nor will I ever again destroy every living creature. (**Gen 8:21**)

God will continue to address human sin, for He immediately lists potential punishment for disobedience to the commands of *Genesis 9:1-7*, but not in the same way, not to the same degree as He did in the Flood. In theological terms God shows His passion for humanity by now being able to look at the same human plight and respond in a different way. He sees the continual sinfulness of humanity and plans for a better future. He acknowledges that the Flood did not remove human tendency toward disobedience, but He promises to be part of making the future different from the past.

The passage adds clarity to the nature of God's heart. God's heart changes. Before the flood His heart is filled with grief and regret over human sin. After the flood, His heart is filled with "never again." In the pre-Flood passage, God's grieving heart prompts the devastating flood. In the post-Flood passage, God's heart prompts a recurring rainbow.

God knows the *human* heart is not changed by the Flood, so God changes *His* heart. The next time every imagination of the human heart turns evil, there will be no devastating flood. God's heart is changed.

That change offers additional insight into the divine heart. Human sin grieves God's heart and makes Him regret making these people. But He is not so grieved that He gives up on the human race. He does not regret the making of all humankind because He continues to make them.

> **God knows the *human* heart is not changed by the flood, so God changes *His* heart.**

The Bible might have ended at *Genesis 7* in the midst of the flood. This hypothetical short version of the Bible starts with God making the good world, creating people in His image and likeness, but ends with bitter disappointment as God decides to end the effort and destroys all He has made. But the Bible does not end at *Genesis 7* because God's grieving and regretful heart decides to continue the human race and to maintain a relationship with them.

God reveals this loyalty in five ways:

1. He blesses Noah and His sons (*Gen 9:1*). This blessing repeats the one given to humankind in *Genesis 1:28* and anticipates the blessing to Abram in *Genesis 12*. A later chapter will show how blessing provides a significant insight into the passion of God.

2. He repeats the command to be fruitful and multiply to Noah (*Gen 9:1,7*). The first couple receives this command in *Genesis 1:28*.

3. He reestablishes humankind's dominion over the animal world (*Gen 9:2-3*). Here God echoes the commands to have dominion and to subdue the earth in *Genesis 1:26,28-30*. Both cases include the use of plants for food, but in the Noachian commandments animals (with restriction) are also given to humans for food.

4. He protects human life (*Gen 9:4-6*). In the wake of the murders by Cain and Lamech, God recognizes that "the inclination of the human heart is evil" (*8:21*) and establishes punishment for those who shed human blood. There is no similar command in *Genesis 1–2*.

5. He continues to see humankind in His image (*Gen 9:6*). God originally created humanity in His image and likeness (*Gen 1:26-27*) and allowed that image and likeness to continue through human propagation (*Gen 5:3*). The post-Flood generation receives the same stamping of God's image.

6. He makes a covenant with Noah not to destroy the earth by a flood (*Gen 9:8-17*). God earlier promises to covenant with Noah (*Gen 6:18*). Now God makes that covenant with Noah, all humanity, and animals with the promise not to destroy the earth by a flood. The covenant has no restrictions or qualifications. All who follow Noah enjoy its benefits. The sign of the covenant is the rainbow. The bow in the sky becomes a symbol and reminder of the promise made in the post-Flood scene by God speaking from His heart.

The Bible does not end after *Genesis 7*, but God uses language from the creation to renew the earth and its people and to continue His own relationship with humanity. We see two aspects of God's heart. On one hand His heart is so deeply affected by human sin that He responds with a destructive flood. On the other hand after the flood His heart remains so loyal to humanity that He blesses, commands fruitfulness, reestablishes human dominion, protects human life, makes human life in His image and covenants never to do again what He just did.

ENCOURAGING WORDS
FROM GOD'S HEART

After that night when I ministered at the murder scene, I did not know what would happen next. How would the grieving wife and mother and her penitent son cope with the new realities? How would she respond to the one who had taken the life of her husband? I tried to put myself in her situation: If two people I loved hated each other so much that one killed the other, could I reach out to the survivor? I was amazed at what happened.

That grieving wife became the chief advocate for her incarcerated son. She made sure we prayed every Sunday for the lawyers, the trial, and the prison environment. She called on people to help, to give her advice. She set about to rebuild her life and especially the life of her son. Eventually, because of her faithful efforts, the young man was released and together they began a new life.

I do not know a single word or phrase that expresses what that woman did. She grieved over a huge loss, but then remained faithful to changing the one who caused that loss. Despite my groping for the right words, the story of that woman and her son offers a concrete parallel to the message about God in the Flood story.

Deeply pained by humanity, God's loyalty seeks to change humanity. God's grieving heart commits to changing the human heart. God makes a decision as a result of the Flood that has ramifica-

God's grieving heart commits to changing the human heart.

tions throughout the rest of the Bible. We who read these words are privy to that decision-making process and witnesses of God's faithfulness to that process. In effect, we have been inside the divine heart.

The Bible opens with a book that concentrates on a God who directs every step. In *Genesis 1–11* He dominates the action with His presence, but in *Genesis 37–50* He controls events in an unseen way. The first 11 chapters are filled with God from beginning to end. Barely six chapters into the Bible, two texts reflect on the heart of the divine being. In both passages God speaks to Himself, allowing humanity to overhear the divine thought processes. In speaking to an eavesdropping world, God reveals sorrow, grief, and a change of plans. God seeks to be known.

This self-revelation of God in *Genesis* lays the foundation for all that follows. God will talk personally with Moses 52 different times in *Exodus*. Through Moses He will share His guidance for living, instructions which are based on who He is. He will send leaders, judges, prophets, and kings. He will commission Hosea to write a treatise on the importance of knowing God. He will reveal Himself in Jesus, who will say that to know Him is to know the Father. Near the end of the Bible in *1 John*, God will commission John to write a shepherding letter on knowing God.

Not only does God reveal His own heart in the Flood narrative, but He exposes the human heart. The Flood story twice juxtaposes the divine heart with the human heart. The Flood narrative is as much about a heart-to-heart discussion as about disaster. The Flood story conveys that God knows the human heart, a quality to which the Bible will repeatedly return.[7]

What we learn about the divine heart is crucial. When God allows us to peer inside His heart, we see a God concerned about and touched by humanity. We might expect the first insight into God's heart in the Bible to be a clear expression of His compassion or love. Framing this volume around the parable of the Prodigal Son where

[7] *1Chr 28:9; Ps 139:23; Jer 17:10; Jn 2:24; 4:39; Rom 8:27; 1Jn 3:19-20.*

God shows compassion, forgiveness, and love may prompt that expectation. The first glimpse into God's heart reveals the unexpected. We find grief and regret. God recognizes humanity's brokenness and it breaks His heart. He is fully aware of human evil. He is pained by human evil. He is moved by human wickedness.

Despite its evil, God remains loyal to the human race. After Adam and Eve's sin, God is loyal. God does not give up on Cain. Perhaps the catastrophic event of the Flood puts God's willingness to continue His relationship with the human race at risk. He knows the Flood did not resolve human evil. Neither does the Flood stop God's loyalty to humankind.

> **The first glimpse into God's heart reveals the unexpected.**

Sin keeps humanity from being all that God had planned. The resulting human brokenness causes God regret and grief. But God continues to seek a relationship with humanity. What we learn about His heart encourages us and explains what we read in the rest of Scripture. Every judge God sends into Canaan, every new prophet who stands to speak, every biblical book that reveals God's Word continues God's loyalty. Whether through the prophet speaking to postexilic Jerusalem in *Isaiah 61* or through Jesus in front of His hometown synagogue in *Luke 4*, God is on a mission to bring better news to the brokenhearted of life.

Ultimately the Flood story speaks of the grace of God's heart. In the midst of titanic evil, God offers grace to the righteous man Noah. After the world's first catastrophe, God places a rainbow in the sky as a sign of a promise to respond with future grace to the same actions that prompted the disastrous flood. God shows His loyalty best in giving grace.

The Flood story surprises the reader with the change in God's heart. God not only decides to take different actions in the future than He had in the immediate past, but He chooses to associate that decision with His heart and to reveal it within that context to those He created. This change need not imply that God's character changed, or that His nature depends on human actions, but rather that His heart holds a deep concern for humanity and promises to be part of their future.

CONCLUSION

Genesis not only begins the Bible, but it lays critical foundations for understanding the heart of God. *Genesis 50* reveals through the words of Joseph that God turns human evil into good. Once Joseph establishes *that* passion of God, to take something wrong and make it into something good, the pattern emerges everywhere. Humanity intends evil from their heart from their youth. But God responds with His own heart to make good what they had made bad.

In the Flood story the reader encounters the first references to the heart of God, learning of His deep passion and concern for humankind. Evil lurks in the human heart. Pain and regret often fill God's heart. The human heart resists change. God's heart is committed to finding a way to change the human heart. Such a heart will take us to Calvary.

WHAT DO YOU SAY?

1. Share a time that you experienced either grief or regret or both.

2. Look at the four key qualities of Noah. How would you explain each of these to another person?

   a. Found favor in the sight of God

   b. Righteous

   c. Blameless

   d. Walked with God

3. What does God know about our hearts?

   a. *1 Chronicles 28:9*

   b. *Psalm 139:23*

   c. *Jeremiah 17:10*

   d. *John 2:24; 4:39*

   e. *Romans 8:27*

   f. *1 John 3:19-20*

4. Read *Genesis 6–9*. List as many ways as you can that reveal God's passion and concern for human kind.

5. Do you think God's heart is the same or different after the flood? What evidence would you point to for your answer?

CHAPTER FOUR

IMMANUEL: GOD ON OUR SIDE OF THE STREET

Begin your study of this chapter by reading Isaiah 7.

amily visits to my grandparents' farm are among my
most pleasant childhood memories. We would play
among the farm buildings, eat grandma's sumptuous
food, and enjoy listening to the family stories. When we got ready to
leave, it was dark. I remember looking out the window of my grandparents' house at the family car parked some distance away next to the
barn. The various farm buildings cast menacing shadows over the path
from the house to the car. The places where I had played a few hours
before now filled me with fear. I thought various monsters inhabited
the shadows. The walk to the car filled me with apprehension.

But every time we got ready to go home, the same thing would
happen. I would resist until my grandfather picked me up in his
strong arms and carried me to the car. The menacing shadows were
still there. I still thought the monsters lurked nearby. But I was no
longer afraid because I trusted the one who
carried me.

Our world is much like that childhood
experience. Darkness prompts fear. Various
kinds of "monsters" threaten us. We all face
menacing shadows that fill us with apprehension. What we want is somebody to go
with us. We need somebody strong to protect us. The next three chapters take up these
concerns.

So far in our study we have learned that God directs our steps and that He takes the evil intent of humanity and turns it into good. Those evil human intentions fill God's heart with grief and regret, but evil does not make Him desert the human race. The rainbow regularly reminds us of His loyalty and restraint.

Yet the look into the heart of God involves God's destruction of most of the pre-Flood world. While we find comfort in God's loyalty to the human race, we wonder about what kind of God can destroy sinful humanity by a flood. Our questions about the ethics of God are compounded as the Bible continues. *Genesis* reveals a God who comes down to interfere with human languages at Babel, to give Abram land that belongs to other people, to annihilate Sodom and Gomorrah, to send a famine to Palestine, and to enslave Joseph in Egypt.

Given this part of His nature, we might be glad that He keeps His distance. We can understand why people think of God as a cosmic highway patrolman. We may be glad He is there, but we do not want any face-to-face encounters. We are content for God to stay at His house as we live in ours.

These and other actions of God raise questions. Can we trust Him not to hurt us? How do we explain God's role in the world's suffering and violence? Why does He interfere with human activity? There is no single response to these questions, but rather the more we get to know God, the clearer we understand how He can allow—and, at times, interfere with—destructive and violent acts.

These next three chapters explore what the Bible says about God's distance from us and His intent toward us. Each chapter takes up a trajectory that begins in *Genesis*, but repeatedly surfaces throughout the Bible. Each trajectory helps us understand the deeper nature of God. The more we listen, the better we understand the heart of our

We begin with a trajectory that might be called the "divine with."

God. We begin with a trajectory that for the lack of a better phrase might be called the "divine with."

The biblical view of God might be compared to a street. God lives on one side of the street and we live on the other. God's side of the street is what we call heaven. There is no crime or poverty. God controls every word and thought. Our side of the street is what we call earth. Crime and poverty seem everywhere. At times God seems to not have much control at all. A broad, multilane avenue separates God's side of the street from the human side. This illustration reveals two ways of understanding God.

First, at times humans gaze across the street at God. Sometimes, as mentioned above, we look with apprehension, concerned that God might come to our side of the street. We are glad when He stays home because we fear the potential destructive nature of His power and might. His divine qualities of holiness, righteousness, and power separate Him from our side of the street. When we see His holiness, we realize our sin. His might makes us feel small. His justice exposes our unfairness. His righteousness burns into our sinful nature. We look across the street sometimes with fear and apprehension, other times in worship and praise. In one sense, the Bible opens and closes with God on His side of the street. *Genesis 1* depicts Him creating our side of the street from His world of holiness, righteousness, and power. At the end of the Bible, *Revelation* speaks of heaven, God's side of the street, and calls us to leave our world and enter His, to move across the street to God's side.

Second, at other times God leaves His side of the street to join us on our side. In *Genesis 2–11* God repeatedly visits the human side of the street. The One who is holy visits the sinners. The Mighty comes to see the small. The Just One comes into the territory of the wicked. We will spend the next few chapters pondering God's visits to our side of the street.

> **God leaves His side of the street to join us on our side.**

The Bible regularly explains the concept of God crossing the street to visit us on our own side with five single-syllable words built around a common preposition. The preposition is "with." Repeatedly in Scripture, the God from the other side of the street says, *"I will be with you."* This chapter ponders over those five words, and the variations of that phrase, asking, "What does that simple affirmation say about the complex being we call God?" Those five words form a trajectory through Scripture, one that varies only slightly, running from Genesis to Revelation.

THE BREADTH OF
THE "DIVINE WITH"

Tracing a trajectory takes us through both familiar and unfamiliar territory. Generally, more people read Matthew than Malachi, but both books are the Word of God. In following a trajectory, we take up how the biblical writers borrowed language used by their predecessors to convey their own material. Many NT writers frequently cite the OT for the words they use to express truth. On other occasions, the language they use is so woven throughout Scripture that citing the OT text is unnecessary. We trace the trajectories in two ways: First, we will survey the use of the "divine with," noting briefly how frequently and persistently this "divine with" appears first in the OT and then in the NT. Second, we probe more deeply into several passages that use the phrase. We might probe any of the occurrences of the "divine with." Hopefully, these will be the most productive as we seek the heart of God. In the following citations, the "divine with" is bolded for clarity.

A SURVEY OF THE "DIVINE WITH"
IN THE OT

The first occurrences of the "divine with" in the Bible appear in *Genesis*. God speaks to Isaac only twice, but on both of those occasions, God first makes this oft-repeated promise:

> ²The LORD appeared to Isaac and said, "Do not go down to Egypt; settle in the land that I shall show you. ³Reside in this land as an alien, and **I will be with you**, and will bless you; for to you and to your descendants I will give all these lands, and I will fulfill the oath that I swore to your father Abraham." (**Gen 26:2-3**)

> And that very night the LORD appeared to him and said, "I am the God of your father Abraham; do not be afraid, for **I am with you** and will bless you and make your offspring numerous for my servant Abraham's sake." (**Gen 26:24**)

In the first passage, God gives Isaac the same promise He first made to Abraham, telling him not to migrate to Egypt but to stay in the Promised Land. When Isaac remains, he comes into conflict with Abimelech over wells. In the midst of their quarrel, God repeats the promise to Isaac a second time. Note that God's words vary slightly. In the first statement, God renews the covenant first made with Abraham now with his son Isaac in words that personalize God's promise, *"I will be with you."* Then in the trouble with Abimelech over the wells in the second passage, God returns to Isaac, not with a promise, but with His presence: *"I am with you."* God oversees a solution to the conflict over the wells.

Moses receives the same promise at the beginning and end of his work with God. Early in *Exodus*, Moses flees to the wilderness where he receives a call from God. At the burning bush, God laid out His mission for Moses with the promise, ***"I will be with you"*** (*Ex 3:12*). As Moses nears the end of his life, on the edge of the Promised Land, Moses passes the same promise on to his successor Joshua: *"It is the LORD who goes before you. **He will be with you**; he will not fail you or forsake you. Do not fear or be dismayed"* (**Deu 31:8**). ***Deuteronomy*** ends with the death of Moses. Just before the end, Moses passes the promise of God's presence on to Joshua. Moses hears the divine promise at the beginning of his work and then transfers it on to his successor.

After ***Deuteronomy***, the book of ***Joshua*** opens with the preparations to cross the Jordan in order to enter the Promised Land. Joshua seeks confirmation of the loyalty of the tribes settling on the east side of the Jordan. They pledge themselves with these words: *"Just as we obeyed Moses in all things, so we will obey you. Only may the **LORD your God be with you,** as he was with Moses!"* (***Josh 1:17***). The promise of the "divine with" moves from Isaac to Moses to Joshua and now to all the people claiming their new home.

The Israelite monarchs continue to speak of the same promise. The book of *1 Chronicles* provides details about David's preparations to build the temple. Now elderly, David instructs young Solomon about temple construction: *"Now, my son, **the LORD be with you**, so that you may succeed in building the house of the LORD your God, as he has spoken concerning you"* (***1Chr 22:11***). Years later, Solomon builds that temple and in a long prayer he dedicates the completed structure with these words: ***"The LORD our God be with us,*** *as he was with our ancestors; may he not leave us or abandon us"* (***1Kgs 8:57***). Both David's preparations for the temple and Solomon's dedication of the structure include reference to God's presence.

> Not only is the "divine with" used in connection with the temple, but so is a reference to God's heart:
>
> continued on next page ➡

> The LORD said to him, "I have heard your prayer and your plea, which you made before me; I have consecrated this house that you have built, and put my name there forever; my eyes and my heart will be there for all time." (*1Kgs 9:3*; cf. the parallel in *2Chr 7:16*)
>
> God not only promises to be with the people, but the temple will be a focal point of that "with-ness" in that God will give it His name, His eyes, and His heart. As long as the physical temple stood, it served as a physical marker of the intersection between the divine and human worlds, a concrete expression of the "divine with." The NT understands that God still dwells in a temple, not a physical one in Jerusalem, but an eternal one of His spiritual people.

God's prophets also used the "divine with." In the eighth century, Amos passes the promise on to the people of North Israel: *"Seek good and not evil, that you may live; and so **the LORD, the God of hosts, will be with you**, just as you have said"* (*Am 5:14*). Amos, from Judah, speaks to the people of Samaria, informing them of God's displeasure at their disregard for justice and righteousness. He calls them to return to God's ways so that He may continue to have a presence with them.

A century later, hearing Jeremiah's reluctance to become a prophet, God twice offers His presence. Both of these promises come during God's call to Jeremiah to be His prophet. First, God said, *"Do not be afraid of them, for **I am with you** to deliver you, says the LORD"* (*Jer 1:8*), and shortly afterwards, after predicting resistance to Jeremiah's ministry, God speaks again to Jeremiah, *"They will fight against you; but they shall not prevail against you, for **I am with you**, says the LORD, to deliver you"* (*Jer 1:19*). Although God twice promises Jeremiah *"I will be with you,"* the prophet often felt abandoned and neglected by God (see the confessions of Jeremiah in *chs. 12–20*). Yet over a lifetime of ministry, Jeremiah found God's promise more reliable than any other source of strength in life.

About one hundred years after Jeremiah, the postexilic prophet Zechariah, in the midst of responding to questions about fasting, turned to talk about the future: *"Thus says the LORD of hosts: In those days ten men from nations of every language shall take hold of a Jew, grasping his garment and saying, 'Let us go with you, for we have heard that **God is with you**'"* (*Zec 8:23*). Zechariah recalled the ongoing biblical promise of God that He would be with His people as a means of motivating the residents of Jerusalem to faithfulness.

Even the common people picked up on the assurances of the "divine with." In a wheat field outside Bethlehem, Boaz greeted his farm workers: *"The LORD be with you."* They answered, *"The LORD bless you"* (**Ruth 2:4**). God's words to His people had become a daily greeting of blessing.

A SURVEY OF THE "DIVINE WITH" IN THE NT

Jesus, the ultimate expression of God being with us, also promised that He would be with those He had discipled. He included a variation of the "divine with" in His great commission and in His prayer of unity:

> *¹⁹Go therefore and make disciples of all nations, baptizing them in the name of the Father and of the Son and of the Holy Spirit, ²⁰and teaching them to obey everything that I have commanded you. And remember, **I am with you always**, to the end of the age.* (**Mt 28:19-20**)

> *Father, I desire that those also, whom you have given me, **may be with me** where I am, to see my glory, which you have given me because you loved me before the foundation of the world.* (**Jn 17:24**)

The promise from the lips of God finally passes on to all who participate in the mission of God.

The promise given throughout the OT, from the lips of God to the mouths of prophets, kings, and common people, finally passes on to the disciples of Jesus and through them to all who participate in the mission of God.

No wonder the same promise ends many NT books:

> *The God of peace **be with** all of you. Amen.* (**Rom 15:33**)

> *Finally, brothers and sisters, farewell. Put things in order, listen to my appeal, agree with one another, live in peace; and the God of love and peace **will be with you**.* (**2Cor 13:11**)

Strikingly, the Bible's last verse states, *"The grace of the **Lord Jesus be with** all the saints. Amen"* (**Rev 22:21**).

SUMMARY

Those 16 occurrences of the "divine with" do not exhaust the appearances of the promise in Scripture, but clearly show that God consistently seeks to cross the street to be with humanity. Perhaps the sheer consistency of God's promise reveals how significant He considers this role. He comes to our side, regularly and in all kinds of situations. The biblical record of the occurrences of the "divine with" show God's intent to be loyal to humanity, to be present with people in a wide variety of circumstances and over a long period of time. While we may think that God always stays on His side of the street, the biblical record is clear: God regularly comes across the street to be with us. Now we turn to a significant question: How does the "divine with" reflect who He is and what He desires? The depth of God's concern with the "divine with" becomes clearer in a deeper investigation of four other uses of the phrase.

A less frequently used expression that is roughly equivalent to the "divine with" is God setting His heart on the people.

> I will rejoice in doing good to them, and I will plant
> them in this land in faithfulness, with all my heart and
> all my soul. (*Jer 32:41*)

> What are human beings, that you make so much of them,
> that you set your mind on them? (*Job 7:17*)

> ¹⁴If he should take back his spirit to himself,
> and gather to himself his breath,
> ¹⁵all flesh would perish together,
> and all mortals return to dust. (*Job 34:14-15*)

These three passages come from a wide variety of contexts. Jeremiah writes in the "book of hope" (*Jer 30–33*) of glorious days in the future when God will put all His heart and soul into the people. We will consider this passage in more detail later in this book. Job speaks in *Job 7* and Elihu in *Job 34* of God's presence. When Job speaks of God setting His "mind" on them, the Hebrew uses the word for heart. Likewise, when Elihu mentions the phrase *"his spirit to himself,"* he uses a combination of the Hebrew words for heart and spirit. Job's reference is most parallel to the "divine with," while Elihu refers to a biblical concept that God is necessary for the human soul to be sustained.

THE DEPTH OF
THE "DIVINE WITH"

Four additional passages using some version of the phrase *"I will be with you"* include *Isaiah 7:14; 41:10; 43:1-7* and *Matthew 1:23*. These poignant verses fall into two related groups. We will consider *Isaiah 41:10* and *43:1-7* together and then turn to *Isaiah 7:14* and its citation in *Matthew 1:23*.

> **How does the "divine with" reflect who He is and what He desires?**

ISAIAH 41:10 AND 43:1-7

Few biblical books pose more difficulties than *Isaiah*, but not many sections of the Bible produce a more in-depth understanding of the divine world than this 66-chapter prophecy. The entire book argues that God's Word is trustworthy. Watts (**105**) points out that God speaks using the first person personal pronoun "I" in *Isaiah 40–52* more than anywhere else in the Bible. These chapters emerge as some of the most significant biblical texts about God.

In the middle section of the book the prophet addresses people who question the trustworthiness of God's promises. As the prophet addresses their doubts, he uses what Westermann (**Oracles**, **42**) and VanGemeren (**79**) call "salvation oracles." These oracles offer significant statements of affirmation during periods of distress and great doubt. One of these salvation oracles appears in *Isaiah 43:1-7*:

¹ But now thus says the LORD,
    he who created you, O Jacob,
    he who formed you, O Israel:
Do not fear, for I have redeemed you;
    I have called you by name, you are mine.
² When you pass through the waters, **I will be with you**;
    and through the rivers, they shall not overwhelm you;
when you walk through fire you shall not be burned,
    and the flame shall not consume you.
³ For I am the LORD your God,
    the Holy One of Israel, your Savior.
I give Egypt as your ransom,
    Ethiopia and Seba in exchange for you.
⁴ Because you are precious in my sight,
    and honored, and I love you,
I give people in return for you,

> nations in exchange for your life.
> ⁵ Do not fear, for **I am with you**;
>> I will bring your offspring from the east,
>> and from the west I will gather you;
> ⁶ I will say to the north, "Give them up,"
>> and to the south, "Do not withhold;
>> bring my sons from far away
>> and my daughters from the end of the earth—
> ⁷ everyone who is called by my name,
>> whom I created for my glory,
>> whom I formed and made."

The bold print reveals that God twice affirms His presence with Israel. God begins (*v. 1*) and ends (*v. 7*) by reminding Israel that He created them and that He has called them by His name. Characteristic of the salvation oracles are regular assurances not to fear (*vv. 1,5*) and reference to the exchanges God made to secure Israel (giving Egypt, Ethiopia, and Seba for Israel in *v. 3* and the nations in exchange for Israel in *v. 4*). The text uses explicit theological terms to describe God's concern for Israel: He created, formed, redeemed, called, loved, and made Israel. The most visual part of the oracle comes with the water and fire in *verse 2*, which may refer to events at the first Exodus[1] or just be metaphors referring to obstacles and difficulties in life. The whole text suggests that God brings His ample strength to a seemingly insignificant and miserable group of people because He loves them and wants to be with them. The God who creates, forms, and rescues people from water and fire looked at the small remnant of Israel as *"precious in my sight."*

> **God brings His ample strength to this group of people because He wants to be with them.**

The context of the double appearance of *"I will be with you"* shows the depth of divine concern. That concern begins at creation, continues through flood and fire, overtakes financial restriction (God trades productive nations for unproductive Israel), and circles back to how He owned them from the beginning.

This text echoes an earlier salvation oracle in *Isaiah 41:10*:

---

[1] Isaiah will repeatedly call the return from Babylonian captivity a second Exodus: *"bring my sons from far away and my daughters from the end of the earth"* (*Isa 43:6*).

*Do not fear, for **I am with you**,*
   do not be afraid, for I am your God;
I will strengthen you, I will help you,
   I will uphold you with my victorious right hand.

Isaiah 41 describes God's hand holding up Israel while *Isaiah 43* describes God's eye on Israel. *Isaiah 41* promises God's strength and help while *Isaiah 43* affirms God's bringing them back from exile and paying all the expenses for the exchange. Both texts call Israel not to fear and reaffirm God's promise to be on the human side of the street.

The context of the *Isaiah* salvation oracles gives clearer understanding of the depth of God's desire and concern to be with His people. *"I will be with you"* must not be regarded as a socially acceptable but empty phrase. When God affirms that He will be with His people, He means that when they find themselves in the midst of the river, lose their footing, feel the current, and begin to drift downstream, He will pull them up with a strong hand. When the house catches on fire, the exits are blocked, and the lungs fill with smoke, God will be there to rescue them.

Harve Smeltzer, one of my close friends, serves as a hospice minister in Kansas City. He told one of my classes of university students about the day when his younger brother, Paul, died in a terrible car crash. Many people told him, "If you need anything, let me know." We know it as the socially acceptable, but often empty, phrase people offer in times of flood and fire. But then Harve recalled how his friend, John Hinton, came over to the house and sat on the couch. He did not order pizza, or read Scripture, or discuss theology, or hand out tissues. He just sat on the couch all day. Harve, who now ministers to people in desperate situations, could not remember the name of a single person who promised "If you need me, let me know," but he found tremendous comfort in John Hinton sitting on the couch.

The issue of suffering and brokenness is close to the heart of God, as we will see in a later chapter. While this book looks at the heart of God, other books focus on the issue of suffering. A companion volume in this series, *Where Is God When We Suffer? What the Bible Says about Suffering* by Lynn Gardner explores the human perceptions that God does not keep the promise *"I will be with you."*

This story shows the human significance of somebody being with us. Many understand the sense of comfort my friend found in the man who was "with him." Although God being "with us" takes a different form than the story of the two men, the significance of one being present for another is clear.

Isaiah 41 and *43* reveal the depth of commitment and concern behind the simple promise, *"I will be with you."* While it is easy to say "If you need me, let me know," God intends more than just a simple social promise. His eye watches over, His hand reaches down, His will

God intends more than just a simple social promise. | paves the way, and His heart gives strength. God also acts when we need him. He pulls us out of the water and fire when we need rescuing, and He sits on the couch when we need comfort.

ISAIAH 7:14

Most of the long book of Isaiah uses poetry to express God's Word to Israel. A small section of prose in *Isaiah 6–8* takes up the call of the prophet (*Isaiah 6*) and then Isaiah's encounter with King Ahaz (*Isaiah 7–8*). In *Isaiah 7* the prophet speaks with Ahaz during an international crisis. Two neighboring states war against Judah. Ahaz seeks an alliance with a distant superpower in order to protect his small kingdom from destruction. Isaiah urges him to trust God, *"If you do not stand firm in faith, you shall not stand at all"* (*Isa 7:9*). In order to convince Ahaz to rely on God rather than political alliance, Isaiah offers him a sign: *"Therefore the LORD himself will give you a sign. Look, the young woman is with child and shall bear a son, and shall name him Immanuel"* (*Isa 7:14*). Matthew cites this verse as being fulfilled in the virgin birth of Jesus Christ. Considerable controversy revolves around the translation of "young woman," which other versions render as "virgin." I fully affirm the virgin birth, but want to move beyond the controversy to ask the questions, "What does this significant text tell us about God? What insight do we gain here about the heart of God?" We will first look at how Isaiah and Ahaz understood this statement and then how Matthew uses this passage.

Isaiah's promise of a sign to Ahaz involves God's intervention in the political life of Ahaz and the at-risk world of Judah. Ahaz, facing the armies of two neighboring states massing on his borders (*Isa 7:1;*

2Kgs 16:5), can only think of calling the superior military strength of the distant Assyrian military machine (*2Kgs 16:7-9*). Isaiah, through this sign, promises that God will take care of international politics (*Isa 7:7-9*). The birth of the child in nine months shows God's power in two ways: First, shortly after the baby's birth, the threat of the two nations will be over. God will take care of the threat if Ahaz will only trust. Second, the baby's name will be a message of what God did with Ahaz. Immanuel means, "God is with us."

Other children had symbolic names in this narrative section of *Isaiah*. When Isaiah meets Ahaz outside Jerusalem, he takes his son Shearjashub (which means "a remnant shall return"), whose name announced a message of hope (*Isa 7:3*). Each time his family and friends pronounce the name Maher-shalal-hash-baz (which means "the spoil speeds, the prey hastes"), they announce that the capitals of the two warning nations will be sacked by a God-guided military power (*Isa 8:1-4*).

Scripture never reveals whether Ahaz practices monarchy according to the instructions in *Deuteronomy 17:18-19*, where the law orders the king to read a copy of the law *"all the days of his life"* or whether Ahaz knows of God's repeated promise *"I will be with you."* The passages about Ahaz in *Isaiah* and *2 Kings* imply that Ahaz is not a Bible-reading king. Isaiah says no more about this mother and child, but it seems clear that a young child in Jerusalem known as Immanuel has a name that reminds all who hear his mother say his name that God's Word is absolutely true, because they know that the enemy who was at their gate nine or so months earlier is now defeated in an unexpected and God-guided way, and the threat against Judah that so worried faithless Ahaz no longer exists. What does exist, expressed in the little boy's name, is a clear affirmation that God's presence with His people is again clearly and powerfully demonstrated.

> **God's presence with His people is again clearly and powerfully demonstrated.**

The people of eighth-century-BC Jerusalem in the times of Ahaz the king and Isaiah the prophet witness the mighty hand of God working internationally and in the lives of a young mother and her son. We can only imagine what Ahaz might have thought about Isaiah's predictions about this young mother. "I need swords, and you send me an infant. I need chariots, and you deliver a cradle. I need strategy, and you talk about symbolic names. I need an army and navy, and you bring diapers and formula!"

But a child is born. The birth announcement says "God is with us" has been born. The midwife comes out to the family to announce that "God is with us" is here. The proud grandmother tells her friends that he was born last night. "'God is with us' is my grandchild." The news spreads all over Jerusalem. The attackers are gone. The threat is over. Peace has returned. "God is with us."

With Immanuel, God again announces that He cannot stay on His side of the street. He cannot watch from a distance. He cannot stay between the cherubim—He must come down. God wants to be among His people, near us, by us, next to us, with us. He seeks to be at our side, share our company, and be present. To stretch the image, God seeks to hold our hands, rub our shoulders, pat our backs, mop our brows, steady our arms, walk at our sides, stop our shaking knees. He looks into our eyes, whispers in our ears, lifts our chins, wipes away our tears, and renews our spirits. He shepherds our souls, guides us through the valley of the shadow of death, leads us beside still waters, and restores our soul. God is with us. Immanuel.

But God has greater plans for this highly significant name. In fact, one might say all that God said and did in the OT points forward to it, and all He says and does in the NT points back to it.

MATTHEW 1:23

Throughout Scripture, God has promised *"I will be with you."* From the patriarchs to the prophets, from monarchs to mothers, from the ancestors to the apostles, the phrase reveals something of the heart of God. As part of that trajectory of God's concern through Scripture, the Bible uses the name "Immanuel" twice, once in *Isaiah 7* to announce a miracle of God and again in *Matthew 1* to declare God's greatest work:

> **God has greater plans for this highly significant name.**

²²All this took place to fulfill what had been spoken by the Lord through the prophet: ²³"Look, the virgin shall conceive and bear a *son, and they shall name him Emmanuel," which means, "God is with us." (**Mt 1:22-23**)* [2]

The first time God made this promise was to a king; the second time was to a sleeping carpenter. The name needs no interpretation in *Isaiah*, but Matthew translates the meaning of Emmanuel for his readers. What God had first done in the eighth century BC finds its ultimate fulfillment in the first century AD. Isaiah's words reminded people for nearly 800 years that God was with them, but the complete story would not be known until a virgin named Mary bore a son who would be the Son of God himself.

The first Immanuel did not convince Ahaz. He joined the ranks of those who believed that God stayed on the other side of the street and never comes to this side. Maybe he believed nobody could cross such a wide street, or that a being so holy, just, right, and powerful had no interest in crossing.

God took His coming to our side of the street to its ultimate and sublime conclusion. One day He placed His Son, Jesus, inside a woman named Mary. She gave birth to God's Son on our side of the street, not His. Jesus was born in one of our houses, not in God's house. He was delivered on earth, not in heaven. They called Him by a name that revealed what His birth did: Immanuel.

> **God took His coming to our side of the street to its ultimate and sublime conclusion.**

Through Jesus we learn that God is with us because He wants to be with us, because He loves us, and because He seeks us out. *"For God so loved the world that he gave his only Son, so that everyone who believes in him may not perish but may have eternal life" (**Jn 3:16**).* Immanuel comes because of God's love. Immanuel comes out of God's desire to be with us and to ultimately be with us forever by granting us eternal life.

CONCLUSION

The title of this book promises to discuss "What the Bible Says about the Heart of God." The occurrences of the "divine with" never mention God's heart or refer to His intent or what gives Him delight.

---

[2] The name Immanuel is the same as Emmanuel. The former reflects the Hebrew form of the name while the latter represents the Greek form.

Yet the repetition of this simple promise at significant places in the Bible points to an important aspect of God. Why is the promise so often repeated, and what might that say about God? Our understanding of God through the promise of the "divine with" might be viewed in three different ways, one from a human point of view and two from the divine point of view. All three of these outlooks contribute to our perception of God.

Reading and absorbing the implications of the promise of God being "with us" often prompt a human-centered interpretation. The long period where God seems hidden in the story about Joseph in *Genesis* mirrors the experience of many people. In the midst of discouragement and tragedy, God seems nowhere to be found. We need reminders about many things in life. Clearly we need a chorus of voices in the Bible that say repeatedly and in all kinds of circumstances that God is with us. We find the assurance of God's companionship reassuring. We find God's presence on our side of the street a source of hope and strength.

> **Clearly we need a chorus of voices that repeatedly say that God is with us.**

The appearance of the often repeated promise of a divine presence responds to this human need. Just as God understood human dependence on food and water and so provided them, God similarly knew the human need for reassurance of divine presence and made it available. Yet simple response to a human need does not exhaust what the "divine with" means about God's nature. We now turn to two divine perspectives.

The many repetitions of the "divine with" appear in Scripture because He is a God who wants them to be there, who is motivated to persistently repeat the promise to be with His people. God is willing to be known as a God who promises to be with His people.

But it is not just God's willingness to make this promise that prompts the many occurrences of the "divine with" but rather it is His desire to actually be with His people. The repetition of the phrase throughout the biblical story is there primarily because God is a God who *is* with His people. It is part of who He is. He is not a God who stays on His side of the street.

The assurance of God being with us raises other issues about this aspect of God. How do we recognize His presence? Harve could see his friend John on the couch being "with him," but how do we identify God's presence? Beyond that is the question of what kind of intent God has in being with us. We take up those questions in the next two chapters as we investigate two additional trajectories about God which begin in the book of Genesis and run throughout the Bible: "He comes" and "He blesses."

At the birth of Immanuel in Bethlehem, the promise of *"I will be with you"* reaches its grand crescendo. The trajectory of the "divine with" makes its clearest statement. But in the birth of Immanuel another biblical trajectory about the divine heart also reaches its clearest statement. Both trajectories intersect in the birth of Immanuel. The next chapter takes up that second trajectory.

WHAT DO YOU SAY?

1. Have you experienced someone being "with you" in a great time of need? What was most significant about their presence?

2. How is God present with us today? Consider the question in light of these scriptures:

   a. *John 14:15-21*

   b. *John 15:26*

   c. *John 16:7-15*

3. What differences (if any) are there between the presence of God in the OT and the presence of God in the NT?

4. What does God promise to do as the "divine with"?

   a. *Genesis 26:2-3,24*

   b. *Exodus 3:12*

   c. *Deuteronomy 31:8*

   d. *1 Chronicles 22:11*

   e. *1 Kings 8:57*

   f. *Jeremiah 1:8,19*

   g. *Matthew 28:19-20*

h. *John 17:24*

i. *Isaiah 41:10*

j. *Isaiah 43:2*

5. Look at question 4. Does this give you further insight into the heart of God?

6. Write a short prayer recognizing and being thankful for God's presence.

CHAPTER FIVE

MISSION: GOD IN OUR NEIGHBORHOOD

Begin your study of this chapter by reading: *Isaiah 40*.

W hen our sons were growing up, our family often took vacations to the northeastern United States. We took in amusement parks and historical sites, and went to see family and friends. During that time I also became an enthusiastic family genealogist. Several distant relatives and I were tracing the Shank family tree only to get stuck about three generations back. We knew our family came from Shanksville, Pennsylvania, but one particular ancestor, my great, great, great grandfather Jacob Shank, remained a mystery. So each family trip became part vacation, part genealogical research. I had to find out about Grandpa Jacob.

On our summer journeys we would spend a couple of days at an amusement park and then two afternoons in a cemetery or the basement of a small town historical society. In fact, to this day, when our family is all in the car and we pass by a burial ground, one of my sons will say wryly, "Dad, there's a graveyard, do we need to stop?" We had good family time and made a host of great memories. From tombstones and old documents, I gathered names and dates of distant relatives all in the interest of finding the crucial details about Jacob Shank.

Genesis 1–11
Descriptions of
God come to Earth

Judges 5
Deborah's Song:
God comes to fight
for Israel

Micah 1
God comes to
punish Samaria
and Judah

Habakkuk 3
God comes to
punish Babylon

Isaiah 40
God comes to
comfort His people

Matthew 1–2
God's coming
announced
as Immanuel

Luke 1–3
God's coming
announced with
praise

Philippians
God's coming
exalted as
ultimate humility

You might say I was on a mission. We were on a family vacation to Maryland, but I was on a quest to find Jacob's birthplace. We had fun at King's Dominion, but for me it was on the way to the Daughters of the American Revolution Historical Library. Every turn had a purpose. Each destination was part of the quest.

Just as most families make vacation trips to visit places away from home, so God travels to places away from His home. We understand that God does not travel in the same sense we do, but the Bible does record that He visits the earth. In fact, the Bible indicates that God visits the earth often. If God had come just once or twice, those appearances would be striking by their rarity. The frequency of the divine visits reveals something about God Himself.

There are some families where the vacations are not just random trips to distant places, but they are driven by somebody on a mission, such as a father looking for a distant ancestor. As we look at God's journeys to the earth, we will find He came on a mission. Once we understand God's mission, we come closer to understanding His heart.

God's trips to the earth begin in *Genesis*. From there these visits appear regularly in the Bible. We can follow them like a thread throughout the Bible. We call that thread a trajectory. The map of the trajectory we will follow in this chapter is in the margin. Of God's many visits to the earth, we will mention four rather briefly and then look into the final two in more detail. After the investigation into God's visits, this chapter will reflect on how these appearances of God on earth lead us into God's heart.

GOD VISITS THE EARTH

During those genealogical journeys in quest of my great, great, great, grandfather Shank, I found myself in many different places focused on dissimilar activities. In an antique shop-junk store near where my distant ancestors lived, I sorted through a pile of old photographs searching hopelessly for the image of a past relative. In Shanktown, Pennsylvania (which has five houses and is not even on the map), I boldly knocked on the door of a home with "Shank" on the mailbox to see if they had any information about what I hoped was our common heritage. In Maryland, I searched through boxes in a basement in Frederick City, and searched the phonebook in Hagerstown. In other places I read old obituaries and ordered books of state history. On the surface the activities varied widely, but underneath there was a common purpose. Someone observing my activities might have concluded that I was engaged in widely different tasks, but in reality it was all to find Jacob.

> **As we look at a few of His visits, we will find one common denominator.**

Observing God's visits to the earth may prompt the same response from us. As we look at a few of His visits, we might initially see no link between His trips. He seems to be engaged in widely different, almost random, tasks. But we will find one common denominator ties them all together.

HE COMES IN PERSON— GENESIS 1–11

In *Genesis 1–11* God frequently appears in humanlike form on the earth: He forms the first human from the dust of the earth, gives the human instructions about garden care, performs surgery on the man to make the woman, finds the couple in the garden after the sin, dialogues with them about their actions, makes them clothes, drives them out of the Garden of Eden, watches Cain offer his sacrifice, warns Cain about his response, visits with Cain about Abel's death, puts a mark on Cain, gives Noah instructions about ark building, shuts the door of the ark, smells the odor of Noah's sacrifice, visits the Babel construction sight, and decides to confuse human languages. In each case, God operates not from a distant heavenly home but takes care of business on earth.

As pointed out in a previous chapter, in the remaining material from the book of *Genesis* the appearances of God on earth become less frequent. God eats dinner at Abraham's tent in *Genesis 18* and wrestles with Jacob at Peniel in *Genesis 32*. For the most part, God is content to communicate through dreams and visions or work in a hidden way to interact with humanity. The reason for these human-like appearances of God in *Genesis 1–11* becomes clearer in light of the changing way that God relates to humanity in the book of *Genesis*. In the context of the entire book of *Genesis* (as noted in chapter two on God being in charge) God relates to humanity in different ways: directly and personally in *Genesis 1–11*, directly but in a more distant way with Abraham and Jacob, and finally only indirectly with Joseph.

Although no explicit statement of God's purpose in visiting the earth appears in *Genesis 1–11*, He does play the role of a deliverer to Adam and Eve by providing them with clothes, to Cain by giving him the mark, and to Noah and his family by saving them from the flood through the ark. Von Rad (*Genesis,* 152-155) and Westermann (*Promises,* 44-56) understand God's visits in *Genesis 1–11* as God on a mission to respond to the spread of sin with His powerful spread of grace.

He Comes to Defend His People— Judges 5

Numerous OT texts describe God's arrival on earth. Scholars often call these visits an epiphany or theophany. I've picked three of them for a quick look: *Judges 5, Micah 1* and *Habakkuk 3*. Then we will probe more deeply into God's appearances in *Isaiah* and the NT.

> The word "theophany" comes from two Greek words meaning "the appearance of God" while the term "epiphany" derives from Greek words meaning "to show forth." Westermann (*What Does the OT,* 20-22) divides God's appearances on the earth into these two categories: Epiphany refers to God's coming *to act.* In God's visit in *Judges 5,* he does not speak, but acts to save. Westermann defines a theophany as God coming *to speak. Exodus 19–34* is the Sinai theophany where God speaks repeatedly. *Genesis 2–11; Exodus 3:1-22; Judges 5:4-5; Psalm 68:1-2,7-9; Isaiah 40; 63:1; 64:1-3; and Habakkuk 3:13-15* are among the most often cited cases of theophany and epiphany.

The narrative of the book of *Judges* tells the stories of 12 judges in Israel. *Judges* comes as a sequel to the unfinished land conquest outlined in *Joshua* and as a prelude to the coming monarchy in *1 Samuel*. It was a period of time when God was quite active in human history.

One of the most theologically explicit statements in the book of *Judges* reflects on God's role during the times of the judges:

> [18]Whenever the LORD raised up judges for them, the LORD was with the judge, and he delivered them from the hand of their enemies all the days of the judge; for the LORD would be moved to pity by their groaning because of those who persecuted and oppressed them. [19]But whenever the judge died, they would relapse and behave worse than their ancestors, following other gods, worshiping them and bowing down to them. They would not drop any of their practices or their stubborn ways. [20]So the anger of the LORD was kindled against Israel; and he said, "Because this people have transgressed my covenant that I commanded their ancestors, and have not obeyed my voice, [21]I will no longer drive out before them any of the nations that Joshua left when he died." (*Jdg 2:18-21*)

In this scene we see the heart of God, moved with pity, filled with hurt, and then torn by anger. In response to the relapse of the people into sin, God generally worked indirectly by sending judges. In the case of *Judges 5*, God came in person to accomplish the same purpose.

One of the major judges was Deborah, who along with Barak led an army to defeat one of the enemies of Israel. It takes two chapters to tell the story. *Judges 4* is like a newspaper report of the battle and victory. God's role is only cited in passing. The next chapter records a song from the victory celebration. It describes the same battle, but God's role plays a much higher profile. The victory song pictures God actually coming to participate in the battle: God visits the earth to win the battle in person.

> [4] LORD, when you went out from Seir,
>   when you marched from the region of Edom,
> the earth trembled,
>   and the heavens poured,
>   the clouds indeed poured water.
> [5] The mountains quaked before the LORD, the One of Sinai,
>   before the LORD, the God of Israel. (*Jdg 5:4-5*)

The song describes God's arrival in the land from the southeast. God's appearance in Edom prompts earthquake-like conditions along with severe weather. As God marches toward the battle, His coming is accompanied by upheaval in the sky and on the ground. *Judges 4* describes a God-supported Israelite army defeating the Canaanite chariots, while *Judges 5* depicts the same events as a divine visit to earth with catastrophic upheavals.

The appearance of two versions of the same event is not a contradiction, but rather an attempt to explain Deborah's belief that her victory was not due to her leadership ability or to Barak's army, but that the cause of victory was the divine intervention and support explained as God's visit to the earth. God frequently intervenes in Israelite affairs during the book of *Judges*. Most often He raises up human leaders to lead the people to overthrow their oppressors. In *Judges 5*, the song pictures God's personal appearance for the same reason. God is intent on protecting His people. He comes in *Judges 5* in support of His people against their enemies.

> **God is intent on protecting His people.**

Initially, God's frequent appearances in *Genesis* have little in common with the warlike God coming to defend His people in *Judges 5*, just as a man paging through a phone book in Hagerstown seems completely unconnected to knocking on a door of a home in Shanktown. But, as we shall see, God's visits actually have much in common.

HE COMES TO DEFEAT HIS PEOPLE— MICAH 1

The eighth-century prophet, Micah, grew up in a small town, but moved to Jerusalem to speak on behalf of God to the people in the capital city. In fact, this country boy opens his short prophecy by talking about two capital cities: Jerusalem and Samaria. He warns of the reality and the reason for the coming destruction for both capitals. *Judges 4–5* describe the battle; Micah only warns of the coming battles. The narrative of the fall of both cities appears in *2 Kings*, where the Bible tells of the destruction of Samaria in 721 BC by Assyria and the fall of Jerusalem to Babylon in 586 BC. What Micah provides, however, is a visit of God to earth on a mission to destroy the two capital cities:

> ³ For lo, the LORD is coming out of his place,
>   and will come down and tread upon the high places
>   of the earth.

> ⁴ Then the mountains will melt under him
> and the valleys will burst open,
> like wax near the fire,
> like waters poured down a steep place.
> ⁵ All this is for the transgression of Jacob
> and for the sins of the house of Israel.
> What is the transgression of Jacob?
> Is it not Samaria?
> And what is the high place of Judah?
> Is it not Jerusalem?
> ⁶ Therefore I will make Samaria a heap in the open country,
> a place for planting vineyards.
> I will pour down her stones into the valley,
> and uncover her foundations. (**Mic 1:3-6**)

Deborah describes God invading Israel from Edom, but Micah pictures God arriving on earth from heaven. As He arrives on earth, His visit causes physical upheaval. Mountains and valleys experience devastation as a result of the divine visit. The passage identifies Samaria and Jerusalem as the object of the visit. Micah uses the destruction of Samaria to warn of danger to Jerusalem.

Micah reveals the fractured nature of the relationship between God and humankind and helps us to see His heart's desire for reconciliation. One theme of *Micah 1–3* is how the people of Jerusalem are unaware of their distance from God. They cannot understand why their city might be destroyed. They fail to comprehend that the way they treat each other is part of the relationship that the whole community has with God. Their oppression of the vulnerable, which the leaders apparently condone, prompts the discipline of God. Micah's description of God's visit seems, in part, to be a way of breaking through the denial and to affirm that the destruction is by the divine hand and not the result of the international political situation.

Micah begins his book with the image of God visiting the earth to punish His people. While other images of God come later in the book (for example, Micah reminds the people of the importance that God places on justice, mercy, and humility in *6:8*), Micah's opening image is of a God on a mission of punishment, not against the wicked nations around Israel and Judah, but to both kingdoms themselves. The same God who comes to defend His people in *Judges 5* now arrives to punish His people in *Micah 1*. On the surface, the two visits seem to go in opposite directions, but we will see they have more in common than we first realize.

He Comes to Crush Evil—
Habakkuk 3

Habakkuk wrestles, as do all people, with the troubling question of theodicy. The term describes the issue of whether or not God's actions, or lack of activity, are fair and just. Habakkuk asks why God uses evil world powers to punish Jerusalem. He wonders, "What is in God's heart? And why does He punish the very people He so loves? How can God use other nations like Babylon, which is more wicked than Judah, to punish Jerusalem?" Using a dialogue format, God responds to each of Habakkuk's inquiries. Then God breaks off the dialogue by giving the prophet a peek into the future when God comes to visit to the earth:

> ³ God came from Teman,
>> the Holy One from Mount Paran.
> His glory covered the heavens,
>> and the earth was full of his praise.
> ⁴ The brightness was like the sun;
>> rays came forth from his hand,
>> where his power lay hidden.
> ⁵ Before him went pestilence,
>> and plague followed close behind.
> ⁶ He stopped and shook the earth;
>> he looked and made the nations tremble.
> The eternal mountains were shattered;
>> along his ancient pathways
>> the everlasting hills sank low.
> ⁷ I saw the tents of Cushan under affliction;
>> the tent-curtains of the land of Midian trembled. (**Hab 3:3-7**)

In the context of the book, the passage describes God's coming destruction of the Babylonian empire, an event anticipated by many of the prophets (e.g., **Isaiah 13–14; Jeremiah 50–51**). The prophet describes the effects of God's visit on the earth in striking poetic language. God's journey to the earth is accompanied by bright light, an outbreak of disease, earthquake-like conditions, and fear among the nations. God announces that He will make a personal visit to deal with the injustices about which Habakkuk complains.

As Habakkuk hears about the pending visit of God, he tells of his own reaction: *"I tremble within; my lips quiver at the sound. Rottenness enters into my bones, and my steps tremble beneath me"* (**Hab 3:16**). The proposed visit shakes Habakkuk to the core. In response the prophet writes one of the great biblical confessions of faith (*Hab 3:17-19*).

God promises to right the world's wrongs, but Habakkuk wonders what he is supposed to do until God makes the correction. God counsels Habakkuk to be patient and to watch for the actions of God. In God's corrective visit to the earth, Habakkuk sees a vision of the future. God's coming with its terrible effects will certainly right the world's wrongs. Theophany answers theodicy.

Like the previous appearances, God's visit is violent. God comes on a mission to punish. In the case of Habakkuk, the focus is on the wicked nations that God uses to

> **Theophany answers theodicy.**

punish Israel. *Micah 1* depicts a destructive visit on Samaria and Jerusalem; *Habakkuk 3* foresees the destruction of Babylon. At this point, this brief survey of four passages that tell of God visiting the earth reveals that God comes to the earth on different occasions, but the purposes seem widely varied. God is busy. It is still unclear if these visits have any consistent purpose and if they say anything about His heart.

BEHOLD HE COMES

GOOD NEWS: HE'S COMING—
ISAIAH 40

While reading a history of Somerset County, Pennsylvania, I learned that my distant ancestors had settled in Shanksville after moving from Woodsboro, Maryland. One clue led to another which uncovered another. That same sort of domino effect is at work in *Isaiah 40*. What Isaiah speaks about eventually leads us to Bethlehem.

The authorship of *Isaiah 40–55* is a debated issue in OT studies. Most conservative Christians understand the entire book to come from eighth-century Isaiah. Others argue for a second Isaiah or Deutero-Isaiah as the author of this portion of the book. Since this study centers on the heart of God, some debates must be set aside in order to attend to the issue at hand. This study takes the view that a single eighth-century prophet wrote the entire book.

One of the longest sustained descriptions of God in Scripture comes in *Isaiah 40–55*. Although the passage never attempts to *prove* the existence of God, some of the anti-idol passages come as close to an apologetic approach as any text in the Bible. Isaiah seeks to persuade his readers to place their faith in God. The intended audience lives in Babylon (*Isa 43:14; 48:20*) as exiles (*45:13; 49:21*) where Babylonians call Israel to worship their gods (*46:1-5*). Isaiah's readers are afraid, homeless, doubting, tempted by idolatry, and defeated. They feel unloved and have stopped worshiping. Isaiah tells them about a trustworthy, caring God who deserves their worship. The salvation oracles offer affirmation that God loves and cares for them.

B.W. Anderson (**417-418**), the well-known OT scholar, argued that the question contemporary people most often raise about God is, "Does He exist?" Much of the literature of the past century about God seeks to prove His existence. Anderson points out that Scripture never raises the question of God's existence. People in the ancient world would not have understood the inquiry. They would have thought, "Of course, God exists." Polytheism, not atheism, was the issue in biblical times.

This 16-chapter description of God opens in *Isaiah 40* with basically two separate prophetic lessons about God. In effect, Isaiah preaches two three-point sermons about God, the first one in *40:1-11* about the heart of God and the second one in *40:12-31* about the nature of God. At the core of Isaiah's first

Isaiah preaches two three-point sermons about God.

description of God stands the remarkable claim that God Himself comes to earth on a mission.

Different voices speak in *Isaiah 40:1-10*:
God speaks in *verses 1-2.*
A first voice responds in *verses 3-5.*
A second voice speaks in *verses 6-8.*
A third voice reacts in *verses 9-11.*

The voices are not identified in the passage but some suspect that at least one of the voices is the prophet himself. The whole scene takes place around God in heaven where God seems to have called a council to discuss His plans for the exiles in Babylon.

God begins the council when He announces comfort for His people (*40:1-2*). This comfort anticipates God's decision to bring the

> The OT describes other scenes that appear to take place around God in heaven. One parallel passage is *Genesis 1:26-28* where God's words *"let us create"* suggest that God is not alone. *Genesis* does not indicate who God is speaking to in *Genesis 1*. Many biblical scholars see all these texts as taking place in heaven where God speaks to other heavenly beings. There are other passages where God speaks to those around him in a heavenly context including *1 Kings 22*, *Job 1–2* and *Psalm 82*.

exiles home to Jerusalem. God uses the long exile to punish them for their sins. The first voice (*40:3-5*) announces that God is about to visit the earth, the second voice (*40:6-8*) explains the power that will make it happen, and the third voice (*40:9-11*) describes the visit. The third voice describes God's visit in this way:

> ⁹ Get you up to a high mountain,
>> O Zion, herald of good tidings;
> lift up your voice with strength,
>> O Jerusalem, herald of good tidings,
>> lift it up, do not fear;
> say to the cities of Judah,
>> "Here is your God!"
> ¹⁰ See, the Lord GOD comes with might,
>> and his arm rules for him;
> his reward is with him,
>> and his recompense before him.
> ¹¹ He will feed his flock like a shepherd;
>> he will gather the lambs in his arms,
> and carry them in his bosom,
>> and gently lead the mother sheep. (**Isa 40:9-11**)

The third person is told to go to the top of a high mountain where he is told *"lift up your voice"* to *"herald good tidings."* The content of the good news comes in three parts: 1) God is mighty; 2) God is gentle; 3) God is here!

> The voice announces the "good tidings" or "the gospel" for the first time in the Bible, prompting some to call *Isaiah* the first Gospel or the fifth Gospel. Isaiah speaks about "good news" or "good tidings" seven times in *chapters 40–66*. Matthew, Mark, Luke, and John present the gospel in its fullest form. Paul articulates the "good

news" in *1 Corinthians 15* as Jesus dying on the cross, buried in a tomb, and rising from the dead. Isaiah offers an earlier version of the "good tidings."

1. **God is mighty.** *"His arm rules for him"* may refer to the regular refrain in the Pentateuch that God brought Israel out of Egypt with a strong arm and an outstretched hand. Isaiah regularly describes the return from Babylonian captivity in terms first used with the Exodus out of Egypt. Clearly the God who defeats Pharaoh, splits the Red Sea, and delivers the land of Canaan to Israel is a mighty God, a God mighty enough to free them from exile.

2. **God is gentle.** Isaiah joins *Psalm 23* in comparing God to a shepherd and perhaps reflects on the fatherlike image in *Deuteronomy 1:31*, in which God carries His son Israel out of Egypt. Isaiah knows that the prophets attribute the destruction of Jerusalem to the mighty hand of God, and so shows that the God He describes has not only the strength to free them from exile but also the gentleness to care enough to do it and protect them on the way.

3. **God is here!** Twice, Isaiah makes the good news announcement: *"Here is your God!"* The mighty and gentle God comes. *"See the* LORD *comes with might."* The heavenly scene of *Isaiah 40:1-3* will soon switch to the earth. The incomprehensible, incomparable, inexhaustible God will visit earth. The God of might and gentleness will make His presence known on earth. *"Here is your God!"*

> The incomprehensible, incomparable, inexhaustible God will visit earth.

God comes to bring the exiles home to Jerusalem. God cares about the people who thought that no one in heaven even knew their pain. The Babylonians who hold the Jews captive are no match for this powerful God. Yet those He plans to rescue are assured that the deliverance will be gentle. Isaiah writes to people whose last major experience with God includes the destruction of Jerusalem and the displacement of their entire way of life. This section of Isaiah, addressed to those in exile, begins with a strong affirmation that He is powerful enough to carry out His plans, that He has commitment to bring His own people home, and that He is indeed coming.

Isaiah does not dwell here on God's arrival in Babylon, the journey from Babylon to Jerusalem with God in the lead, or the arrival of God's caravan in Jerusalem. Instead, Isaiah launches into his second lesson (see the boxed text) which stresses the power of God to accomplish His goals with the exiles. A God who is incomprehensible, incomparable, and inexhaustible will accomplish the mission for which He comes.

Isaiah 40's Second Sermon

In the last half of *Isaiah 40*, the prophet preaches a three-point sermon on God. Isaiah addresses the people who witnessed God's destruction of Jerusalem and who experienced the loss of all they held dear—statehood, king, homes and farms, temple and priesthood, and an entire way of life. Living in a foreign land, forced to live by a different set of customs and laws, they question whether the God they worshiped in Jerusalem will be up to the task of being their God in exile. Isaiah responds with three points:

1. **God is incomprehensible**—*40:12-17*. Isaiah opens the second sermon in chapter 40 with a series of Job-like questions to which no human then had a response and to most of which we have no satisfactory response today. Who taught God knowledge? Where did He get His sense of justice? We do not know. Isaiah argues that although we cannot fully understand God, He fully understands us. He has solutions to issues we have not solved. Just because the collective human wisdom sees no way out does not mean that God does not have a solution.

2. **God is incomparable**—*40:18-24*. In order to show that no other being compares with God, Isaiah offers a set of comparisons in which the competition fails to measure up to God, leaving Him in a category all by himself. When Isaiah compares God with idols or animals or kings, none of those entities finds equal footing with God. A God who towers over the competition must be a God worth trusting.

3. **God is inexhaustible**—*40:25-31*. Humans routinely experience exhaustion. Isaiah argues that God never wears out, breaks down, or gives up. God cannot be compared to even the fittest humans, youths who run races, for even they face limits on how far or how fast they can run. God must be more like the eagle who seems, from a human standpoint, to reach unreachable heights without wearing out. A God who never wears out can be trusted with the future.

Isaiah announces that something is about to happen, then reveals the source of the power to make it happen, and finally relates the good news of it actually happening. Isaiah's words take on a double fulfillment. God comes to bring His people home from exile. Later the NT will understand Isaiah's words to announce the coming of the Messiah. The good news is again associated with God's coming. This time He comes in the incarnation.

GOOD NEWS, HE'S HERE—
INCARNATION

The NT declares that God comes to the earth. He comes in human form as Jesus. *Matthew 1–2* and *Luke 1–3* announce the coming of God as a human infant. God—who walks the earth in *Genesis 1–11*, who regularly appears in theophanies and epiphanies, who announces His coming in *Isaiah 40*—comes as a baby. Both *Matthew (3:3)* and *Luke (3:4-6)* borrow from *Isaiah 40* to cite the role of John the Baptist coming to prepare the way. Matthew states that Jesus *"will save his people from their sins"* (*Mt 1:21*) and then cites His coming as a fulfillment of the *Isaiah 7* prophecy about Immanuel (*Mt 1:22-23*). When Mary reflects on Jesus' birth, she too borrows language of exaltation from *Isaiah 40* (for example, *Lk 1:51* cites *Isa 40:10*). Even the father of John the Baptist, Zechariah, reaches back to *Isaiah 40* in his praise to God, recounting the things God has done to show his faithfulness (*Lk 1:69-70,76*). The angels who make a nighttime announcement to the shepherds draw on Isaiah's *"good tidings"* and identify the child as Savior and Messiah (*Lk 2:10-11*).

John's Gospel also focuses on God's coming. John's opening language links His coming with the OT. John draws on God's speaking the world into existence in *Genesis* in order to connect it with the Greek idea of wisdom, or *logos*. John explains that the Word existed at the creation but that the Word has now become human flesh. God's coming *"enlightens everyone"* (*Jn 1:9*) and offers *"power to become children of God"* (*1:12*). John likely uses *Exodus 34:6* to indicate that Jesus will be filled with grace and truth. Then John announces the nature of the visit: *"And the Word became flesh and lived among us"* (*1:14*). The term for "lived" has roots in the Old Testament word for "tabernacle," the temporary and moveable meeting place of the divine and human worlds, but John re-forms it into a long-term residence. *The Message* version of the Bible puts it in vivid vernacular: *"The Word became flesh and blood and moved into the neighborhood."*

The Gospels thus unite two biblical trajectories—the "divine with" and God's visits. The "divine with" comes to a crescendo with Immanuel. In Jesus, God moves across the street. In Immanuel, God is "with us" in the fullest sense. God's visits come to a climax when God moves into the neighborhood. God coming in the form of the son is the climax of all God's visits to the earth. The two trajectories fully overlap in Jesus.

> **The "divine with," comes to a crescendo with Immanuel.**

John writes about Jesus so that people will come to faith. God sends His son so that the entire world will know of God's love and come to faith (*Jn 3:16*). The Gospel begins by stating that God incarnate will interact with people face to face, one on one, in their world and on their time, and ends with a statement of the purpose of drawing them to faith (*Jn 20:30-31*). We recognize this language as evangelistic. Evangelism simply takes the Greek word *euaggelizo*, which means "preaching good news," and anglicizes it. It is God reaching out, seeking humankind, striving to draw us to Him by every means. The God who brought *"good tidings"* in *Isaiah 40* brings *"good news"* in *John*.

In a sense, God is the original evangelist. God is the world's first missionary, leaving His home to go to a foreign country. He visits with a greater purpose in mind. God is not a tourist just sightseeing in our land. In Jesus, He takes up full residence and does so for a purpose. He is here to give dead people life, to make blind people see and to find people who are lost. He comes to our world. He visits us. He speaks our language. God's heart seeks relationship with human hearts, which prompts Him to make the move toward us.

Philippians 2 presents the case for incarnation in hymn form. The Bible opens with an almighty, cosmic God speaking the world into existence, making humankind out of dirt, sending a destructive flood, and placing a rainbow in the sky. Now, near the close of the Bible, that same God has become a humble carpenter. The full sacrifice and commitment of God to humanity is explained in hymn language:

> ⁵*Let the same mind be in you that was in Christ Jesus,*
> ⁶ *who, though he was in the form of God,*

> did not regard equality with God
>   as something to be exploited,
> 7 but emptied himself,
>   taking the form of a slave,
>   being born in human likeness.
>   and being found in human form,
> 8   he humbled himself
>   and became obedient to the point of death—
>   even death on a cross. *(Php 2:5-8)*

This passage offers a careful look at God coming to earth, describing what He left behind, what form He took and the legacy to which He committed himself. This passage is a clear statement of God's coming and the mission to which He dedicated himself.

Paul uses this text in the book of **Philippians** in two ways. First, this passage presents God's good news for the world in succinct form. Paul uses the word "gospel" nine times in the book of **Philippians**. In this passage Paul explains the core gospel of God's coming to earth. Secondly, this passage shows that God has already done what Paul and others now do. Paul dedicates himself to the spread of the gospel. In this passage Paul uses Jesus' example to lay a foundation for his message to the Philippian church, in which he cites their partnership with him in the spread of that gospel. In effect, Paul cites God's mission as a model for the Philippian church and himself.

Few words better express the distance God travels than Isaiah's announcement *"Here is your God"* or John's proclamation *"The Word became flesh and blood and moved into the neighborhood."* Paul's poem contains words that seem at odds with any description of a distant, uncaring, deity: emptied, slave, humbled, death. God's willingness to place Himself in a vulnerable position, to empty Himself, to humble Himself into a human shape, reveals His true heart.

> **God's willingness to place Himself in a vulnerable position reveals His true heart.**

GOD COMES ON A MISSION

Working on finding the key ancestors in one's family tree takes commitment. I remember how tired my eyes were after reading pages of the 1840 US census on microfilm. When we moved recently, I opened a box in the attic that held the six large notebooks that contained all the documents I had photocopied at the height of my genealogy passion. Even though I finally gave up on finding any information about Jacob K. Shank beyond the fact that he was born in Maryland in about 1774 and died in Pennsylvania in 1866, I recall those years of my search with fondness. I enjoyed the hunt. I was passionate about making a breakthrough. I desperately wanted to be one of those people who could trace their family tree back to a dozen or more generations.

Mission is part of the heart of God. It is His passion. Each purposeful visit arose from His heart. God's repeated visits and especially His climatic visit in the incarnation reveal how much His coming is part of who He is. Passion drove me to put up with microfilm census records and long trips to basement rooms in small town historical societies. Passion drove God to come and then return again and again. Mission is a quality of God's heart, a passion of God.

God visits the earth for a reason. Each of His repeated appearances on earth in *Genesis 1–11* is purposeful. His theophanies and epiphanies in the

> **God's repeated visits reveal how much His coming is part of who He is.**

OT reflect something He hoped to accomplish. In *Isaiah*, God came to set the exiles free. The incarnation aims to show God's love and draw all people to Himself. The incarnation completes the biblical trajectory of God's journeys to the earth. The biblical story, of course, anticipates a second coming of Jesus to the earth at the Judgment Day.

The trajectory showed that each visit by God is purposeful. God is not content to create the world and govern it from afar. God does not visit the earth and leave it without making some adjustments. God did not visit once and then decide not to come back. The purposefulness of God's coming indicates He is a God on a mission. Although the word "mission" implies one who sends and one who goes, in God the two roles are collapsed into one. God sends Himself on a mission.

Schwarz (125-131) claims that it was Karl Hartenstein who coined the phrase *"Missio Dei."* It comes from the Latin meaning "the sending of God." It is a way of saying that God is one who comes on a mission. In theological circles, *Missio Dei* came to mean that the Christian mission derives from God and that the church is not a mission of its own, but on a mission of God. Bosch (9-11) explores how

Missio Dei has become a significant concept in biblical studies and Christian ministry. It may be we have used the word "mission" so long to describe our human efforts, such as our response to the Great Commission and organizational mission statements, that we perceive the term to be human in origin, but the biblical trajectory of God coming to the earth reveals that He is a missionary God, that He comes in a purposeful way because of who He is.

This quality means that whatever lies in the heart of God is not content to remain in His heart. A divine being might have a particular trait but keep that trait to Himself. Mission indicates that the quality within God's heart cannot remain in His heart.

We might make a rough parallel with a wealthy man. We not only have a notion of "wealthy man" but the additional concepts of "miser" and "generous." A wealthy man who also happens to be a miser is a different person from a wealthy man who is generous. Whatever qualities God has, He shares them. He is not just a God of love, but a God who comes to us with that love; not just a God of mercy, but a God who comes to us with mercy. It is one thing to be a rich person, but quite another to be charitable. We call a man who shares his money generous. We call a God who shares His love a missionary God.

God's persistence is notable. I have stored all my family tree research in the attic. If God had only come a few times, we might not be able to see His passion for coming, but the substantial number of His appearances reveals his consistency. He does not give up. He comes. He keeps coming. He promises to come again.

God's coming in the form of Jesus represents the highpoint of the biblical narrative and the central focus of all Christian theology. The Christian faith does not revolve around a philosophy or ethics or organizations, but around a relationship with a God who comes. He seeks us out. God does not hide from humanity or sit in a distant place waiting for us to find Him. Neither does He force us to enter His world before He enters our world. God's regular coming provides the foundation for God's entrance into the world in Jesus Christ.

He comes. He keeps coming. He promises to come again.

Just as God walked on the earth in *Genesis 1–11* seeking some connection with early humanity, just as Deborah, Micah, and Habakkuk pictured Him visiting the earth with punishment in mind that would prompt their hearts toward Him, just as Isaiah described God coming personally to lead His exiled people home to Jerusalem, so in Jesus Christ God hopes to draw all people to Himself. Behind all the biblical narrative, at the core of every biblical doctrine, inherent in all the information about God is the divine desire to be close to human hearts. The visits of God to earth imply something about His heart.

CONCLUSION

William Lawrence Bragg, winner of the Nobel Prize in Physics in 1915 became a well-known scientist in England in the twentieth century. One of his hobbies was gardening. Crick's biography of Bragg (53) describes how, when he became the director of the Royal Institution in London in 1953, Bragg had to leave his Cambridge garden behind. Restless, unable to garden in his city apartment, Bragg dressed up in old gardening clothes, put his shovel on his shoulder, and wandered around the rich neighborhoods until He found a pleasing garden on an exclusive street in South Kensington. He rang the bell and introduced himself as Willie, an odd-job gardener with an afternoon free each week. The woman of the house hired him and he turned her garden into a showplace. Some time later during an afternoon tea on the day "Willie" was working in the garden, one of the wealthy guests looked out the window and exclaimed, "My dear, what is Sir Lawrence Bragg doing in your garden?"

The story speaks of the unexpected. The wealthy woman at tea did not expect a world-famous, award-winning physicist to be on his knees pulling weeds. The only explanation was that Bragg had a heart for gardening that went beyond what people expected of a man in his position.

God creates the world by voice command in *Genesis 1*. He controls the planets and the plants, the asteroids and the animals. We do not expect to find Him breathing into the nostrils of a clay man or see Him walking in the garden in the cool of the day or inspecting a construction project at Babel. *Isaiah* describes Him as powerful, incomprehensible, incomparable, and inexhaustible. We expect such a being to be divinely busy at divine things. We do not expect Him to come to the rescue of a small group of people living in captivity. Jesus gave up a position in heaven to take the form of a human slave. We might well say to Adam and Eve or to the people in Babylonian captivity or to Paul's readers, "Good heavens, what is the LORD God doing in your neighborhood?"

Our word to describe what prompts God to do the unexpected is "mission." He comes. He visits. He moves into the neighborhood. He does it because it is part of who He is. He is at heart a God on a mission.

The Christian hymn tells us "joy to the world, the Lord is come." Although the hymn correctly refers to the incarnation, it is based on the foundation of God coming into the world. We have traced what we call a biblical trajectory of God making significant visits to earth, each with a purpose in mind which reveals Him to be a God on a mission. He comes to the earth to tend to the divine-human relationship. Those visits culminate in the dramatic work of Jesus Christ.

> **"Good heavens, what is the LORD God doing in your neighborhood?"**

Jesus models God's love, dies as expression of God's love, and sacrifices Himself to reunite us with God.

Joy to the world, the Lord is come!

WHAT DO YOU SAY?

1. When Israel is in Babylon, they feel like God has forgotten them. Name other people in the Bible who felt God had forgotten them. Has there been a time in your life when you felt as if God had forgotten you?

2. John's Gospel focuses on God's mission through the incarnation. Who, in the Gospel of *John* is a recipient of God's mission by coming to faith? In what ways did people come to faith in John?

3. Reflect on this chapter. What did you learn about:

   a. God's coming and caring for His people

   b. God's coming and His mission

   c. God's coming and the incarnation

4. Define and give an example of:

   a. Theophany

   b. Theodicy

5. God visits with a purpose. What are the implications for evangelism, as we reach out to others?

CHAPTER SIX

BLESSING: GOD DOING PEOPLE A WORLD OF GOOD

Begin your study of this chapter by reading *Genesis 12:1-3*.

O ne of my jobs in high school was securing advertisements for the program we sold at the home football games. I went uptown to call on the local merchants about buying ads. In nearly every store, the people out front would send me to the office in the back where the owner or manager conducted business.

As I walked to the back and knocked on the door, I was always filled with dread. Would I get a gruff, "We're not interested" or a "Get out of here, I'm busy" or "I bought one last year and it didn't do any good"? I often thought, "He owns this business and I'm just a high school kid intruding on his time." Worse yet, I feared she might ask me, "Do you have a license to do business on Main Street?"

I remember how relieved I was when the authority figure behind the desk smiled, welcomed me in, and bought a bigger ad than I had hoped. Pretty soon I started making a list of the "good prospects" so that the next year I could approach the businesses where I had a positive experience and encouraging results.

People in positions of authority and power can make our lives miserable or happy. Until we know their intent toward us, we are often suspicious.

We know God is in a position of authority and power. He can make our lives miserable or happy. We want to know "Is He good?" All that we've studied so far indicates the answer is "Yes, He is good." He uses His control of the world to turn evil human actions into good. His heart is affected by human sin, but it does not turn Him against us. He's not a God who stays far away, but promises to be with us. He comes on a mission to win our hearts. All that points to the reality that God is good. He smiles, welcomes, and gives us more than we expect. The word the Bible uses to describe God doing just that is "blessing."

Blessing often receives little serious theological attention. Although it is used frequently in the Bible, it is commonly given little significance. When the full meaning of blessing is understood, it reveals a God who has our best interests in His heart. So we begin by deepening our understanding of blessing which will enable us to see several cases of God's blessing and God's heart in a new light.

> Much contemporary theology provides scant reflection on the concept of blessing. Many theological dictionaries either omit the word entirely or treat it briefly. Religious writers have written few books or articles on the idea. Although entire volumes exist on love, faith, and hope, the literature on blessing is scarce.

BLESSING— A PACKAGE WORD

Those who study the Bible tend to read over the word "blessing." They mentally substitute the word "affluence" or some cultural version of the good life, without completely absorbing the theological implications of the concept associated with the word in Scripture. For example, many recite the Aaronic blessing, "The LORD bless you and keep you . . ." (*Num 6:24*) without understanding the full importance of what the words mean. Others, for instance, read the Beatitudes with their "blessed are the . . ." (*Mt 5:3-9*) openings for what they say about poverty of spirit, grief, or mourning, without significant regard for the implications of blessing.

The concept of blessing appears in the Bible over 400 times. Blessing occurs in both *Genesis 1* and *Revelation 22*. God is frequently the one doing the blessing and often the one who is blessed. Many of the best known verses in the Bible include the word "blessing." The promise to Abraham in *Genesis 12:1-3* uses various forms of the word five times. The famous Aaronic blessing in *Numbers 6* has been set to music and framed for dining room walls. *Psalms* begins with the well-known, "Blessed is the man . . ." and each of Jesus' opening four points in His Sermon on the Plain in *Luke 6* begins with "blessed are. . . ."

> Contemporary uses of the words "bless" and "blessing" capture a portion of what blessing is all about, but often lack awareness of the deeper biblical implications of the concept of blessing. Frequently people thank God in prayer for "all their blessings." If pressed to describe what those blessings are, most would point to signs of financial affluence, good health, and beneficial relationships. Family members often punctuate their farewells with a "God bless you," by which they seem to mean a wish for safety, well-being, and relationship with God. Many seem to use the word "blessing" in a vague religious sense, but ascribe little theological content to the word.
>
> Following a sneeze, people often say, "Bless you" which seems to indicate something like "I hope you are not getting sick and that you are in good health." The origin of that practice reportedly came about several centuries ago when it was believed that one's spirit might leave the body if the person sneezed too hard. As such, they said "God bless you" in hopes that God would not allow the person's spirit to leave. This idea is probably connected to the concepts of the Hebrew word *nephesh* and the Greek word *pneuma*, which can mean spirit, wind, or breath. People mistakenly thought the breath leaves the body, and thus so does the spirit.

Biblically, blessing is rooted in God. It is associated with the good of life, with satisfaction and fulfillment. Westermann (*God*, **44**) defines blessing as "a quiet, continuous, flowing and unnoticed working of God which cannot be captured in moments or dates." Blessing makes no noise. Blessing never stops. Blessing flows constantly from God to humanity. *Blessing is a theological way of describing all the provision, all the good, all the grace, all the mercy, all the love, all that God does for humanity.* Blessing is being valued, worthwhile, and accepted. Westermann (**ibid.**) continues by noting "blessing is realized in a gradual process." Perhaps that is why the word blessing is popularly connected with the good things of life including possessions, health, and relationships, because they are the result of a gradual process of God's work in our lives. When we look out and sense that life is good, we often think, "I'm really a blessed person." Westermann (**ibid.**) goes on to say that blessing comes "in the process of growing, maturing, and fading." We will shortly see the central role that blessing plays in the lives of children growing up, but Westermann's point is that blessing touches us from the beginning of our growing until we finally fade away at death.

> Blessing is difficult to define. One way of probing the meaning of this word is to read the biblical texts where it appears. Many of those references are included in this chapter. A second avenue involves looking up "blessing" in a Bible encyclopedia or word study book. A third, more in-depth approach, entails looking at Westermann's work, *Blessing in the Bible and the Life of the Church*. Additionally, I talk about the word "blessing" as it applies to children in my book *Children Mean the World to God* (**29-44**).

Blessing describes such a substantial quality of life that its significance may be missed due to its immensity. Just as we might go days without looking at the sky or thinking about the air we breathe, both the sky and air are essential components of life. Blessing is to the soul what air is to the body. Without blessing and air, life comes to a halt.

God is significantly involved with blessing in the Bible. The importance of blessing can be illustrated with a triangle. The points of the triangle are love, grace, and blessing. The triangle depicts God's holistic intent toward humanity. Love describes the *duration*. God will not stop or wear out in His intent toward us. Grace depicts the *cost*. Our relationship with God does not depend on us, it depends on Him. It is by His grace that we have a relationship. Without that grace, none of us could be His friend. Blessing describes the *quality* of God's intent toward us. Blessing encompasses the well-being and spiritual and physical prosperity God has in mind for us.

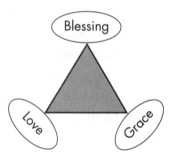

God is not the only one who blesses in the Bible. As we shall shortly see, He gives us the ability to be part of passing on the blessing to other people. Blessing refers to the value of what is being given and is often used in the Bible to transfer the good things from one generation to the next. Indeed, many uses of blessing are associated with fertility (**Gen 1:28; 9:1; 17:16; Deu 1:11**, etc) and with parents' intentions for their children's future (**Gen 27:1-4**). By blessing, God stays in relationship with us, and we stay connected with each other. Blessing is a form of solidarity in which people of significance transfer all that is good one to another.

> Blessings are transferred in different ways. Not all blessings in the Bible flow from God to humanity. In fact, blessings flow in three different ways: 1) People bless other people, 2) God blesses people, and 3) people bless God. All three means of blessing, rendered here in bold, appear in **Genesis 14:17-20**. This meeting takes place after Abram returns from war.
>
> > *[17]After his return from the defeat of Chedorlaomer and the kings who were with him, the king of Sodom went out to meet him at the Valley of Shaveh (that is, the King's Valley). [18]And King Melchizedek of Salem brought out bread and wine; he was priest of God Most High. [19]He **blessed** him and said,*
> > > *"**Blessed** be Abram by God Most High,*
> > > *maker of heaven and earth;*
> > *[20]and **blessed** be God Most High,*
> > > *who has delivered your enemies into your hand!"*
> > *And Abram gave him one tenth of everything.*
>
> Blessings flow in three different ways in this text. See the accompanying diagram which illustrates these three ways.
>
> 1. People bless people. Although there is some ambiguity about the subject of the pronouns in *verse 19* "He blessed him," the passage suggests that Melchizedek blessed Abram. This blessing flows from *one human to another*. The priest of Salem offers his blessing to Abram. Through sharing Melchizedek's bread and wine, he and Abram participate in the passing on of a blessing.
>
> 2. God blesses people. Melchizedek then refers to another way blessings are transferred by referring to *God's blessing of the man*, Abram. The priest may have knowledge of God's verbal blessing of Abram in *Genesis 12* or may deduce from Abram's wealth (cf. **Gen**

14:15) that God had blessed him. In fact, Melchizedek implies that the blessing he passes on to Abram originates with God.

3. People bless God. In *verse 20*, the priest of Salem blesses God. This third means of blessing is from *humans toward God*. Often when humans wish good for God, it is translated as worship. For example, the NIV of *Ephesians 1:3* reads, *"**Praise** be to the God and Father of our Lord Jesus Christ, who has blessed us in the heavenly realms with every spiritual blessing in Christ,"* while the NRSV renders, *"**Blessed** be the God and Father of our Lord Jesus Christ, who has blessed us in Christ with every spiritual blessing in the heavenly places."* The blessing Paul intends toward God is, in effect, praise of God.

Means of Blessing

Blessing, and God's heart toward us, takes on deeper significance as we explore God's blessing of humanity. This blessing includes the first blessing from God to humanity in *Genesis 1*, the special blessing to and by Abram in *Genesis 12*, the Aaronic blessing in *Numbers 6*, and the blessing of Jesus to children in *Mark 10*.

The focus of this study is not the complexity of blessing in the Bible, but rather what God's blessing of humanity tells us about the heart of God. But we must understand that not only does the word "blessing" encompass all that God does for good toward us, but the words for blessing are used in a wide variety of contexts:

God blesses people in *Gen 1:22; 1:28; 5:2; 9:1; 12:2,3; 17:16,20; 22:17; 24:1,35; 25:11; 26:3,12,24; 28:3; 30:27,30; 32:26,30; 35:9; 39:5; 48:3,16; 49:25; Ex 20:24; Num 6:24,27; 23:20; 24:1; Deu 1:11; 2:7; 7:13; 12:7; 14:24,29; 15:4,6,10,14,18; 16:10,15; 23:20; 24:13,19; 26:15; 28:8; 30:16; Josh 17:14; 24:10; Jdg 13:24; Ruth 2:4; 2Sa 6:11,12; 7:29; 1Chr 4:10; 13:14; 17:27; 26:5; 2Chr 31:10; Neh 8:6; Job 42:12; Pss 5:12; 28:9; 29:11; 45:2; 67:1,6,7; 107:38; 109:28; 115:12,13; 128:5; 134:3; 147:13; Prov 3:33; Isa 19:25; 51:2; 61:9; Jer 31:23; Hag 2:19.*

God blesses things in: *Gen 2:3; 27:27; Ex 20:11; 23:25; Deu 28:12; 33:11; Job 1:10; Pss 65:10; 132:15.*

GOD—A BLESSING GOD

GOD'S FIRST ACTION TOWARD NEWLY CREATED HUMANITY—GENESIS 1:28

When I was selling ads to the business owners in our little town, I desperately wanted some assurance that I might get a positive response. I hoped to be greeted with a smile. I also found assurance in a handshake. Best yet, I was overjoyed when the busy person behind the desk set his work aside to give me his full attention.

We want the same assurance from the powerful creator God. We do not have to wait long in *Genesis 1*. In the midst of the making of light and placing all the planets in orbit, that assurance comes in three often overlooked words. As we work our way past the newly created day and night, beyond the freshly formed plants, and on to the animals taking their first breath, we hear the words of assurance: *"God blessed them"* (*Gen 1:28*). *After God creates the first two people, His first action toward them is blessing.* Those three words represent the Creator's smile. It is His handshake to the human race. He sets aside all His other work to give the new people His full attention.

We easily read over those three words. Most of the commentary about the creation of humankind in *Genesis 1:26-28* is about what it means to be created in God's image and likeness. In effect, we read the passage that says, *"God blessed them"* and we think, "That's nice, but I want to talk about what it means to be made in His image." I suggest that we ponder those three words as a means of understanding what God is doing in this final creative act.

God's blessing of humankind offers the first insight into the heart of God toward humanity. God's holistic approach is represented by the triangle of love, grace, and blessing. God's love toward humanity is not mentioned until *Exodus*, and His grace is first announced to Noah, but His blessing appears in the opening words of the Bible. With that blessing,

God's holistic approach is represented by the triangle of love, grace, and blessing.

God announces His good intent toward humanity. The blessing is a smile on God's face. He begins a "quiet, continuous, flowing and unnoticed working" to use Westermann's words, that will continue through until the end of the book of **Revelation**. All of the provisions, all the good, all the mercy, all the love that God will give are wrapped up in these simple words.

The first occurrence of God blessing comes in the context of what **Genesis 1** says about God. The chapter might be summarized as the *Creator creating creation*. God dominates from beginning to end. He alone acts and speaks. He makes, inspects, and evaluates. In the process of creation He gives each part of creation its function. The first blessing (**Gen 1:22**) goes to the sea creatures and birds. After blessing the animals of sea and sky, God offers His first blessing to humankind. Thematically, the high point of creation comes in **Genesis 1:26-28**:

> ²⁶Then God said, "Let us make humankind in our image, according to our likeness; and let them have dominion over the fish of the sea, and over the birds of the air, and over the cattle, and over all the wild animals of the earth, and over every creeping thing that creeps upon the earth."
>
> ²⁷ So God created humankind in his image,
> in the image of God he created them;
> male and female he created them.
>
> ²⁸God blessed them, and God said to them, "Be fruitful and multiply, and fill the earth and subdue it; and have dominion over the fish of the sea and over the birds of the air and over every living thing that moves upon the earth."

This complex text describes God making humans, identifying their functions, blessing them, and giving them commands. God speaks about creating the humans in His image and likeness. Like the other parts of creation, God assigns functions to the humans: they are to have dominion and to subdue. What happens if we think about the God of this passage in light of the blessing? How do these three words deepen our understanding of God's heart?

Humans occupy a central place in the created order. Trible (15) points out that God speaks in the first person to only the humans and gives dominion only to them. Additionally, God created only humans in His image and likeness. Despite the fact that God is later called light (**Ps 27:1; 1Jn 1:5**), it is not light that God made in His image. Although the sun, moon, and stars share in God's power to rule the universe, the luminaries are not made in His image. *Hosea 14:8* compares God to a tree, but in *Genesis 1* the trees are not like God. Only the humans come out of the mind of God as copies of the Divine. To them God offers His image and likeness.

Students of Scripture usually assign one of three meanings to image and likeness:
1. Some suppose that the image is the unique human qualities of will, intellect, and soul or spirit;
2. Others suggest that image refers to humans as relational creatures imitating God's relational nature;
3. Most OT scholars rely on how the words "image" and "likeness" were used in the ancient Near East. Monarchs created images of themselves in order to maintain control. As a parallel, God uses humans as His representatives to maintain control. Humans have dominion over the earth as God's representatives.

If the image and likeness are considered in light of the blessing, then we see God in a clearer light. The powerful Creator, who speaks things into being, who evaluates all that He makes, is immediately associated with "it is good." God does good work. He makes good things.

But when God calls the light *"good"* (*Gen 1:4*), the good associated with light is not moral good or good in the sense of satisfaction or fulfillment, but rather one of good function and efficiency. Light works well. It removes the darkness. It provides illumination.

When God calls the vegetation *"good"* (*Gen 1:12*), God does not give trees a sense of fulfillment or make turnips satisfied or apples happy. Vegetables are not morally good. God's judgment of the plant kingdom, rather, implies that the system of plant life works well and functions the way He intends for it to function.

When God creates the sea creatures and birds, He blesses them. We do not understand this blessing to mean that fish and birds have some sense of receiving the love and mercy of God, but that they are part of God's plan to make the earth a good place. Fish and birds will be involved in the "quiet, continuous, flowing and unnoticed working of God."

However, with humankind, God both makes them in His image and blesses them. Like God, they have the ability to find satisfaction

Of all creation, only humans can fully appreciate God's good, grace, mercy, and love.

and the spiritual good of life. Of all the pieces of creation, only humans can fully appreciate God's good, grace, mercy, and love. Only humans fully connect with being valued, worthwhile, and accepted. Being in God's image points to the human capacity to fully understand and appreciate the blessing. The creation story thus reveals not only a God who blesses, but a God who creates beings who can fully experience the blessing, beings like Himself. Being created in God's image and likeness is itself part of the blessing. Blessing is God's embrace of humankind as beings that reflect Him.

By making humans in His likeness and offering them His blessing, God reveals Himself to be in solidarity with the human race. He welcomes humanity. He makes a connection with people. He seeks their good. He values and considers them worthwhile. God is not a distant CEO issuing orders to the universe in an uncaring manner. God is not a general far behind the front lines, moving troops in and out of battle. Rather, blessing makes the creator God personal, caring, and intimately involved with those made in His image.

In *Luke 20:20-26*, the Pharisees come to Jesus with a query about money: should Jews pay taxes to the emperor or not? Jesus, however, sees it as a theological question: what is the emperor's and what is God's? His answer is also theological. He asks whose image is on the coin and simply tells them to *"give to the emperor the things that are the emperor's and to God the things that are God's"* (*Lk 20:25*). In asking about the image, Jesus was referencing the imprint of Caesar's face on Roman coinage. He was, however, also alluding to the statement in *Genesis* that people are made in the image of God. The matter is not actually a financial issue but a spiritual one: Caesar may have claim to the coins because they have his image, but God has claim to people because they have *His* image.

Jesus was encouraging his listeners to give themselves back to God. God can use us to be a blessing to others if we allow Him to do so. God's intent to do good to humanity is accomplished through us when we give ourselves over to Him.

Digging a bit deeper, we observe that both the image and the blessing come without conditions. We do nothing to reflect God's image. That image is His gift to us. We do nothing to receive this

> **Both the image and the blessing come without conditions.**

blessing. Blessing is also His gift to us. This blessing requires no human cooperation, demands no obedience. Wherever humankind goes, they carry the spiritual DNA of God's blessing with them. Blessing comes before covenant, prior to law, ahead of gospel. The God who creates light for the eyes, air for the lungs, food for the stomach, creates blessing for the soul. All humans have equal access and right to the light and to the blessing. God will later add other dimensions to the blessing (a blessing to all the earth through the descendants of Abram in *Genesis 12*) and even stipulations to some of the blessings (obedience from Israel in *Deuteronomy 28*), the first blessing comes within the total human situation. Regardless of historical period or human cultural particulars, all humanity participates in the blessing of the progression of the human race.

Genesis 1:28 does not describe a God who makes a single gift to humanity and then returns to His distant home, shunning further contact. Instead God's blessing continues "in the process of growing, maturing and fading," to recall Westermann again. In fact, God includes in the creation a means of continuing the human race: they are to reproduce and multiply, and they are to subdue and have dominion over the earth. Blessing is often associated with fertility and children. The blessing is associated with the sexual act, the establishment of the family, and the propagation of the human race. The fruitfulness and multiplication of the human race cannot be considered outside of the blessing. God blesses the man and woman, and then gives them the ability to reproduce themselves as a means of passing on the blessing of life to the coming generations.

Blessing is the theological word that is regularly linked with children. Consider these uses:

Parents or other adults pass on a blessing to children: *Gen 17:20; 24:60; 25:11; 27:4-41; 28:14; 31:55; 48:9-20; 49:25-28; 1Chr 16:43; Ps 37:26; Heb 11:20.*

Chapter 6 A World of Good

> God makes promises of blessing that include children: *Gen 1:28; 9:1; 17:16,20; 22:17; 26:3-4,24; 28:14; 39:5; Pss 107:38; 112:1-2; 127:5; Prov 5:18; Isa 51:2; 61:9; 65:23; Lk 1:45; 2:34; 11:27; Acts 3:25; Heb 6:14.*
>
> Blessing is associated with people having children: *Deu 1:11; 7:13; 28:2-6; 30:19; Josh 17:14; 1Chr 13:14; Eze 44:30; Lk 23:29.*
>
> Those who give attention to orphans and at-risk children are linked with blessing: *Deu 24:19; Ps 41:1; Prov 14:21.*
>
> God blesses children: *Jdg 13:24; Job 29:4; Isa 44:3; Mk 10:16.*

God desires to bless the human race, not just once but regularly. In fact, He sets in motion a process of passing the blessing on through human reproduction. The propagation of the blessing in God's heart is fixed in the way the human race works. I could not imagine one of those business owners telling me, "Not only will I buy a full-page ad this year, but put me down for a full-page ad as long as there are students at the high school." God is a blessing God and ensures that His blessings will continue to flow.

God is a blessing God and ensures that His blessings will continue to flow.

Genesis 1:28 simply states that, despite all that will take place in the biblical story and in human history, it all begins with God's blessing of the first humans, a blessing that was to travel with human reproduction, a blessing that originated in the heart of God passed on to those made in His image and likeness, indicating His good intent toward all human beings. God is at heart a blessing God.

GOD STRATEGIZES ABOUT BLESSING— GENESIS 12:1-3

Our high school newspaper staff published the football programs. When I joined the paper staff, the football advertising income was almost nonexistent. Our sponsor called a meeting to work out a plan. I did not know it then, but we were strategizing about how to turn the advertising revenues around. We needed a plan.

By *Genesis 12*, God announces a plan. Despite His initial blessing of the human race, they had responded with a long string of sinful activities recorded in *Genesis 1–11*. The flood punished one generation of evildoers, but did not change the reality that humans sinned from their youth. In *Genesis 12*, God returns to His intent to bless the human race. This time He spells out His plan. The word blessing in several forms appears five times (all bolded):

> ¹Now the LORD said to Abram, "Go from your country and your kindred and your father's house to the land that I will show you. ²I will make of you a great nation, and I will **bless** you, and make your name great, so that you will be a **blessing**. ³I will **bless** those who **bless** you, and the one who curses you I will curse; and in you all the families of the earth shall be **blessed**." (Gen 12:1-3)

God calls Abram, whose name is later changed to Abraham, to leave his home, move to a new neighborhood and to let God use him to influence humanity. God blesses Abram, makes Abram a blessing to others, promises to bless those who bless Abram, and through Abram pledges to bless all the earth. The blessing of *Genesis 1:28* leads to the blessings of *Genesis 12:1-3* and gives us additional insight into God.

The promise to Abram is an oft-discussed passage. Most scholars point to a significant juncture between *Genesis 11* and *Genesis 12*. The primeval history ends, and the long narrative about the ancestors of Israel begins. The expanding sin of humankind encounters God's increasing response of grace in *Genesis 1–11*. Clearly the passage plays a pivotal role in the unfolding of Genesis and much of the OT story. Despite the importance of this passage, we do well to ponder the significance of blessing. God intends good. Blessing is a package word that describes much of God's merciful and gracious gifts to humankind. What does this passage tell us about God's desire to bless?

The promises to Abram are complex. Scholars configure the promises in a variety of ways. One of the most frequently cited outlines comes from Clines (29), who sees three different themes:

1. a promise to give Abram *descendants*, a theme taken up in the book of *Genesis* where the lineage of Abram is constantly threatened, and again in *Numbers* where his descendants reach sizeable numbers;
2. a promise of *relationship*, a theme taken up in *Exodus* and *Leviticus* where there are explanations of the necessary circumstances for a divine-human relationship;

> 3. a promise of *land*, a theme taken up in *Numbers* and *Deuteronomy*, finally reaching fulfillment in *Joshua* and *Judges*.
>
> This configuration, as in many ways of outlining the promise passage, gives little weight to the fivefold appearance of blessing, subsuming it under the larger issue of relationship. Clines' reading of *Genesis 12* makes the passage a table of contents to the Pentateuch, but at the expense of the teaching about blessing.

Indeed, *Genesis 12* is remarkable in its focus on God. The divine first person pronoun appears five times: "I will show," "I will make," "I will bless," (twice) and "I will curse." God is the blessing expert and here makes Abram into an expert like Him. In His declaration to Abram, God expands on His intent to do good in four ways:

First, God blesses Abram. He wants Abram to have a full life and to enjoy satisfaction. God intends good toward Abram.

Second, God uses Abram as a medium of His blessing: *"you will be a blessing."* The divine intent to do good now works through human contact with Abram. Others will experience God's good intent through their encounters with Abram. The divine intent to do good is, in a sense, franchised. God acts so that His good intent will be more fully, and perhaps more easily, experienced. Abram becomes a local outlet for God's goodness. Abram is the first of many human faces to represent the divine nature, a sequence that will culminate in the coming of Jesus, who is God's presence in the world to accomplish His good intentions toward humankind.

Third, God establishes a reciprocal nature to blessing: *"I will bless those who bless you."* The passage imagines someone such as Melchizedek blessing Abram. Men like Melchizedek who learn how to bless and then bless Abram will find themselves blessed by God. Individuals who bestow good on others, who cast that goodness on Abram, will find God's good intent working in their lives. It is not a reciprocation that demands blessings for Abram before blessings are received, as if the blessing of God worked in a rigid system. It is not a childish "you let me play with your toys and I'll let you play with mine" scenario. Rather, the intent is peda-

God does good with the hopes that humans will imitate that good intent toward other humans.

gogical. God does good with the hopes that humans will imitate that good intent toward other humans.

The negative side of blessing is equally reciprocal: *"him who curses you, I will curse."* Not only does God add to the good that humans do, but God responds in kind to those who pursue evil intent. When we read of God's good intent toward us, we cannot help but wonder about the issue of evil. If God is intent on good, why does He allow evil? How can the evil in the world be reconciled with God's blessing? *Genesis 12* hints at how this dilemma will be resolved. God will curse those who curse Abram.

Fourth, God makes the blessings worldwide.[1] God's blessing in *Genesis 1:28* pertained to all humanity through the first couple. *Genesis 12* makes God's method more explicit. He informs Abram that He will bless all people *"by you."* Through Abram and his great nation, God will deliver His blessings to all the families of the earth. God does not simply intend good to the first couple or to Abram and Sarai or to the nation of which Abram is the father, but through this family/nation God intends good toward the entire human race

The death, burial, and resurrection of Jesus Christ are the perfect expression of God's good intent to Abram in *Genesis 12*. God's ultimate act of doing good to the world is accomplished at the cross. All the families of the earth are within reach of the blessing of God. God's desire to do good to humanity does not waver, but culminates in the death of the divine son of God.

With Abram God reveals the intensity of His desire to bless. He blesses Abram. God wants the entire world to see what it is like to be blessed by God. Abram will be a walking example of a person

God's ultimate act of doing good to the world is accomplished at the cross.

living in God's blessing. But Abram also becomes a warehouse for God. Others will find God's blessings through Abram. God is not willing for the human race to go on its sinful way, so well established in *Genesis 1–11*, but rather God intentionally plans for Abram and all

---

[1] Some versions take the final use of blessing in this passage as reflexive, *"all the families of the earth shall bless themselves,"* rather than as the NRSV's *"all the families of the earth shall be blessed."* While the theological implications of the reflexive translation might point to another element of God's blessing, I use the NRSV translation.

who follow to experience God's quiet, persistent, ever-present distribution of grace, mercy, and love.

GOD'S BLESSING IS PERSONAL— NUMBERS 6:22-27

One of the most famous statements of blessing comes in the often overlooked book of **Numbers**. The opening ten chapters of Numbers tell of preparations for the departure from Mount Sinai. Integral to those provisions are the duties of the newly appointed priests. One of their roles was to pass on the blessing. The task is assigned to Aaron and his sons. In assigning them the duty of blessing, God also provides the words with which to bless. It is perhaps one of the most enduring statements of God's intent toward humankind:

> [22]The LORD spoke to Moses, saying: [23]"Speak to Aaron and his sons, saying, 'Thus you shall bless the Israelites: You shall say to them,
> [24] "The LORD bless you and keep you;
> [25] the LORD make his face to shine upon you, and be gracious to you;
> [26] the LORD lift up his countenance upon you, and give you peace."'
> [27]So they shall put my name on the Israelites, and I will bless them." (**Num 6:22-27**)

The content of the blessing comes from God Himself. While most biblical statements of blessing simply contain the word "bless" (as in "God blessed them" **Gen 1:28**), this blessing has substantial content made up of six parts: bless, keep, shining face, grace, lifted up countenance, and peace. Nowhere else in the Bible is blessing given such significant content. The blessing uses significant and frequently used theological words: grace (used nearly 200 times in the Bible), peace (about 360 times), and the dual mention of God's face ("face" and "countenance" being the same Hebrew word). Blessing thus includes God's guarding and preserving, His shining face implies grace, and His lifting of His countenance provides peace. The phrase "make his face shine upon you" appears frequently in the Bible,[2] while "lift up his countenance upon you" is unique to this passage. Here "face" means "presence." Blessing includes the presence of God.

[2]These texts all seem to allude to **Num 6:25: Pss 4:6; 31:16; 67:1; 80:3,7,19; 104:15; 119:135; Ecc 8:1; Dan 9:17; 2Cor 4:6.**

Blessing is given substantial meaning and significance. That content includes God keeping watch over and protecting the ones being blessed and also giving them spiritual gifts

God is at heart a blessing God.

that include His presence, grace, and peace. The oft-repeated phrase *"make his face shine"* is typically associated with rich spiritual concepts including the good of life, love, grace, blessing, salvation, and restoration. Blessing, in effect, becomes a code word for many of God's spiritual gifts to humanity. God is at heart a blessing God.

The placement of this blessing in the midst of the law known for its long lists of stipulations and human obligations comes as a surprise, but serves to keep the law in perspective. God chooses Israel because of His love (*Deu 7:7-8*) and gives Israel grace prior to giving the law (*Ex 20:2*). This Aaronic blessing in the midst of the law reminds those reading about the preparations for leaving Sinai of God's good intention toward the people.

This blessing has no conditions. Unlike *Deuteronomy 28*, where the blessings come to the obedient and the curses to the disobedient, here the blessing is simply given. Aaron and his descendants are charged with the role of telling the people of God's intent to bestow good on their lives. In the last line of the blessing, God affirms that He will keep His promise. He values His people, seeks a relationship with them, will be with them, and will bring good into their lives. The blessing is accompanied by striking personal references to God.

The conditions on blessings in *Deuteronomy 28* might be compared to similar conditions on blessing in *Psalm 1* and *Matthew 5*. The one who obeys the law in *Deuteronomy 28* will be blessed. The one who meditates on the law in *Psalm 1* will be blessed. While some read these statements as a rigid system where obedience triggers God's release of a blessing, it is easier to understand these teachings as pointing to the reality that God's good intent for Israel is partially contained in the law. The law is instruction or guidance about how to best live life. Those who recognize the blessing of this instruction will find a blessing in walking in these kinds of paths, not to legalistically trigger the release of a blessing for each act of obedience, but to find the way God intended for people to live to the fullest.

Chapter 6
A World of Good

> Jesus echoes the same thinking in the Beatitudes. While some
> read the Beatitudes as a rigid system whereby the one who prac-
> tices poverty of spirit is rewarded with the blessing of a place in the
> kingdom, it is clearer to understand Jesus pointing to ways of living
> life that result in happiness and satisfaction (i.e., blessing). The
> Beatitudes themselves are a blessing from God that allow humans
> insight into the qualities of life that when cultivated result in a more
> fulfilled existence.

The God whose first act toward the newly created humans is to bless them (*Gen 1:28*), and who, after a long series of rebellious human acts (*Genesis 3–11*), commits Himself to bless the whole earth through Abram (*Gen 12:1-3*), continues to bless humanity by assigning the transfer of the blessing to the Aaronic priesthood. In giving the priests the words to say, the content of blessing is associated with God's good intent toward His people. God is at heart a God who blesses.

Blessing is the theological term most often associated with children in Scripture. The first blessing of God on humans in *Genesis 1:28* immediately takes up the blessing in the context of human reproduction and the next generation. Blessing frequently occurs in contexts related to children.[3] It is appropriate that our last text focuses on God's blessing to children.

JESUS BLESSES THE CHILDREN— MARK 10:13-16

The central section of Mark (*8:22–10:52*) links the earlier part of the Gospel where Jesus is presented as the powerful Son of God with the conclusion of the book where Jesus faces conflict and death. In this middle section Jesus discusses the meaning of His life and death (*10:45*) and the nature of discipleship (*8:34-38; 10:42-45*). In that context, Jesus uses a child to explain the nature of his work:

> [13]People were bringing little children to him in order that he might
> touch them; and the disciples spoke sternly to them. [14]But when
> Jesus saw this, he was indignant and said to them, "Let the little
> children come to me; do not stop them; for it is to such as these
> that the kingdom of God belongs. [15]Truly I tell you, whoever does

[3] See the side discussion of this on pp. 121-122.

not receive the kingdom of God as a little child will never enter it." ¹⁶And he took them up in his arms, laid his hands on them, and blessed them. (Mk 10:13-16)

The disciples do not consider children within the realm of Jesus' ministry and seek to bar them from access to their Master. Jesus thinks otherwise; He scolds the disciples and welcomes the children. He uses their presence as occasion to focus on the nature of God's kingdom and to physically touch them and verbally give them a blessing. The synoptic Gospels each present two stories of Jesus dealing with children, but the blessing occurs only in Mark.[4]

The text tells us that Jesus sees the children. The God whose face is associated with blessing in *Numbers 6*, now incarnated in the divine Son of God, turns His face ("when Jesus saw") to children. The God who blessed the first humans, who blessed Abram and those He encountered, and who blessed through Aaron and his sons, now blesses through Jesus.

Jesus is not being *sentimental* about children, but He is being *theological* about children. The good intent that God has for humankind is now expressed directly to these

The God who blessed repeatedly before, now blesses through Jesus.

children. Jesus passes on God's good intentions to them. Jesus' action is consistent with the biblical connection between blessing and children. What God first did in *Genesis 1:28* Jesus continues in *Mark 10:16*. Jesus is not doing something new, but continuing something deep within the context of the God of Scripture. God's intent to do good to humanity is not allowed to die with the ones who receive the original blessing, but that blessing, that intent of God to do good, must be and is passed on to those who come after. God blesses Abram, but the blessing does not end with Abram. It continues. God assigns Aaron the task of blessing the people, but the blessing does not stop with Aaron's death because his sons continue giving the blessing. Jesus joins a long line of those who fulfill God's heart to pass on the good things to people, especially to the newest members of the human race. God is at heart a God of blessing.

Chapter 6
A World of Good

---

[4] See the first case in *Mt 18:1-5; Mk 9:33-50 and Lk 9:46-48* and the second instance in *Mt 19:13-15; Mk 10:13-16 and Lk 18:15-17*.

GOD'S HEART—
POURING OUT BLESSING

The concept of blessing, often used in sentimental ways or emptied of any significant theological meaning in contemporary usage, actually conveys a considerable theological intent. Blessing carries within it the intent to do good. When this concept retains its full meaning, the texts where it is used contain significant revelation about God.

God's first action toward humanity was to reveal His intention to do good. In blessing the first humans, God was not engaged in an empty ritual nor filling space with meaningless words, but He was stating the first fundamental piece of how He intended to relate to those created in His image. He intended to do them good. His heart is filled with blessing.

> **Blessing carries within it the intent to do good.**

God intended for this blessing to be passed on throughout human history and provided means for that blessing to be passed on. God's intent did not expire at the deaths of the first humans. It was not taken back after the first sin. It was not buried in the waters of the flood. It was not destroyed by human sin or human rebellion or human ignorance. He established blessing with no expiration date and with means of permanently and consistently ensuring that each new generation of humans could learn and experience the blessing: the intent of God to do good toward them, just as He had expressed on the sixth day of creation. God's concern for passing on the blessing speaks to the strength of this desire within His heart. God's heart is so filled with a desire to do good to humanity that it was not only His first act toward us, but an act that He ensured would be consistently maintained. The blessings continued to flow out of His heart.

The blessing of God especially concerned the weakest members of the human race, its offspring. From the beginning, God's concern to wish the human race well involved the process of continuing that interest in human children. Not only did God plan for the blessing to continue, but He sought ways for it to be established in the lives of the youngest of humans. God's plan to pass the blessing on to children speaks to how this desire resided deep in His heart.

God intends good for all of us. It runs through Scripture from beginning to end. As the Bible closes, it cites the blessing of those dressing for their heavenly home. When we sin, God overcomes that evil with good. Perhaps the most succinct summary of God's heart is the often repeated, but often misunderstood, phrase: God bless you.

To say He is a God of blessing often seems empty of meaning and inconsequential. We would rather have a powerful, all-knowing, everywhere-all-the-time God. But stress on blessing shows us the intent of that power, the result of God's all-knowing, and the evidence of that omnipresence. The fact that good continues to happen even in the most evil of places, that good occurs when we are good, and good happens when we are bad, is evidence that Somebody puts goodness into the human experience. Let me illustrate the issue in this way.

It is clear that Somebody puts goodness into the human experience.

Imagine God above the earth with a large watering pot. The pot is filled not with liquid fertilizer or water, but with blessing. God pours it down on the human race in all times, all places, and all circumstances. Nothing can stop it, hinder it, or prevent it. We may not see it, get it exactly when we want it, appreciate it, or use it, but it is there. Not only does God stand at heaven's door with His watering pot, but He uses people to pass it on to others.

Just as plants receive the blessing, they pass it on to us. Animals get the blessing and pass it on to us. Fathers and mothers obtain the blessing and pass it on to children. Each baby represents the potential of God making good things happen between man and woman.

I use this image because so many of our images of God describe Him in the wrong way. Some imagine Him as the cosmic policeman or the uncaring miser off counting His money. But the God who blesses conveys a decidedly different image. He wants His face to shine upon us. The way He does that is through blessing.

Where is God's blessing in the bad times? Jeremiah gives us a vivid answer.

Jeremiah 30–33 is often called the Book of Hope, containing some of the most expectant words in the Bible. The passages are written during the Babylonian siege of Jerusalem, which ends with the collapse of the Jewish state and the burning of the capital buildings, including the temple of God. The poems of the book of *Lamentations* describe the revolting human conditions during the siege. The last days of Jerusalem are among the most dismal of Israelite history.

During the siege, the prophet Jeremiah is in prison. During his incarceration God tells him to buy a field from his cousin. Not only is it clear that the entire city and its environs is about to fall into enemy hands, making any real estate transaction an act of fiscal doom, but it is likely that the land Jeremiah purchased is at the time of closing occupied by the Babylonian army. Incredibly, the land Jeremiah purchases might have been the site of the officer's latrine or the feed lot for the war horses. The point of the purchase, recorded in *Jeremiah 32*, is to assure the people of Jerusalem that even on the darkest of days, there is reason to hope, that God would restore the land.

Jeremiah stresses that the calamity pressing on Jerusalem is brought by God in response to the people's disobedience. God speaks of how the behavior of the Judeans arouses His anger (*32:30-31*) and that nothing is too hard for God to accomplish. Then, with His prophet buying land he will never possess, from the prison cell of a doomed city, doomed by the power of its own God, God Himself speaks, revealing crucial information about what was going on in the heart of God during the black days of Jerusalem: *"I will rejoice in doing good to them, and I will plant them in this land in faithfulness, with all my heart and all my soul"* (*Jer 32:41*). These are unlikely words considering the circumstances. In them God reveals His heart. He tells them what is in His heart and soul while the people are experiencing the blackest hour in their history. With all His heart and with all His soul He seeks to do them good. The word "blessing" is not used. Nobody in the city feels particularly blessed. But even in this dark hour, God's heart beats with good intent for His people.

CONCLUSION

One day while selling ads for that high school program, a business owner turned me down in a gruff manner and returned to his work without even showing me the door. As I left, I lost all enthusiasm for my task. How could I go to the next store to ask them to buy an ad in the football program on the heels of such a negative experience? I gave up my work for that afternoon, went home to lick my wounds, and decided to return to the task another day.

To many people God seems as inaccessible and uncaring as the boss in the back office with the door closed and a scowl on his face. We approach the door with apprehension uncertain about what response we will receive. The biblical teaching about God as a blessing God puts all of that in a different perspective.

When we wonder what makes God smile or ponder what He is passionate about, we must think of blessing. God loves to bless. We often understand the word "bless" in a shallow way, but when we fully understand that blessing includes all that God does for us, all the provision, the good, the grace, and the mercy He sends our way, then understanding a God whose heart is filled with blessing becomes a significant insight into who He is and a means of knowing Him.

As the prodigal son knelt before his father, he sensed forgiveness and mercy. He felt worthwhile, valued, and accepted. With his ear pressed against his father's chest, he heard his father's heart beating. What he experienced in his father's care was his father blessing him.

When we seek out the heart of God, when we listen to Scripture as a means of putting our ears against God's chest, we too will learn that we are loved, valued, accepted, that God has good intent toward us. When we hear that blessing, we have heard the heart of God.

> **Understanding a God whose heart is filled with blessing becomes a significant insight into who He is.**

WHAT DO YOU SAY?

1. Recall a time when a person in a position of authority made you happy or made you miserable.

2. In your own words, how does God show His intent to do good in *Genesis 12:1-3*?

3. Look up the word "blessing" in a Bible encyclopedia. What do you learn? Write your own definition of blessing.

4. If God intended for humans to pass the blessing on to other humans, including children,

   a. How is that done in the Bible?

   b. How is that done in our churches?

   c. How is that done in our families?

5. Has someone ever blessed you? How?

6. Is blessing physical? Spiritual? Or both? Explain.

CHAPTER SEVEN

JEALOUSY: THERE CAN ONLY BE ONE

Begin your study of this chapter by reading *John 14*.

During the collapse of Communism, I was part of a team of preachers invited by officials in the old Soviet Union to travel to Moscow and Kiev. The invitation came from one of the state television stations in Kiev. They wanted to host a public forum to respond to questions raised by programs about Christianity airing on their superstation.

During that and subsequent visits I came to love the Russian and Ukrainian people. I remember our knowledgeable and friendly guide at the Kremlin. He treated us with dignity and kindness. He overlooked our ignorance of his country, its culture, and history and answered questions that must have seemed childish to him.

One thing that puzzled me about the guide was his clothing. He wore a business suit during the days that he escorted us around Moscow. His blue dress shirt went nicely with a light gray coat. I remember the dress shirt was frayed at the collar, and the cuffs on his pants were worn out from dragging on the Kremlin concrete. I did not think much about it until the next morning. When we met him the second day, he was wearing the same clothes. It seemed odd to me that the guide at the leading cultural institution in the country did not take more pride in his dress. Later in the trip, I more fully understood his situation. It was the only suit of clothing he owned. He didn't have another choice.

I. The God Named "Jealous"
II. Explaining Exclusivity
III. One Way in the NT
    A. Jesus and the Shema
    B. Jesus and Discipleship
    C. Jesus and the Way
    D. The Monotheistic Church
IV. Exclusively Yours
V. Conclusion

135

That explanation came to me when I was later visiting the première shopping center on Khreschatyk Street in the Ukrainian capital. As I went from floor to floor looking at all the consumer items from kitchenware to clothing, I noticed that there were no choices. There was one style and color of men's dress shoes. In the kitchen department there was a single kind of flatware. In hardware they sold one hammer, not multiple hammers of different weights and handle options, but just a hammer. I realized that one result of economic collapse is the absence of choices.

I have always had options. In the morning I have to decide which shirt and pants to wear because I have multiple choices. At lunch I must choose between several different sets of dishes that we own. In my garage I have six hammers, each one made for a specific task.

Our culture thrives on choices and competition. We not only have

> **Our culture thrives on choices and competition. Being able to pick what we like is part of our DNA.**

to choose between a Ford and a Toyota, but then between a SUV or a sedan, and furthermore between a small or large SUV, and on the choices go right down to multiple shades of red for the exterior.

We in the U.S. not only thrive on competition, many of us demand it. Nothing is more unpopular in our society than situations where there is no choice. Being able to pick what we like is part of our DNA.

Our love of choices makes this chapter quite difficult. The Bible tells us that when it comes to divine beings, there is no choice. There is one God. There are no others. Clearly the Scriptures acknowledge that people believe in other gods, but the Bible also states unequivocally that to believe in the God of the Bible means to accept the reality that those other gods do not exist but are simply human inventions.

Monotheism lies at the core of the Christian faith. Christians believe that one of the fundamental qualities of God is that He is the only God. Monotheism runs from Genesis to Revelation. It is a non-negotiable conviction of our belief system.

I suggest that monotheism is not just something we believe about God, it is also something that God Himself maintains. In fact, God's uniqueness is at the core of who He is. It is in His heart. That is, a single God is not simply a doctrine or a policy maintained by God or a quality of God, but it is His passion.

As we think about this topic, our task is not simply to call for *adherence* to monotheistic belief, but rather to explore *why* God makes such a demand. I am not saying that we should just announce our demand, "there is just one choice when it comes to divine beings, so take it," but rather I am urging us to get into God's heart to understand why there is just one choice.

What we find is this truth: God devotes Himself to us. He's in control of the world even to the point of making good out of human evil. He knows our evil well and it affects Him deeply, but His heart does not give up on us. He does not stay far away from our world, but regularly makes His presence known among us. He repeatedly comes on a mission to win our hearts. All that He intends for us comes in the package of blessing which contains all the provision, all the grace, all the love, all the good of life. All of that is exclusively ours when we become exclusively His. Because of who He is in His heart, there can be no other way.

We are not shopping for a god. We are not going from store to store to see which divine being has the best features. The reason we are not on a shopping

> **We are not on a shopping trip for a god because God has already chosen us.**

trip for a god is because God has already chosen us. He is the one making the choice. He picked us. We are His and nobody else can have us. This reality comes out in one of the names God uses for Himself, in the way He gives instructions, and most clearly in His son, Jesus Christ.

THE GOD NAMED *"JEALOUS"*

God is jealous. In fact, one of His names is *"Jealous."*[1] God reveals this unusual name in the book of *Exodus*. After God gives the law and the people accept the covenant, the nation sins with the golden calf. In the dialogue between God and Moses after the sin, God forgives and makes a grand self-disclosure in *Exodus 34:5-7*. Before a list of ten ceremonial commandments in *Exodus 34:17-28*, God tells Moses to warn the people about the temptation of idolatry in the land He is

---

[1] When jealous refers to the name of God, I will put it in quotes and italics, as in *"Jealous,"* to make the use of this word as a name of God clearer, even though translations of the Bible, such as the NRSV, do not follow this practice.

giving them. He instructs them about what to do about the places and means of idol worship. Then God tells them why He opposes idolatry:

> *¹³You shall tear down their altars, break their pillars, and cut down their sacred poles ¹⁴(for you shall worship no other god, because the LORD, whose name is Jealous, is a jealous God). ¹⁵You shall not make a covenant with the inhabitants of the land, for when they prostitute themselves to their gods and sacrifice to their gods, someone among them will invite you, and you will eat of the sacrifice.* **(Ex 34:13-15)**

The NRSV places *"Jealous"* as a name of God in English parentheses, but there is no such syntactical form in Hebrew. This particular translation simply uses the parenthesis as a place to put the reason for the warning against idolatry. Two reasons are given: the LORD's name is *"Jealous"* and one of His qualities is that He is a jealous God. In Hebrew both of the appearances of jealous are in adjectival form.

This particular Hebrew word *qanna'* appears in its various forms over 80 times in the OT, 33 of which describe God in some way. God is jealous

For His name (**Eze 39:25** in a context of mercy)

For His land (**Joel 2:18** in a context of pity)

For Jerusalem and Zion (**Zec 1:14; 8:2**)

For His people in times of battle (**Isa 37:32=2Kgs 19:31; Isa 42:13; 63:15**)

God's jealousy also makes Him

Oppose some people (**Deu 29:20; Ps 79:5; Isa 26:11; Eze 5:13; 8:3,5; 16:38,42; 23:25; 35:11; 36:5,6; 38:19; Zep 1:18; 3:8**).

Be zealous for righteousness and justice (**Isa 9:7**).

In Isaiah's description of the armor of God, which Paul quotes in **Ephesians 6**, God wears zeal as a cloak (**Isa 59:17**). Another striking occurrence of the word "jealousy" is in James: *"Or do you suppose that it is for nothing that the Scripture says, 'God yearns jealously for the spirit that he has made to dwell in us?'"* (**Jas 4:5**). Each of these could prove profitable avenues for seeking out the heart of God, but must be set aside to attend to one other use of this word.

I do not think that if I were God, I would choose *"Jealous"* as a

name. It seems inappropriate to use what is commonly a negative human emotion to describe the holy God. We have all met people whose jealousy is a weakness in their personality. To take that kind of image and apply it to God insults God. We must begin by exploring the other passages that describe God as jealous.

> The Hebrew word for jealous, *qanna'*, is thought to come from a root that means to become intensely red, as with dye. Apparently the word came to reflect how the face flushed when the heart was filled with this emotion. It has the same range of meanings as the English word jealousy.

The adjective "jealous" appears eight times (in two different forms) referring exclusively to God. Aside from the two appearances just mentioned in *Exodus 34:14*, here are the other passages. I have made the word "jealous" bold to make it easier to see the consistent use of the term:

The adjective "jealous" appears eight times referring exclusively to God.

> You shall not bow down to them or worship them; for I the LORD your God am a **jealous** God, punishing children for the iniquity of parents, to the third and the fourth generation of those who reject me. (*Ex 20:5*)

> ²³So be careful not to forget the covenant that the LORD your God made with you, and not to make for yourselves an idol in the form of anything that the LORD your God has forbidden you. ²⁴For the LORD your God is a devouring fire, a **jealous** God. (*Deu 4:23-24*)

> You shall not bow down to them or worship them; for I the LORD your God am a **jealous** God, punishing children for the iniquity of parents, to the third and fourth generation of those who reject me. (*Deu 5:9*)

> ¹⁴Do not follow other gods, any of the gods of the peoples who are all around you, ¹⁵because the LORD your God, who is present with you, is a **jealous** God. The anger of the LORD your God would be kindled against you and he would destroy you from the face of the earth. (*Deu 6:14-15*)

> ¹⁹But Joshua said to the people, "You cannot serve the LORD, for he is a holy God. He is a **jealous** God; he will not forgive your transgressions or your sins. ²⁰If you forsake the LORD and serve foreign gods, then he will turn and do you harm, and consume you, after having done you good." (*Josh 24:19-20*)

*A **jealous** and avenging God is the LORD, the LORD is avenging and wrathful; the LORD takes vengeance on his adversaries and rages against his enemies. (**Nah 1:2**)*

Even a quick reading of these texts reveals that God's jealousy is associated with two things: violence and idolatry.

First, violent images abound: His jealousy drives Him to punish; to being a devouring fire; to being angry; to destroying His people; to turning, harming, and consuming His people; to taking vengeance and to raging against His enemies. We will discuss the broader implications of God's violence in a later chapter, but note here that it is difficult to ignore the violent side of God's jealousy. Well-known Bible stories such as Noah's flood, the destruction of Sodom and Gomorrah and the deaths of Ananias and Sapphira tell us of God's use of violence and punishment. Jesus repeatedly talks about hell in terms that make it a place of violence and punishment. God's acts of violence and punishment arise from His jealousy. The reason for His jealousy lies in the second matter taken up in these texts.

Second, these passages associate jealousy with idolatry. God's jealousy will not permit His people to bow down to idols, to make idols, to worship idols, to follow other gods, to go after foreign gods. In this sense the jealousy is associated with exclusivity. God wants the total loyalty of His people. He will not share their worship with any other being.

God wants the total loyalty of His people.

All of this material may suggest that God is like a child who gets angry when he does not get his own way or that God is like a spurned wife who lashes out in anger against her unfaithful husband. Jealousy seems beneath God. Mills (**46**) says these texts suggest a "possessiveness which is far from healthy."

Beyond the negative connotations of jealousy, we also wonder about a God who does not want competition. Culturally, many of us find it difficult to be told there are no choices. We cannot understand a God who does not want or even permit opposition. We want to shop for a divine being, not be the object of His shopping.

I suggest that the jealous language about the God named *"Jealous"* goes in a different direction. *"Jealous"* tells us that He is in a category all by Himself. He is unique. He is the only one of His kind. It is not that He merely rejects competition; there *is* no competition. It is not that He objects to us having a choice—there simply *are* no equivalent choices.

Ironically, our culture values things that are unique. We go to great lengths to protect our identities because we do not want anybody pretending to be us. We are not willing to share a Social Security number with a person two states away or even next door. We will pay more money for a unique work of art than we will for a mass-produced piece. We do not want to wear the exact same clothes as other people at the party.

God has Social Security number 1. According to the Bible, God was the only being in the universe. He then created us. We then created other gods. He is not one of the mass produced divine images. He is a unique divine being. Nobody is clothed like God.

God uses the name *"Jealous"* to explain His situation when we respond to Him in a way that denies His uniqueness. When we turn to an idol and give that idol God's Social Security number, God is alarmed. He, in effect, says, "That's *my* number!" When we buy one of the mass-produced gods to put on the altar of our lives, thinking it is the real thing, God sees the error we have made. We have mistakenly built our lives around a fake. He tells us we have purchased a forgery. What we think is a god is not a god at all! He is so devoted to us that He notifies us of our blunder. *"Jealous"* wants our attention. When we take an idol and dress it up in clothes that God normally wears, He resists. He informs us of our error. He warns us of the implications of our slip-up. When humans fail to respond, at times, He comes down and burns up the idols we have dressed up in His clothes. Jealousy is part of who He is. He is serious about being the only God in our lives.

Jealousy is a word of passion. God takes the name *"Jealous"* as an expression of that passion. The passion is rooted in His unique

> God is serious about being the only God in our lives.

nature. When that uniqueness is challenged, God's jealous nature responds. He cautions. He alerts us of our mistake. Sometimes He destroys.

When we read in Scripture about *"Jealous"* and about a jealous God, we are hearing God warn us about the way things really are. He does not want us to make any mistake because He is devoted to us.

God repeatedly teaches and emphasizes the positive aspects of this exclusive relationship.

He does not want us to believe a lie. The word "jealous" comes in the desperate context of violence and idolatry, because God senses that our false beliefs have brought us to a desperate place. Before God takes the passionate name *"Jealous"* and before He claims to be a jealous God coming in destruction, God repeatedly teaches and emphasizes the positive aspects of our exclusive relationship to the exclusive God. To more fully understand the God whose name is *"Jealous,"* we turn to the larger context of law in which most of these uses of God as a jealous God appear. We will limit ourselves to the treatment of the law in Deuteronomy.

EXPLAINING EXCLUSIVITY

Some of the most widely recognized lines from Deuteronomy are the Ten Commandments, referred to in *Deuteronomy 4:14* and *10:4* and listed in *5:7-21*. Readers of the Ten Commandments have long divided them into two major concerns.[2] The first four commandments deal with the *divine-human relationship*, offering direction about the *vertical* relationship between God and humanity:

1. Have no other gods.
2. Fashion no images of God.
3. Make proper use of the divine name.
4. Remember the Sabbath.

Vertical Relationship between God and Humanity

5. Honor parents.
6. Do not kill.
7. Do not commit adultery.
8. Do not steal.
9. Do not bear false witness.
10. Do not covet.

Horizontal Relationships among People

The last six commands focus on *relationships within the human community*, offering instruction about the *horizontal* relationships among

---

[2] The Bible does not put numbers with the commandments. Students of Scripture have assigned their own numbers with the result that there are three different systems for numbering the Ten Commandments, often identified by the names Jewish, Catholic, and Protestant. This numbering reflects the Protestant division of the Ten Commandments. Breuer (**291-330**) explains the issues involved.

people. The first grouping of the Ten Commandments centers on the vertical divine-human relationship in which each of these commands rests on the exclusivity of God:

1. There are no other gods. Monotheism claims the existence of only one God. Henotheism admits the existence of other gods, but worships only one God. Any claim of monotheism must speak in language that acknowledges that other gods are represented by idols, have names, and have special days and places of worship. However, monotheism, while making that accommodation in order to speak of exclusivity, does not admit of the existence of other gods. The Ten Commandments insist on monotheism and proceed in such a way as to maintain that view.

2. Not only are there no other gods, but there are to be no images of this one God. Many OT texts forbid the making and worship of idols. Theologically, there can be no situation where there appears to be more than one God. Idols can be easily duplicated and multiplied. The multiplication of idols is inconsistent with the exclusivity of God.

3. The name of God must be respected. It must not be used in such a way that damages God or permits the name of a foreign god or idol to be put alongside the name of the one God. To permit such other names impinges on the exclusivity of God.

4. One day is set aside for the worship of God. No other days belonging to idols or foreign gods are permitted and no other worship of any other foreign deity or idol is allowed because it runs counter to the exclusivity of God. Israel shows its dependence on God alone by not working during the Sabbath and therefore receiving no return for their own efforts.

The first four commandments find a basic premise in the exclusivity of God. There is only one God and these commandments give expression to the implications of monotheism. God is at work explaining reality and the core of His heart. He devotes Himself to these people and to us. Now He explains how that relationship works.

The first four commandments deal with the vertical *divine-human relationship* while the last six commands focus on horizontal *relationships within the human community*. The vertical commandments are the basis of the horizontal commandments. The two major concerns of the Ten Commandments, point to a progression in a theological understanding of the law. *The Ten Commandments demand that the issue of divinity be settled first. Deuteronomy 5:7* and commandments two through four—the representation of His image, the use of His name, the keeping of His day—rest on the premise that there are no other gods, thus tying the first four commandments into a unit. Only then do the Ten Commandments turn to the relationships in the human community. The premise of one God becomes the foundation for the other principles. It is the vision of the one God for the human community that must be maintained: Honor of parents, preservation of life and purity, protection of property, honest communication, and unselfish desires. Our behavior as the people of God is a reflection of

The premise of one God becomes the foundation for the other principles.

who God is: We are faithful to God because He is faithful to us. We do not bear false witness because God is truthful. We do not steal because God is gracious, etc.

The existence of one God dominates the presentation of the law in Deuteronomy. Most of Deuteronomy explores the issues raised in the Ten Commandments. Various proposals have been made showing how the Ten Commandments function as a kind of table of contents for the remaining part of Deuteronomy. One such system is explained in the box.

Some scholars argue that the Ten Commandments in *Deuteronomy 5:7-21* become a table of contents for the entire book of *Deuteronomy* by introducing ten different topics that are taken up in the statutes and ordinances in *Deuteronomy 12:1-26:15*. Olson (67-112) presents one such configuration in which each commandment is the major topic in the indicated passages of Deuteronomy:

1. No other gods or images: *Deu 12:1–13:18*
2. Make proper use of the divine name: *Deu 14:1-21*
3. Remember the Sabbath: *Deu 14:22–16:17*
4. Honor parents: *Deu 16:18–18:22*
5. No killing: *Deu 19:1–22:8*
6. No adultery: *Deu 22:9–23:18*
7. No stealing: *Deu 23:19–24:7*
8. No false witness: *Deu 24:8–25:4*

Two specific examples will illustrate this process.

First, *Deuteronomy 6–13* (**Olson, 50-70**) offers an extended commentary on the first commandment of *"no other gods"* by anticipating those forces which direct human attention away from this God: politics (*Deuteronomy 7*), greed (*Deuteronomy 8*), pride (*Deuteronomy 9*), self-centeredness (*Deu 12:30*), false prophets (*Deu 13:1*), unbelieving family (*Deu 13:6*), and community pressure (*Deu 13:12*). Thus, not only the first four of the Ten Commandments focus on the one God, but so do many of the laws in *Deuteronomy 6–13*.

Second, one line dominates the book of *Deuteronomy*. The Ten Commandments open with that line: *"You shall have no other gods before me"* (*Deu 5:7*). No other line reverberates throughout Deuteronomy like this one. The exclusive worship of God is repeated over twenty times.[3] Miller (**22-23**) argues that the worship of one God is central to *Deuteronomy*.

In a sense the first four Ten Commandments explain the exclusivity of God in negative terms. *"You shall not. . . ."* The next chapter of Deuteronomy provides a positive statement of God's exclusivity: [4]*"Hear, O Israel: The LORD is our God, the LORD alone. [5]You shall love the LORD your God with all your heart, and with all your soul, and with all your might"* (*Deu 6:4-5*).

Translators (**Weinfeld, 337**) offer at least four different options on rendering the first phrase:
1. The LORD is our God, the LORD is one;
2. The LORD is our God, the LORD alone.
3. The LORD our God is the one LORD.

[3] See *Deu 7:4,16; 8:19; 11:16,28; 12:30,31; 13:2,6,7,13; 17:3; 18:20; 19:9; 20:18; 28:14,36,64; 29:18,26; 30:17; 31:16,18,20; 32:15-18,37*.

This passage is traditionally called the "Shema" (pronounced she MAH) after the first word in the passage, translated as "hear." Two issues arise about this text. First, the passage is open to different translations, as explained in the box. Given how God jealously guards His exclusivity and how monotheism is at the core of the surrounding law, it is difficult to understand the passage in any way but as monotheistic. Second, this passage is cited in at least six other verses in the Bible, which are listed in the box below. Later in the chapter we will take up Jesus' use of this exact passage.

There is an important relationship between the first group of the Ten Commandments and the Shema. They stand in connection to each other almost as two sides of a coin. *Deuteronomy 5:7* is one side of the coin, the negative version—have no other gods. *Deuteronomy 6:4-5* is the flip side of the coin, the positive version—love only this God. The exclusive worship called for in *Deuteronomy 5:7* is repeated in *Deuteronomy 6:4-5*.

The Shema connects the exclusivity of God with love. God is unique. There is no being like Him. He has no competition. There are no other choices. The Shema affirms that uniqueness and acknowledges that He is the God of Israel. The one God has chosen Israel. The One who is exclusively God has picked them. Not only has He chosen them, but He has turned their evil into good, not given up on them when they sin, continued to be with them, come to them on a mission, and repeatedly and intentionally blessed them with all the good He provides. Now the Shema calls for reciprocation. God loves you. The one God loves you. Now love Him back. Love Him exclusively.

The centrality of monotheism in the presentation of the law in *Deuteronomy* points to a God behind the laws for whom this ideal is centrally important. The law centers on monotheism because of God. He is the one

> **The one God loves you. Love Him back. Love Him exclusively.**

God. So central is this concept to His divine identity that all the law emerges from it. The law's purpose was to instruct the people about what was real and nothing was more real than the exclusivity of God. Monotheism typically connotes a doctrine that we must believe, but in *Deuteronomy* monotheism also points to a decisive aspect of God's nature. The presentation of the law in *Deuteronomy* leads to understanding something of God's heart. Monotheism is not simply a convenient doctrine or a pragmatic law or a fundamental principle of the Judeo-Christian faith, but rather monotheism arises out of God's very being, out of His heart. So central is this to God's nature that He names Himself *"Jealous."* The exclusivity of God continues to echo in the NT and to that material we now turn.

ONE WAY IN THE NT

For many years I thought my father had every tool ever made. When I would find an item he did not have as a Christmas present, I was the envy of the family. For months they would tell the story beginning with, "Harold found a gizmo Dad didn't have!" So I was delighted to find a flea market in Kiev, Ukraine, that sold old Soviet Union tools. Every time I made a trip to preach in Ukraine, I would find Dad something he did not own. Dad would beam when he opened the box to find a device that he did not even know existed!

Our consumer society loves the choices made possible by mass production, but we also value what is unique and distinctive. I may enjoy the fact that I have a choice of 25 hammers when I go to the hardware store, but the hammer I buy is not my prized possession. We generally treasure the exceptional rather than the ordinary. We more highly value the unique than the duplicate.

I believe that in God we have found the exceptional, not the ordinary. In Him we have something unique, not a duplicate. The mass produced gods of the idol-makers and the catalogs of world views churned out by the world's thinkers do not measure up to the unique God of the Bible.

Jesus thought the same way. He valued the exceptional and the unique. He treasured the exclusivity of God in the NT. He made it clear in His citation of the Shema, through His call for discipleship, in His insistence on being the only way, and by how His followers took up the banner of monotheism.

> **Jesus valued the exceptional and unique and made this clear in His insistence on being the only way.**

JESUS AND THE SHEMA

One day during the ministry of Jesus, religious leaders ask Him to settle a dispute. The argument revolves around the question of which was the first commandment. According to the Mishnah (Makkot 23b-24a), a collection of postbiblical Jewish teaching, the law had 248 commandments and 365 prohibitions for a total of 613 laws. Jesus responds with the top two:

> [29]The first is, "Hear, O Israel: the Lord our God, the Lord is one; [30]you shall love the Lord your God with all your heart, and with all your soul, and with all your mind, and with all your strength." [31]The second is this, "You shall love your neighbor as yourself." There is no other commandment greater than these. (*Mk 12:29-31*)

Jesus quotes *Deuteronomy 6:4-5*, the Shema, for the first commandment and *Leviticus 19:18* for the second. In this passage, Jesus endorses the monotheistic teaching of *Deuteronomy 6:4-5*. Jesus' identification of *Deuteronomy 6:4-5* as the first commandment echoes the above understanding of how the law unfolds in *Deuteronomy* with monotheism at its heart. His use of *Deuteronomy 6:4-5* also places monotheism at the core of His teaching and thus at the center of Christianity. Both the OT and the NT are firmly committed to the ideal of one God. The exclusivity of God is reflected in several other aspects of Jesus' ministry.

> In *Mark 12* Jesus cites the two commandments that best summarize the Ten Commandments. The first four commandments take up the vertical divine-human relationship reflected in the holistic command to love the one God. The last six commandments focus on the horizontal relationships among humankind expressed in Jesus' citation of *Leviticus 19:18* about neighborly love.

Jesus came from the Father. He says exactly what we expect the Son of God to say about God's exclusivity. In citing *Deuteronomy 6:4-5* as the first commandment on which all the law was based, Jesus verifies that God's oneness stands at the center of the law and all the law revolves around it. Jesus' own passion for exclusivity emerges in two other ways.

JESUS AND DISCIPLESHIP

Jesus frequently called for total commitment in terms such as these:

> *34He called the crowd with his disciples, and said to them, "If any want to become my followers, let them deny themselves and take up their cross and follow me. 35For those who want to save their life will lose it, and those who lose their life for my sake, and for the sake of the gospel, will save it. 36For what will it profit them to gain the whole world and forfeit their life? 37Indeed, what can they give in return for their life? 38Those who are ashamed of me and of my words in this adulterous and sinful generation, of them the Son of Man will also be ashamed when he comes in the glory of his Father with the holy angels." (Mk 8:34-38)*
>
> *29Jesus said, "Truly I tell you, there is no one who has left house or brothers or sisters or mother or father or children or fields, for my*

sake and for the sake of the good news, ³⁰who will not receive a hundredfold now in this age—houses, brothers and sisters, mothers and children, and fields with persecutions—and in the age to come eternal life. ³¹But many who are first will be last, and the last will be first." (Mk 10:29-31)

Jesus tells his disciples that they must *"deny themselves"* in order to follow Him. Any other path results in losing their lives. To devote themselves to any other cause is to be ashamed of Jesus. He calls them to leave family and home for His mission. He wants their complete loyalty.

When Jesus said, *"Let them . . . take up their cross and follow me,"* the phrase held special significance for His Jewish audience. The idea of taking up one's cross brought to mind 200-year-old events that had been burned into the Jewish people's memory and preserved by Josephus in his *Antiquities of the Jews* 13.5–14.2.

At the Feast of Tabernacles, the Jews rise up against the offenses of the Greek ruler Alexander Jannaeus. Alexander attempts to make a sacrifice on the altar, a ritual designated only for Jewish priests. The Jews are furious that the pagan who had usurped their land is now trying to take over their worship, so they oppose and publicly humiliate Alexander during the festival. They believe their God is important and they fight for the dignity of His worship.

Alexander, disgraced and enraged, kills 6,000 Jews over the next few days, starts a war with the Jews that lasts six years and takes another 50,000 lives. Alexander consolidates his victory by performing what Josephus calls "one of the most barbarous actions in the world." He orders 800 Jewish men to be led outside of Jerusalem and crucifies them in sight of the whole city. As they die, the men watch their wives and children massacred with the sword. Meanwhile Alexander feasts with his concubines, savoring his complete victory over the Jews.

The day of 800 crucifixions is the Jewish equivalent of the September 11 terrorist attacks on the US: Tragic and unforgettable. The memory of Alexander Jannaeus' cruelty remained fresh on the Jews' minds for generations. Surely most of the Jews in Jesus' day would have known about it. Jesus' statement that His disciples must "take up their crosses" brought to mind stories of whole families lost in one day, shared memories of tragedy and crushing loss. The implication was that they would have to "deny themselves" to the

> highest degree possible. Those who stayed with Him did so with the same conviction of their forefathers: Following their God was important enough to endure a future of suffering.

With these and other similar calls, Jesus echoes the intent of the Shema command, but with different language. Just as the Shema made God the focus of the call for holistic love, so Jesus made Himself the focus of the call for self-denial and cross-bearing.

Every generation, and our current times are no exception, witness young people laying down their lives for causes bigger than themselves. Many make the point that a man who gives himself to a cause must believe in that cause. When a woman lays her life on the line for something outside herself, she values its importance. It is unlikely that men and women will commit themselves to something which is simply one choice among many. Few people will die for freedom if they believe that totalitarianism is an equally acceptable choice. Most people are willing to make the ultimate sacrifice only for something unique and important.

Jesus calls people to give their lives for Him. Those who do believe in Him, accept His message, and commit themselves to spreading the word. They believe He is from the Father, that He is the Son of God, that He offers what nobody else can promise.

Although our culture values choice, it also understands giving one's life to a cause. It recognizes that any cause worth dying for must be something unique and important. That is the crux of Jesus' call to discipleship. Jesus asks people to follow Him because He is unique and important.

The call to discipleship is not simply the methodology of Jesus and the early church, but rather it is rooted in the monotheistic faith. That monotheistic faith was rooted in God, whose passion for exclusivity resided in His heart. Jesus demands loyal disciples because God demands loyal followers. Jesus' disciples could no more follow two masters than the Israelites could worship idols and the God named *"Jealous."* God's passion for exclusivity is reflected in Jesus who makes a similar call among His disciples.

God's passion for exclusivity is reflected in Jesus.

JESUS AND THE ONLY WAY

God the Father sends Jesus the Son to the earth. Jesus treasures God's uniqueness. For Jesus *"the Lord is one" (Mk 12:29)* is central. Jesus understands God's heart for exclusivity. He knew the essence of God His Father. It comes as no surprise, then, that Jesus takes on the same identity. He does not adopt the name *"Jealous"* or use the language of the Shema about Himself, but Jesus claims unique status. Consider these three NT texts that dwell on that subject:

> "And I, when I am lifted up from the earth, will draw all people to myself." *(Jn 12:32)*

> ⁶Jesus said to him, "I am the way, and the truth, and the life. No one comes to the Father except through me. ⁷If you know me, you will know my Father also. From now on you do know him and have seen him." *(Jn 14:6-7)*

> ¹¹This Jesus is
>> "the stone that was rejected by you, the builders;
>> it has become the cornerstone."
> ¹²There is salvation in no one else, for there is no other name under heaven given among mortals by which we must be saved. *(Acts 4:11-12)*

Jesus claimed to be able to draw all people to Himself and that He was a single path to life and truth. The only means of accessing the Father was through Him. All matters of salvation center on Jesus and nobody else.

These texts reflect Jesus' claim to be the One sent by God to fully express His love *(Jn 3:16)*, to provide atonement for humankind *(Mk 16:15-16)*, and to bring all God's plans to fulfillment *(Mt 5:17)*. Jesus and the early Christians did not see Jesus as one option among many, but as the single option. John's Gospel regularly connects Jesus with God with the "I AM" statements. He said, *"I and the Father are one" (Jn 10:30)*, and *"if you know me, you know the Father" (Jn 14:7)*. In both claims, Jesus clearly points out that He is not merely a prophet sent by God—He is God Himself come down to earth. The one God has one Son.

Jesus uses the "I am" (*ego eimi* in Greek) construction in *John* in two ways: First, "I am" is tied to a symbol such as bread or light. Second, "I am" is used without a symbol sometimes translated as "I am he." These passages allude to *Exodus 3:14* where God tells Moses that *"I AM WHO I AM"* (see Ball).

1. *I am the bread. (6:41,48,51)*
2. *I am the light. (8:12)*
3. *I testify on my own behalf. (8:18)*
4. *. . . unless you believe that I am. (8:24, no symbol)*
5. *. . . then you will realize that I am. (8:28, no symbol)*
6. *Before Abraham was, I am. (8:58, no symbol)*
7. *I am the gate. (10:7,9)*
8. *I am the good shepherd. (10:11,14)*
9. *I am the resurrection and the life. (11:25)*
10. *... that when it does occur, you may believe that I am he. (13:19)*
11. *I am the way, and the truth and the life. (14:6)*
12. *I am the true vine. (15:1,5)*
13. *I am he. (18:5, no symbol)*
14. *I am he. (18:6, no symbol)*
15. *I told you that I am he. (18:8, no symbol)*

God maintains a presence on earth. God Himself comes to earth multiple times in the Bible. He repeatedly sends prophets and preachers as His representatives. He ensured that His words were recorded and available to human eyes. God uses these multiple ways to communicate with humanity.

But the Bible makes equally clear that God sends just one Son. That one Son is a unity with the Father. Together God the Father and God the Son are a unity with the Holy Spirit. The stress on oneness, on unity, arises out of the reality of one God.

The God named *"Jealous,"* gives the law which centers on His exclusivity. He comes into the world in the form of Jesus. Jesus quotes the Shema, as the greatest commandment, calls His disciples to full loyalty, and claims to be the only way to God and salvation. Those who followed Jesus continued the same teaching.

THE MONOTHEISTIC CHURCH

The world which received the law presented in *Deuteronomy* and the world into which Jesus came as the incarna-

The stress on oneness, on unity, arises out of the reality of one God.

tion of God both preferred more than one option when it came to divine choices. As a result *Deuteronomy* spends considerable time building boundaries against idolatry. Paul addresses the same circumstance in Corinth:

> [4]*Hence, as to the eating of food offered to idols, we know that "no idol in the world really exists," and that "there is no God but one."* [5]*Indeed, even though there may be so-called gods in heaven or on earth—as in fact there are many gods and many lords—* [6]*yet for us there is one God, the Father, from whom are all things and for whom we exist, and one Lord, Jesus Christ, through whom are all things and through whom we exist.* (*1Cor 8:4-6*)

Far from taking a henotheistic position, Paul simply uses the same language used in the Ten Commandments and the OT law to defend monotheism. In order to speak about competing claims to deity, these texts use accommodative language to refer to those making the false claims. Paul cites the monotheistic teaching of *Deuteronomy 6:4* and the claims of Jesus and the early Christians about the exclusive role of Jesus.[4]

Jesus affirms in His teaching the monotheistic beliefs of the OT and its holistic commands to love God. He parallels the holistic commands in His own call to discipleship and echoes the single nature of God in His claim to be the world's only Savior. In opposition to calls for pluralism, Paul falls back on two fundamental teachings of the faith: Belief in a single God and hope in a single Savior, Jesus.

The rationale behind the call for a single Savior comes from the identity of God as a single God. Perhaps a single God could have sent multiple saviors, but if a single God sent a single Savior, there can be no other options. There are no other options not because of a doctrine or belief system, but because of a God who is jealous about who He is. Because God is a unique God and because that exclusiveness is part of the heartbeat of that God, there can be no other set of beliefs. The doctrines of monotheism and Jesus as the way, the truth, and the life are not arbitrary or products of human thinking or accidents of history; instead, they reflect what lies in the heart of God.

---

[4] One should take notice of the NT comments and prohibitions of idolatry: *Acts 7:41; 15:20,29; 17:16; 21:25; Rom 2:22; 1Cor 5:10-11; 8:1,4,7,10; 10:7,14,19; 12:2; 2Cor 6:16; Gal 5:20; Eph 5:5; Phil 3:18-19; Col 3:5; 1Th 1:9; 1Pet 4:3; 1Jn 5:21; Rev 2:14,20; 9:20; 21:8; 22:15.*

EXCLUSIVELY YOURS

When human jealousy is mentioned, we often think of demanding individuals who place high public priority on what they believe is theirs. Jealousy is often associated with resentment, revenge, and envy.

> God is a unique God — exclusiveness is part of His heartbeat.

Jealous people are often wildly emotional, suspicious, and solicitous. Occasionally, there is a positive side to jealousy in which the word takes on the qualities of being zealous, supportive, or protective of a person or cause. In short, human jealousy, while periodically a positive trait, is often thought to be a weak human quality.

It is difficult to imagine a world without real competition. Consumerist society is founded on competition. Every aspect of life abounds in struggle. Human immersion in competition makes it difficult to ponder an existence where there is no true competition, no one worthy of competition, no other being.

Living among billions of people does not provide many parallels to being completely unique and alone. Trying to think about a divine being who has no peer, for whom there is no competitive being, who need not share anything with anybody may be beyond our abilities. Perhaps our difficulty in pondering such an existence or in imagining such a world makes us conjure up competitors for God.

Part of God's response is to name Himself *"Jealous,"* to proclaim His complete uniqueness, to build barriers against acceptance of would-be competitors, and to send a single Savior. This study suggests that God's uniqueness lies deep within His heart.

In addition to living in a competitive world, those in American culture increasingly value diversity, pluralism, and relativism. Many reject any idea that there is absolute truth or that we can know it. Others demand acceptance of multiple belief systems not based on any value in a particular system, but simply because pluralism is valued. Those who hold to truth must seek ways to communicate to those within this pluralistic system.[5]

This study suggests that the uniqueness of God is not simply a doctrine that we can understand and then repackage in more suitable

---

[5] See Cotham for a recent attempt to point the way with regard to non-Christian faiths.

language. Monotheism is not rooted in a philosophy that can be rethought. God named Himself *"Jealous"* as a reflection of His divine being. Ultimately the doctrines so under attack in today's pluralistic society whether an unwillingness to make Jesus the only Savior, or to accept the Bible as truth, or to argue for the universal kingdom of God, are not negotiable.

Those who demand choices in deity must of necessity put the God named *"Jealous"* into a box, like the one I mentioned earlier. When He is in a box, we can examine Him, control Him, and make our decisions about Him. However, the God whose heart we explore defies being so controlled. We cannot keep Him in our box. Joshua recognized the danger of this kind of thinking.

> **Those who demand choices in deity must put the God named "Jealous" into a box that does not fit Him.**

The book of Joshua ends on a confusing note. Joshua calls the people to renew their covenant with God. Here is their response:

> [16]*Far be it from us that we should forsake the LORD to serve other gods; [17]for it is the LORD our God who brought us and our ancestors up from the land of Egypt, out of the house of slavery, and who did those great signs in our sight. He protected us along all the way that we went, and among all the peoples through whom we passed; [18]and the LORD drove out before us all the peoples, the Amorites who lived in the land. Therefore we also will serve the LORD, for he is our God.* (**Josh 24:16-18**)

When Joshua calls for the people to commit themselves to the One God, they eagerly agree. They say the right words and do the right things. The next line is unexpected: *But Joshua said to the people, "You cannot serve the LORD, for he is a holy God. He is a jealous God"* (**Josh 24:19**). We wonder how Joshua can respond so negatively to people who have acted so positively. Did the people not do exactly as they were asked? Why can they not serve God?

To believe and covenant with God means that we have to have some concept of God in mind in whom we believe and with whom we covenant. Joshua realizes that since the people have conceptualized God, they have something called "God" in mind. They are ready to sign up to follow that God. Joshua sees that they have made themselves little boxes labeled "God." It will not do. It is not

enough.

To explain this dilemma, Joshua tells them, *"He is a jealous God."* He means that God is so unique, so unlike any other being, so exclusive in His nature, so jealous in His identity, that they cannot place Him in their little boxes.

"Jealous" can harm His people or protect them from harm. *"Jealous"* will admit no rivals. *"Jealous"* claims the total allegiance of His people. The divine jealousy expresses God's passion for His exclusivity.

Fortunately, for Joshua and Israel, and by implication for us, God makes a covenant with them that day. Ultimately making the covenant did not depend on them or us completely understanding God. It depends on God. There is no one like Him. He is the only one.

> **Joshua means that God is so unlike any other being that they cannot place Him in their little boxes.**

WHAT DO YOU SAY?

1. *Matthew 6:24* is a passage where Jesus demands exclusivity. What is the natural result of trying to follow two masters? Have you found this true in your own life?

2. We are called to love God with all our heart, soul, mind, and strength. What does this look like practically on a day to day basis?

3. How would you respond (after studying this chapter) to a co-worker who says:

   a. "How can you say there is only one God?"

   b. "What makes you so sure the Jesus of the Bible is the only way to God?"

   c. "You call him God, I call him _____. Aren't we both worshiping the same being just using a different name?"

4. Most Americans do not have wooden or metal idols in their house that they worship. Is worshiping idols just an OT problem? Why or why not?

5. *Deuteronomy 6–13* anticipates those forces which direct humans away from God:

> *Deuteronomy 7*—**politics**;
>
> *Deuteronomy 8*—**greed**;
>
> *Deuteronomy 9*—**pride**;
>
> *Deuteronomy 12:30*—**self-centeredness**;
>
> *Deuteronomy 13:1*—**false prophets**;
>
> *Deuteronomy 13:6*—**unbelieving family**;
>
> *Deuteronomy 13:12*—**community pressure**.
>
> Is this still relevant today? Share a personal struggle in being pulled away from God.

THE INNER CIRCLE
PREVIEW TO THE
NEXT THREE CHAPTERS

W hen we meet somebody new to us, we usually introduce ourselves. We start with our name, and depending on the situation, we may also include where we are from, or what we do, or how we are connected to the person we are meeting. Typically, I say, "I'm Harold Shank from Edmond, Oklahoma. I am on the faculty at Oklahoma Christian University." Often I include a significant fact that links me to the person I'm meeting. "You know my sons, Daniel and Nathan" or "I'm Sally's husband."

God introduces Himself in *Exodus 34:5-7*. He begins with His name and then tells us eight more things about Himself. The initial items are short, like a list. The last items are longer, like an explanation. In this introduction God tells us what is important about who He is. We might expect Him to say, "Hello, I'm God from heaven and I am the creator of the world" or something similar. He does no such thing.

Here is the divine introduction:

> *⁵The Lord descended in the cloud and stood with him there, and proclaimed the name, "The Lord." ⁶The Lord passed before him, and proclaimed,*
>> *"The Lord, the Lord,*
>> *a God merciful and gracious,*
>> *slow to anger,*
>> *and abounding in steadfast love and faithfulness,*
>> *⁷ keeping steadfast love for the thousandth generation,*
>> *forgiving iniquity and transgression and sin*
>> *yet by no means clearing the guilty,*
>> *but visiting the iniquity of the parents*
>> *upon the children*

and the children's children,
to the third and the fourth generation." (Ex 34:5-7)

In this passage, God introduces Himself to Moses on top of Mount Sinai. Denton (**36**) points out that most biblical descriptions of God tell *what He does*, but this passage, and those texts that depend on it, tell *who God is*. Moberly (**"Speak of God," 193**) calls it the fullest description of God in Scripture.

> Postbiblical Jews call *Exodus 34:5-7* the "thirteen attributes of mercy" and use this passage in their preparation for the Day of Atonement. They identify these attributes: 1) the LORD, 2) the LORD, 3) God, 4) merciful, 5) gracious, 6) slow to anger, 7) abounding in steadfast love, 8) faithfulness, 9) keeping steadfast love, 10) forgiving iniquity, 11) forgiving transgression, 12) forgiving iniquity, and 13) cleanses. The rabbis understood the name God to refer to God's justice and mercy, which are otherwise verbally absent from the list. See Hanson (**100**).

Students of this passage often speak about its biblical significance. Brueggemann (**"Crisis-evoked," 95**) labels it the OT's "most characteristic speech" about God. Laney (**36**) claims, "It is the only place where God actually described Himself, listing His own glorious attributes." Bosman (**233**) calls the passage "a credo." For Raitt (**45**), this passage is the most significant statement of forgiveness in the OT.

> Of *Exodus 34:5-7*, Brueggemann (*Exodus*, **946**) writes, "Nowhere before this speech has anyone been privileged to hear directly a disclosure of what is most powerful and definitional in God's own life."

God's introduction of Himself in *Exodus 34* is one of the first and one of the longest revelations about God in the entire Bible. In fact, it is the longest passage in the entire Bible where God talks about God. All of that suggests that what we find here provides us with significant insight into God Himself. We do well to ponder over these words and reflect on what they might say about God's heart.

This text about God comes in the midst of the significant book of *Exodus*. Although *Exodus* is often thought of as just a book of law, it actually takes up the important question of God's presence. How is God with us? Does He ever leave? How can we tell if He is here? How do we worship? *Exodus*, exploring all of those critical questions, includes in the midst of that discussion this significant statement of God's person.

> **Though Exodus is thought of as just a book of law, it takes up the important question of God's presence.**

This passage where God introduces Himself is echoed throughout the rest of the Bible. Other biblical writers quote God's self-disclosure and apply it to new contexts. Many of the words used to describe God in both testaments are found in this text. Even God remembers this conversation later in the wilderness experience. When God speaks to Aaron and Miriam, He recalls His conversation with Moses:

> *⁵Then the LORD came down in a pillar of cloud, and stood at the entrance of the tent, and called Aaron and Miriam; and they both came forward. ⁶And he said, "Hear my words:*
> *When there are prophets among you,*
> *I the LORD make myself known to them in visions;*
> *I speak to them in dreams.*
> *⁷ Not so with my servant Moses*
> *he is entrusted with all my house.*
> *⁸ With him I speak face to face—*
> *clearly, not in riddles;*
> *and he beholds the form of the LORD." (**Num 12:5-8**)*

Although God spoke repeatedly to Moses, the language about *"face to face"* and beholding the form of God suggests that God is thinking about *Exodus 33–34* when He refers to Moses in this conversation with Aaron and Miriam.

God's introduction is a significant passage! Any attempt to listen to God's heartbeat, to probe deeper into the essence and passion of God, must ponder deeply over these words. We must listen again and again to God introducing Himself to us. In making this self-disclosure, God provides a means to know Him at an intimate level.

Yet this text is complex and not easily digested. It is not a simple one- or two-word description of the divine being, but an in-depth revelation. Furthermore, to look at just the passage itself is insufficient, because it comes in a narrative sequence that gives it additional meaning. God introduces Himself to Moses for a particular reason.

The Inner Circle

Apart from the surrounding context, this passage has a life beyond its setting in *Exodus*. Repeatedly quoted and cited in both the OT and the NT, this passage gives us the vocabulary by which we talk about God! How can we absorb such a substantive statement about God?

The next three chapters ponder God's introduction. The investigation will look like three concentric circles.

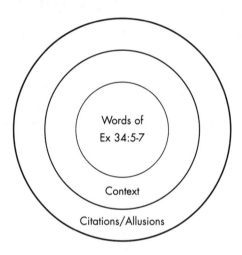

We begin with the inner circle, the passage itself. What do these words mean? How does the introduction unfold? What fundamental truths does it reveal about God? The next chapter takes up the middle circle. There we will think about how the passage functions in the book of *Exodus*. How does the narrative context add depth to these fundamental truths about God? Why did God introduce Himself in this way and that time to Moses? How does the setting amplify the content? The third chapter centers on the outer circle. That chapter contains a chart that analyzes the way other biblical authors use this passage. Some quote most of these words, others just cite a portion. Both the OT and NT repeatedly allude to this introduction. The truths about God were not restricted to Israel during the Exodus but are given to all nations and to all people, even to those in Christian faith. In the look at the outer circle, we will find that God's introduction in *Exodus 34:6-7* has special relevance to Jesus Christ.

That is the plan for the next three chapters as a means of unpacking an important and complex presentation by God of God. We begin by exploring the significance of the words God chooses to use to describe Himself.

CHAPTER EIGHT

GOD'S SELF INTRODUCTION: UP CLOSE AND PERSONAL

Begin your study of this chapter by reading *Exodus 34:5-7*.

The investigation into the inner circle of *Exodus 34:5-7* has two goals: to understand the meaning of these words and to explore what they say about God. In order to understand this complex passage, we will divide it into three parts. After looking at each part in detail, I will then show how the three parts flow together to inform us about God. The passage starts with the name of God, then moves to qualities of the divine being, and then concludes with actions of God.

The Hebrew grammar of this passage provides clues to how the passage unfolds. Note how the grammar divides the passage into three parts:

1. Three Hebrew *nouns*—all names of God.
   a. The LORD
   b. The LORD
   c. God

2. Four Hebrew *adjectives*—all descriptions of God
   a. Merciful (adjective)
   b. Gracious (adjective)
   c. Slow to anger (adjective with a noun)

> d. Abounding (adjective) in steadfast love and faithfulness (nouns)
>
> 3. Five Hebrew *verbs*—all actions of God
>   a. Keeping (participle) steadfast love
>   b. Forgiving (participle) iniquity, transgression, and sin
>   c. By no means clearing (two verbs in Hebrew) the guilty
>   d. Visiting (participle) the iniquity of the fathers to succeeding generations

This threefold division offers a way to investigate a complex passage in an orderly way. It suggests first looking at the identity of the speaker expressed in the names of God, then at qualities of God expressed in adjectival form, and finally at actions of God expressed verbally.

NAMES OF GOD

Names often involve complex issues. Many of us are named for our parents. Some of us name our children after biblical characters with the hopes that they will imitate their namesake. We often have to ask people to spell their names. We quickly learn that Emily, Emma Lee, and Emmalee must be carefully distinguished.

The names of God immediately present a similar number of complex issues about language, translation, and meaning. Despite the complexity, in order to appreciate the significance of what God is doing in this self-disclosure, we must understand some important background material about the names of God.

Two different nouns are used to name God. The last one, translated as "God" is the Hebrew word *'el* which is simply the generic word "god" or "God." The other name is used three times in the passage, but twice in the formal introduction. In the NRSV, God introduces Himself as the LORD. Note that the last three letters have small capitals. It is our way of distinguishing between "Lord" and "LORD." These two English words refer to two quite different words in the Hebrew. The word "Lord" means master; the word "LORD" is God's name. Some versions render this name as Jehovah. Scholars propose Yahweh. Contemporary English versions such as the NRSV follow a long tradition of English translators and Jewish synagogue practice of using the word "LORD" or occasionally "GOD."

> To appreciate God's self-disclosure, we must understand some background on the names of God.

The word LORD must not be confused with the word "lord," that is, "master." The word "GOD" is not the same as the word "God."

Hebrew, the language of most of the OT, ceased to be the dominant spoken language of the Jewish people around the time that the OT historical period ends. In *Nehemiah 9*, for example, Ezra reads the law in the Hebrew language, but the people required interpreters to understand it. During OT times the Hebrew language was written without vowels. The consonants were written down and the people who spoke the language added the proper vowels. For example, I might abbreviate a word this way: "btwn." You might recognize that I mean the word "between," but I just left out the vowels. Text messaging often uses the same process. Ancient Hebrew did that for the whole language. As fewer people actually spoke Hebrew, ancient scholars developed several systems for adding vowels to the language.

Because of the original vowelless nature of written biblical Hebrew, the name of God went through an interesting history. In rabbinic Judaism, which began to develop in the years between the OT and NT, readers of the text were not permitted to pronounce the name of God. Rabbis argued that if one pronounced the name of God, one might use the name in vain, thereby violating one of the Ten Commandments. Instead, they substituted the word "Adonai," which means "lord" or "master." When vowels were added to the vowelless text by the Masoretes in the 7th–10th centuries AD, the vowels assigned to the name of God were not the original vowels of God's name, but the vowels of the Hebrew word "lord" or "master." This practice gave rise to the name "Jehovah." However, the vowels for God's name had not been lost because so many OT names included God's name. Jehoshaphat is one example. His name means "the LORD judges" and includes the first part of God's name. Elijah and Nehemiah also contain elements of God's personal name. From names such as these, scholars are able to reconstruct the original of God's personal name as "Yahweh." Mettinger (14-49) provides a detailed analysis of the origin and the history of the divine name.

According to *Exodus 3:14-15* God's name "LORD" means I AM WHO I AM, or, as the footnote to the NRSV suggests, I AM WHAT I AM or I WILL BE WHAT I WILL BE. Others propose that the name stands for I WILL

CAUSE TO BE. The Hebrew root of the name of God is the word "to be." The various suggested meanings point to God's eternal existence and to His causative powers. Mettinger (41) claims the names express "the conviction of God's active and helpful presence." It speaks to His identity, character, existence, and presence. It proclaims His existence without regard to anything or anyone else. He is self-existent.

Most of our names in English do not describe who we are. "Harold" means "warrior" in some European languages, but I have never been a warrior and I do not like to fight. My name is just a name. In biblical times many names had meanings. Isaiah (see *Isaiah 7–8*) and Hosea (see *Hosea 1*) gave their children names that in effect preached a sermon each time the child was called by that name. God's name, LORD, is one of those names that had meaning.

The double use of the divine name occurs only here in the Bible.[1] Laney (41) suggests it stresses that God is being present. Denton (40) claims the dual occurrence of the divine name indicates that the passage was used as a confession in liturgy since the repetition gives the phrase more emotional strength.

His name is not only a name, but also a reflection of who He is.

God's introduction begins appropriately enough with His name. His name is not only a name, but also a reflection of who He is. Now that we know who is talking, we are prepared to hear Him tell us about who He is.

THE DESCRIPTION OF GOD

Four adjectives describe God. The four adjectives are "merciful," "gracious," "slow to anger" (adjective with a noun), and "abounding in steadfast love and faithfulness" (adjective with two nouns). To begin with, this investigation probes into the meaning of each word and then moves on to how the words function together in a holistic way. We begin with merciful.

---

[1] *Ps 104:1* seems to be another passage that makes double use of the divine name, but the first appearance of the name completes one clause and the second appearance begins the next clause. An abbreviated form of the divine name occurs twice in *Isa 38:11*. The following texts which include the phrase *"Lord, Lord"* may be influenced by *Ex 34:6: Mt 7:21f.; 25:11; Lk 6:46*.

Merciful

The Hebrew word *rachum* can be translated as "merciful" or "compassionate." This adjective appears in the OT thirteen times[2] and only refers to God.[3] The root is often associated with the love of parents toward children or some other nurturing relationship. Laney (**43**) notes *rachum* generally describes the love of a superior to an inferior, while Raitt (**50-51**) stresses that it is a love without conditions, more given than sought. Note the context of the verbal form which appears in bold in the following texts:

> Can a woman forget her nursing child, or show no **compassion** for the child of her womb? Even these may forget, yet I will not forget you. (**Isa 49:15**)

> As a father has compassion for his children, so the LORD has **compassion** for those who fear him. (**Ps 103:13**)

Isaiah writes that even though a rare mother may fail to show compassion to her child, God never fails to show understanding for His people. The Psalmist compares God's interest in humanity with that of a human father's interest in his children. Mackay (**563**) points out that this word reflects a mother's love for her child, a love which knows the child's vulnerabilities and is committed to providing care regardless of the child's behavior or lack of response. The word reflects a kind of sympathy when punishment might be expected.

> **The word reflects a kind of sympathy when punishment might be expected.**

Later in *Exodus 34* a noun form of this word is used: *"All that first opens the womb is mine, all your male livestock, the firstborn of cow and sheep"* (**Ex 34:19**). The word "womb" in this verse has the same root as "mercy." Dyrness (**84-85**) notes that the Hebrew language operates in a synthetic way that it often uses words with concrete roots to refer

---

[2] I will frequently mention how many times a word appears to give the reader some sense of how extensively the word is used in the biblical corpus. For example, using a verb with only God as the subject radically defines the nature of that verb. Additionally, when a word appears in a certain context in a small number of times, I usually include the list of references for the reader's convenience in further study of how the word functions in different texts.

[3] *Ex 34:6; Deu 4:31; 2Chr 30:9; Neh 9:17,31; Pss 78:38; 86:15; 103:8; 111:4; 112:4; 145:8; Joel 2:13; Jonah 4:2.*

to more abstract concepts. In this case, the feminine body part, womb, becomes the basis of the concept of compassion or mercy. The word for "womb" comes to mean "mercy." One might say that God's concern for humanity is rooted in an expectant mother's concern about the new life within her body.

Gracious

The Hebrew word *channun* comes from the root word for grace. A feminine form of this word is the basis of the name Hannah (see *1 Samuel 1–2*). Yamauchi (**202**) notes that grace typically flows from a stronger person who has abundance to a weaker person who has need, while Denton (**42**) defines *channun* as beauty or kindness toward the poor. Like the word for compassion, this adjective is used 13 times in the OT, each time referring to God.[4] A verbal form appears in *Exodus 33:19*, *"I will be gracious."* Graciousness is what makes God hear the cry of the troubled debtor (*Ex 22:27*). The root concept is thought to be associated with yearning. This quality enables one who has everything to be aware of and to give to the one who has little. God is one who out of His ample resources gives to those who need.

> **This quality enables one who has everything to be aware of and to give to the one who has little.**

Slow to Anger

These three English words translate two Hebrew words (*'arek 'aph*) that literally mean "long nose." The two words appear together 13 times in the Bible, with ten of them referring to God.[5] The phrase is an idiom for controlling anger or for having patience. Dahlberg (**135**) points out that the Hebrews considered the nostrils the source of anger; therefore, the longer the nose, the greater the patience, while the shorter the nose, the greater the impatience. The Hebrew language often used body parts to describe human traits: A stiff neck meant stubborn, while high hands pointed to the intentional or premeditated sin.

---

[4] *Ex 22:27; 34:6; 2Chr 30:9; Neh 9:17,31; Ps 86:15; 103:8; 111:4; 112:4; 116:5; 145:8; Joel 2:13; Jonah 4:2.*
[5] God is slow to anger in *Ex 34:6; Num 14:18; Neh 9:17; Pss 86:15; 103:8; 145:8; Jer 15:15; Joel 2:13; Jonah 4:2; Nah 1:3.* Proverbs holds up the patient person with these same words in *Prov 14:29; 15:18; 16:32.*

While the number of times God's long nose is mentioned shows the significance of His patience, the long-nosed person in *Proverbs* is a reminder to imitate that patience. Who knew having a long nose could be so desirable?

In an ironic way, the literal words here are the only physical description of God in the Bible. He has a long nose. However, rather than intending to depict the face of God, the words rather describe Him as longsuffering and patient.

> The only "physical" description of God is actually a description of His *character.*

Abounding in Steadfast Love

These four English words translate two Hebrew words which appear together 13 times in the OT.[6] The first is the word for much or great (*rab*). The second word is one of several Hebrew words translated by the English "love." This word (*chesed*) appears 248 times in the OT with 128 of those in the *Psalms*.[7] The KJV uses ten different English words to render this Hebrew word, most often using "mercy," "kindness," or "loving."

When we uncover the meaning and implications of this word for loyalty or steadfast love, we have probed near to the core of God's heart and why He seeks relationship with us. Laney (47) suggests that God's love is an unmerited loyalty by which God binds Himself to His people. We, who often think we should be loved because of our looks or possessions or talents, find a God who loves the ugly, the needy, and the awkward—all those whom we find difficult to love. The heart of God beats with a love that loves those whom He deems lovable, even if they are those we regard as unlovable. He loves the pretty and the ugly, the "in" crowd and the rejected crowd. God's love for me is not based on who I am or what I look like or where I stand in the human measure of status. Rather, it all depends on Him.

[6] *Gen 24:49; 47:29; Ex 34:6; Josh 2:14; 2Sa 2:6; 15:20; Pss 25:10; 61:7; 85:10; 86:15; 89:14; Prov 3:3; 20:28.*
[7] Scholars generally agree that *chesed* involves a relationship between the two parties. However, they argue over whether *chesed* is given as a result of the relationship (**Glueck, 54-55**) or whether *chesed* is the basis on which the relationship is formed (**Sakenfeld, 121-127**).

Faithfulness

Translated as "truth" or "right," this noun ('emeth) appears 127 times in the OT with 37 of those appearances in the *Psalms*. Of the 127 uses, 26 apply to God.[8] This word shares a common root with the word "Amen," one of the most commonly translated Hebrew words in the world.[9] Just as those praying offer a word of confirmation to the prayer, in a sense God promises to offer a word of confirmation to His people.

The idea of "nurse" comes from the same root. In a striking image, *Numbers 11:12* compares God to a nurse: *"Did I conceive all this people? Did I give birth to them, that you should say to me, 'Carry them in your bosom, as a nurse carries a sucking child,' to the land that you promised on oath to their ancestors?"* God tells Moses that He is faithful just as a nurse is faithful to the child in her care. God's comments in *Numbers 11* express His exasperation with the complaints of the people in the wilderness. Although God declines to be Israel's nurse, He does promise to be as faithful as that nurse. Naomi (*Ruth 4:16*) became Obed's nurse while Mordecai (*Est 2:7*) served as Esther's foster father, both situations using the same root concept.

> **God tells Moses that He is faithful just as a nurse is faithful.**

It is common for the Hebrew language to use more than one word to describe a concept (see "long nose" or "slow to anger" above). This usage (called hendiadys) may be at work in the phrase "abounding in steadfast love and faithfulness." Denton (**40**) considers the words "steadfast love" and "faithfulness" as synonyms used to emphasize the point. Instead of "steadfast love and faithfulness," it is appropriate to translate the Hebrew as "faithful love."

Indeed, what is true of "abounding in steadfast love and faithfulness" combining to form one thought may be true of the four adjec-

---

[8] *Gen 24:27; 32:10; 34:6; 2Sa 2:6; 2Chr 15:3; Neh 9:33; Pss 25:10; 31:5; 40:10f.; 54:5; 57:10; 61:7; 71:22; 86:15; 108:4; 115:1; 117:2; 138:2; 146:6; Isa 16:5; 38:18f.; 39:8; 61:8; Mic 7:20.*

[9] Jacobs (**5-6**) cites the use of "amen" as a liturgical response used in Judaism, Christianity, and Islam. The word has the same Hebrew root as *'emunah* (faith) and is also connected with the word *'emet*, meaning "truth." The idea expressed is of firm trust, acceptance, and reliability. "Amen" is found in a variety of contexts in the Bible (*Num 5:22; Deu 27:15-26* [in each verse]; *1Kgs 1:36; 1Chr 16:36; Neh 5:13; 8:6; Pss 41:13; 72:19; 89:52; 106:48; Isa 65:16; Jer 11:5; 28:6*). Louis Ginzberg describes amen as "perhaps the most widely known word in human speech" (cited in Jacobs).

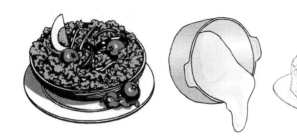

tives and the associated nouns. These are not separate descriptions of God, but overlapping qualities. This description is not like a salad where the lettuce, croutons, and onions are mixed together but still separate, but more like a cake where the sugar, eggs, and flour are integrated to form the final product. As a unit, this description has several shared qualities.

First, these are all relational qualities. Some qualities of God exist within His being independent of His surroundings. He is eternal, powerful, and holy. They describe God isolated from any other thing or being. Mercy and grace, on the other hand, require beneficiaries. Patience and faithful love are words used in relationship. God introduces Himself with qualities that require human interaction.

> Birch (124) observes, "God has no character that matters in the world until there is a community to which God is related and that can give witness to the experienced character of God."

Second, these are all benevolent qualities. These qualities flow from a stronger source to a needy recipient. They are not earned, but given freely. All of them intend good for the beneficiary. This description of God is interwoven with hope and optimism. It suggests that the divine being has human best interests at heart.

Third, God initiates all these qualities. He takes the lead and moves first. In subsequent divine-human interchange, humans often seek these good things from God, but the basis of that seeking is that He first reveals these qualities as part of His nature and that He is a God whose nature involves sharing these good things with humans.

Fourth, there is an ambiguity about these qualities. These adjectives and their associated nouns are general in nature, describing wide concepts which have considerable depth. The list is free of restrictions or

The list is free of restrictions or qualifications. qualifications. God is described without any sense of how He might act in a given circumstance. We know He is merciful, gracious, patient with faithful love, but we remain uncertain about how He might respond to a particular situation. That ambiguity is taken up in the final section.

THE ACTIONS OF GOD

The third section of *Exodus 34:5-7* revolves around five verbs which describe God in actions. The verbs with their objects are listed below:

Keeping (Hebrew participle) *steadfast love for the thousandth generation*

Forgiving (Hebrew participle) *iniquity and transgression and sin*

By no means clearing (two verbs in Hebrew) *the guilty*

Visiting (Hebrew participle) *the iniquity of the parents upon the children and the children's children, to the third and the fourth generation*

Of the five verbs, the first takes up the quality of steadfast love mentioned earlier. The last four deal with sin. The following material investigates these four verbal phrases.

KEEPING STEADFAST LOVE FOR THE THOUSANDTH GENERATION

The Hebrew original here has the same word for *"steadfast love"* as used in *Exodus 34:6*. In the previous case it is modified by the concept of "much" or "abounding." There the depth of God's steadfast love is emphasized. In the current situation the word is preceded by *"keeping,"* a Hebrew word meaning the one who watches the vineyard, guards the city, and especially connected to the one who perseveres with fidelity. God plays this role 15 times in the OT.[10] Just as the trusted military personnel keep watch over a city, so God keeps watch over His steadfast love. Just as the night watchman guards the security of the vineyard, so God preserves His steadfast love.

But God does not just spend one night watching over His loyalty— He guards it for a thousand generations. The number for thousand is

---

[10] *Deu 32:10; Pss 12:7; 25:21; 31:23; 32:7; 40:11; 61:7; 64:2; 140:1,4; Prov 2:8; 22:12; Isa 26:3; 42:6; 49:8.*

often understood literally, but it is also the word for infinite or without number.[11]

The two appearances of *"steadfast love"* in the passage emphasize different aspects of God's loyalty. *"Abounding in steadfast love"* expresses the depth and abundance of God's love, speaks to its quality, its present availability. *"Keeping steadfast love for the thousandth generation"* describes the width and coverage of God's love, speaks to its quantity, its future availability.

Forgiving Iniquity and Transgression and Sin

The Hebrew word for forgive (*nasha'*) means "to lift off, to carry, to take away." Hebrew words often take a literal action and give it a symbolic meaning. Just as a mother lifts a burden off her child, so here God lifts sin off the sinner. Just as the garbage truck carries away the refuse, so God carries away the iniquity.

Iniquity (*'awon*) conveys the idea of making a straight thing crooked. Instead of walking in a straight line toward God, the iniquitous person walks in a crooked line. Transgression (*pashats*) refers to a broken relationship between two people. Two parties face conflict. It may be two neighbors at odds or two nations at war. The two parties in the case of this transgression are God and the human. The third term (*chata'ah*) means to miss something. Here the reference is to a person who misses living up to God's ethical standards.

As mentioned earlier, Hebrew often uses more than one word to

> **God is able to forgive whatever kind of disobedience humans try.**

convey a single concept. It may be here that the three words simply refer to all possible wrong doing (**Cassuto, 440**). The emphasis is not on the fact that humans have not left a single kind of disobedience untried, but rather that God is able to forgive whatever kind of disobedience humans try.

The last two verbal phrases are considered together.

[11] See these texts: *Ex 20:6; 34:7; Deu 5:10; 32:30; Ecc 6:6; Jer 32:18.*

Yet by No Means
Clearing the Guilty

Visiting the Iniquity of the
Parents upon the Children and
the Children's Children, to the
Third and the Fourth Generation

The last phrases are often left off the list of God's qualities.[12] Perhaps some considered the matters too difficult to discuss. Others may have found these last lines too complex. Rather than being a single word or a short phrase, this quality of God contains 15 words in Hebrew.

The word *"clearing"* (*naqah*) refers to plundering a city in war or purifying water, but many of its 44 occurrences in the Hebrew Bible refer to taking away sin. Here, the Hebrew uses an emphatic form of the verb (using the verb *naqah* twice) to indicate the intensity of God's intent. The word *"guilty"* does not appear in Hebrew, but is implied from the previous phrase.

The Hebrew word (*paqad*) for *"visiting"* has a variety of meanings, including "to attend to" and "to visit," but also "to muster," "to appoint," or "to punish." The *"iniquity"* that is not forgiven here is the same word used of the "iniquity" that is lifted off in the previous trait. The meanings of this word *paqad* may seem contradictory and often vary with the translator and the context.

One of God's actions is to punish succeeding generations for the sins of the parents. There are at least four different ways to understand this last trait.

1. *God does not forgive unconfessed and unrepentant sin.* This understanding suggests interpreting the phrase as "God pays attention to the unrepentant sins of the parents, remembering them for several generations." Earlier, God promises to forgive all possible human sins. This statement qualifies that earlier promise by affirming that God does not forgive sin which is unconfessed. Sin which has not been forgiven cannot simply be forgotten with the passing of time. Raitt (**40, 56**) claims there are forty biblical occasions when God does not forgive sin and 140 promises of forgiveness.

---

[12] For example, this last phrase in *Ex 34:7* is not considered as part of the Thirteen Attributes of Mercy used by postbiblical Jews in the Days of Awe prior to the Day of Atonement.

2. *God forgives sin, but does not remove the consequences of sin.* This interpretation of the phrase suggests that "God forgives sins, but some sins have consequences which God does not remove until several generations have passed." To use language made popular by Dietrich Bonhoeffer, God's grace offered in this passage is not "cheap grace." Forgiveness does not remove consequences (**Birch, 131**). Although God is willing to forgive any sin, God reveals that the consequences of a particular sin may continue to affect descendants of the sinner in a negative way.

3. *The decision to forgive sins is God's alone and is not dictated by human wishes.* In this view, God asserts, "I will forgive those I want to forgive and not forgive those I choose not to forgive, and I even have the freedom to punish succeeding generations for the sins of their parents." Raitt (**44-48**) suggests that the passage juxtaposes a forgiving pole and a punishing pole as a means of explaining God's identity. God claims the right to balance the two poles out of His steadfast love and mercy. God is not subject to human whims.

> **God is not subject to human whims; He is free to do what He wants to do.**

God is free to do what He wants to do. He can forgive sin or He can refuse to forgive sin. He can forgive it now or generations in the future. He is not bound by the list of His traits.

4. *God's justice demands that some sins be punished, even for generations.* According to this understanding God makes this promise: "When injustice is done to an individual, and the person inflicting the injustice does not make it right, I will stay with that situation for the succeeding generations until the wrong is made right." To forgive the sins of those who have oppressed and hurt others does not address the oppression or the hurt. In the last trait God promises that even if it takes three or four generations to address the wrong, He will continually right the world's wrongs.

There may be still other ways of understanding God's concluding words in His divine introduction. At this point, we only explore the possible meaning of the words themselves. Ultimately, God's actions in human history define this final promise by God. We will explore this matter more fully in coming chapters.

HOW THE THREE PARTS
FLOW TOGETHER

God's introduction in *Exodus 34:5-7* contains rich material for exploring the essence of God. Using the grammar of the passage as a clue to its structure, this investigation has looked at the names of God (the nouns), the description of God (the adjectives), and the actions of God (the verbs). Having dissected the passage, the chapter concludes by stitching it back together to see how it works as a unit.

This divine introduction is often called God's self-disclosure. The passage presents not what people think about God or what they conclude or see about the divine being, but what God Himself chose to reveal. God tells us what He thinks we need to know about Him. He cuts to the core. He gets to the point. He answers our questions before we ask them. He tells us exactly what we need and want to know.

> **God tells us what we need to know about Him, answering our questions before we ask them.**

The language of the introduction is not in the expected first person, but in the third person. It claims to be spoken by God, but as God reveals Himself He does not say "I am merciful" but *"He is a merciful God."* It may be that the language allows humans to write, read, and recite the words without the unusual situation of assuming God's point of view. God reveals Himself in such a way that the words are easily adaptable as a confession of faith.

As God reveals Himself, the description narrows much like a funnel. It begins with the divine name with all its implications for God's power, self-existence, and creative ability. The one about to be described stands beyond the human sphere. After establishing the self-existent nature of God, the passage turns to how God relates to the human sphere. The relationship is hopeful and beneficial, but without specific application. Then the description turns to God's love: That love abounds and lasts for generations. It prompts God's offer to forgive all sin. Ultimately His love is qualified by His refusal to forgive all that sin brings on humanity.

Many conclude that the passage describes two different divine beings. Van Leeuwen (32) believes this passage presents two opposing poles of God's nature. Tribble (1) notes that the passage describes

"God the lover and God the punisher." Moberly (**"Speak of God,"** 200) concludes, "We thereby have a clear tension within the text: the one whose nature is insistently merciful, even to Israel in its faithlessness, is the one whose nature it is to require exclusive faithfulness." This reading of the passage implies a God of contradictions. The inconsistency Moberly feels is not new, nor is it easily explained. Indeed, McCann (**208**) argues that this tension is the basic interpretative issue for all of biblical theology. However, there is another reading of the passage that removes the tension.

Rather than seeing the passage as a salad where the parts of God remain distinct, I suggest that the text is more like a cake where the ingredients mix together to form a whole entity. In this reading, the last section of the passage defines and refines what is said before. The merciful, gracious, patient God of faithful love and forgiveness must not be read as a God that ignores what is wrong or unjust about life. The first section which stresses divine mercy is refined by the verbal phrases which point out that mercy does not mean anything goes.

> **The ingredients in this passage mix together to form a whole entity.**

Fretheim (*Exodus*, 302) takes this second view and informs the discussion here. The final line indicates that forgiveness is not leniency. It is real forgiveness, not indifference. When people repent, God removes the sin. When they do not repent or continue in sin, God does not clear them of guilt in a lenient way (changing the rules in midstream) or with indifference (as if God were saying it does not matter), but He punishes them.

Seeing the passage as an unfolding holistic description of God does not necessitate seeing God as contradictory, but rather each line of the passage adds to what precedes, offering refinement and definition. When the final line is omitted, as is often done in treatments of this passage even in the Bible itself, something substantial about the nature of God is removed.

CONCLUSION

The importance and complexity of this passage for understanding God prompts a threefold examination of this material. God introduces Himself by giving His name, telling of His merciful essence which is capable of complete forgiveness of human sin but which treats human wrongdoing with great seriousness. That brief statement reviews the inner circle of this investigation, what we hear when we examine the words and the unfolding of this passage. Yet this inner circle does not stand alone. It stands in a particular context in the book of *Exodus*, a sort of middle circle, and this passage is quoted and alluded to in both testaments, what might be called an outer circle. Our investigation now moves to the second circle.

WHAT DO YOU SAY?

1. If you are studying with a group, share with the group either

   a. the meaning of your name, or

   b. why you gave your children their names.

2. Pick one of the adjectives that describe God in *Exodus 34:5-7* (merciful, gracious, slow to anger, abounding in steadfast love and faithfulness) and draw an artistic representation of the description.

3. God does not remove the consequences of sin. A particular sin may continue to affect descendants of the sinner. Have you observed this to be true? How?

4. Write a sentence or two reflecting what you have learned about:

   a. The names of God

   b. The description of God

   c. The actions of God

5. The author gives four different ways of understanding God's action of punishing succeeding generations for the sins of the parent.

   Which of the four do you believe most accurately represents God's action? Why?

   Which of the adjectives that describe God in *Exodus 34:5-7* attracts you most?

   What are some other ways that God introduces Himself in the Bible?

CHAPTER NINE

GOD'S SELF-INTRODUCTION: THE DIVINE RESPONSE–
FAITHFUL TO THE UNFAITHFUL

Begin your study of this chapter by reading *Exodus 32–33*

Imagine this conversation:

"Have you met the new president?"
"Yes, but only briefly. What do you think?"
"I think heads are going to roll. I see lots of changes and many unhappy people."

What is going on in this conversation? The brief dialogue does not give us any context. It could be a conversation between two U.S. Senators reflecting on the effect the new President of the United States will have on the legislative branch. Or it might be two lawyers at corporate headquarters thinking about who might lose their jobs due to the new C.E.O.

But our imaginary conversation could also be two university students fearing that the new sorority president would impose a curfew or a ban on parties. The two people could easily be members of the local model railroaders club sensing that under new leadership meetings would now start on time and there would be penalties for hobbyists who left the layout running without supervision. Context makes a difference!

We are in the midst of a three-chapter look at a real dialogue, a brief conversation between God and Moses in which God offers a significant self-disclosure. We have looked closely at the words God uses and how His revelation unfolds. Now we look at the con-

As we witness what God says about Himself, we begin to understand Him at a deeper level.

text in which this dialogue takes place. As we witness what God says about Himself in the face of His rebellious people in the middle of the book of Exodus, we begin to understand Him at a deeper level.

Outline of the General Context of Exodus 34:5-7

Genesis 37–50—Through Joseph God's people move to Egypt
Exodus 1–2—Egypt enslaves Israel
Exodus 3–19—Moses leads the people out of bondage
Exodus 20–23—Ten Commandments and the Covenant Code
Exodus 24—Covenant ratified
Exodus 25–31—Plans for the tabernacle
Exodus 32–34—Sin with the golden calf and the aftermath
Exodus 35–40—Construction and erection of the tabernacle

RISING UP TO REVEL

Let me tell you about Sean. In thirty-two years of being a minister, I heard variations on Sean's story repeatedly, so while these events are all true, they represent a combination of a couple of different situations. Although I had seen Sean occasionally at church, I did not know much about him except that he ran a substantial company in our city, seemed to have a wonderful family, and was obviously quite wealthy. He appeared to be interested in spiritual things, but hovered around the edge of the church community, never really taking an active part. Then he came to see me.

Sean told me about his frequent business trips to a couple of nearby cities where he engaged the services of expensive call girls. He was so careful and secretive about his sexual exploits that he had continued this activity for about five years before his wife, Sarah, answered the telephone at their house at the same time Sean did and she overheard his conversation planning an encounter with a woman in another city. With his double life exposed, he came to see me.

As we talked in my study, Sean had many concerns. Most of them revolved around Sarah's response. Would she divorce him? Could she take him back? Was there some way she could forgive him? What future did they have together?

Later when I visited with Sarah she was bitter and angry. She hired a private detective to investigate Sean's activities to see if he was telling the whole truth. On top of that she had engaged an attorney who urged her to divorce Sean and promised her most of the family assets. Initially I was not hopeful that the relationship could be restored.

The Sean–Sarah saga mirrors the events that unfold in *Exodus 32–34*. God and Israel form a relationship much like Sean and Sarah built a marriage. Israel gathers around Mount Sinai, hears the words of God's covenant with them, and agrees to become His followers (*Exodus 20–24*). Then, while Moses is atop Sinai to receive the instructions about building the tabernacle (*Exodus 25–31*), the people turn to sin. They make a golden calf and worship it. But they are not done with the festivities:

> They rose early the next day, and offered burnt offerings and brought sacrifices of well-being; and the people sat down to eat and drink, and rose up to revel. (*Ex 32:6*)

When Moses delays coming back down the mountain (*Ex 32:1*), the people press Aaron to make them a god they can see. Soon the people are busy creating the golden calf. Once it is made, they plan a day of worship and celebration. Then they begin to revel. The word "revel" means to "laugh," but it is also associated with sexuality. The NRSV translates the same word as "fondling" in *Genesis 26:8*. God's evaluation of the people's activity comes in His comment to Moses: "Your people . . . have acted perversely" (*Ex 32:7*). The word "perverse" often refers to moral failure.

Cecil B. DeMille's epic movie, "The Ten Commandments," now over fifty years old, may be the source of the visual image many people have of this scene in *Exodus 32*. DeMille called the scene "an orgy Sunday-school children can watch." Simon Louvish's biography of the director's life is, ironically, called *Cecil B. DeMille and The Golden Calf*.

God responds with anger, sends Moses to investigate, and plans to rid Himself of Israel:

> ⁹The LORD said to Moses, "I have seen this people, how stiff-necked they are. ¹⁰Now let me alone, so that my wrath may burn hot against them and I may consume them; and of you I will make a great nation." (*Ex 32:9-10*)

God announces the end of Israel. Instead of reading about the Israelites we might have easily been reading about the "Mosesites." God redeems Israel from slavery, promises them a land of their own, and offers them guidance for life, but they respond by rejecting Him. God's response here is much like a wife who finds out that her husband has been unfaithful. Israel's worship of the golden calf violates the relationship that God seeks with these people. The passage calls to mind the God who takes on the name *"Jealous."* When Israel worships another being as god, it contradicts all that God stands for and all that He is.

He told them: Have no other gods. Do not make any idols. Do not use My name in vain. Israel agrees to the relationship. Then as God spends time with Moses explaining the construction of the tabernacle (*Exodus 25–31*), the people seek another god (*Ex 32:1*). Strike one.

No wonder God is upset and plans to rid Himself of such fickle followers.

They make an idol of that god (*Ex 32:4*). Strike two. Then they call the idol by God's name (*Ex 32:5*). Strike three. No wonder God is upset. No wonder He plans to rid Himself of such fickle followers.

After my conversation with Sarah, I sensed the same anger, uncertainty, and tension. Her husband's sexual unfaithfulness prompted her anger. The future of their relationship was blurry. Their bond was stressed to the point of collapse. The issues facing God and Israel seemed to be the same ones confronting Sean and Sarah: Would the relationship continue? Was forgiveness a possibility? What did the future hold?

WORKING TOGETHER
TO REBUILD

Exodus 32:7-14 gives a detailed report of the post-golden calf conversation between Moses and God. God is intent on the destruction of the people, but Moses intercedes. God relents from a total destruction (*v. 14*), but He still calls for a reprisal: The Levites kill three thousand men as punishment (*v. 28*) and God sends a plague (*v. 35*). At the end of *Exodus 32*, the relationship between God and His people is unclear and precarious. As *Exodus 33* opens, God instructs the people to continue on their journey to the Promised Land, but the ambiguity deepens. God says, *"Go up to a land flowing with milk and honey; but I will not go up among you, or I would consume you on the way, for you are a stiff-necked people"* (*Ex 33:3*). Those words alarm the people. They perform acts of repentance hoping God will continue with them. Moses intercedes again by meeting with God.

Previously God spoke to Moses on Mount Sinai, but *Exodus 33:7-11* explains that now God meets Moses in the "tent of meeting" located outside the Israelite camp. Perhaps the new meeting place is some distance from the main body of the Israelite people so that God will not consume them. The God named *"Jealous"* has the potential to punish those who violate His fundamental being.

Moses goes to the tent of meeting to consult with God. Moses is concerned about two things: Does he know God? Will God be present with the people? In response, God makes two additional appearances to Moses: First Moses stands in the cleft of the rock and sees God's back (*Ex 33:17-23*). Second Moses returns to the top of Sinai where God offers His introduction (*Ex 34:1-7*).

THE RELATIONSHIP SURVIVES

God's self-introduction comes in a significant section of Scripture that asks questions about God's presence. Moberly (*Mountain of God, 62*) calls *Exodus 33* the most extensive presentation of the presence of God in the entire Bible. The question of God's presence unfolds in three ways:

1. God had explained to Moses that He will be present in the tabernacle located in the middle of the camp. *"Have them make me a sanctuary, so that I may dwell among them"* (*Ex 25:8*). The tabernacle will be the physical location of God's presence among Israel. The story of the erection of the tabernacle comes in *Exodus 35–40*. But in *Exodus 33* after the sin with the golden calf, God meets with Moses at the tent of meeting outside the camp. God's promised presence in the future tabernacle now seems in jeopardy.

2. God tells the people to go to the Promised Land. He indicates He will send an angel but not go Himself (*Ex 33:2-3*). God seems unwilling to be present with the people.

3. Moses goes to the tent of meeting to ask God directly if He will be present with them (*Ex 33:12-16*). God replies that He will be present, but Moses seems unsure. God speaks and Moses responds:

[14]He said, "My presence will go with you, and I will give you rest." [15]And he said to him, "If your presence will not go, do not carry us up from here." (Ex 33:14-15)

We wonder, "Is Moses hard of hearing? Does he not believe God?"

This dialogue between God and Moses is most unusual. We wonder, "Is Moses hard of hearing? Does he not believe God when He promises to be present?"

God had been present with Israel. After the sin with the golden calf, He seems to move away. His future presence with them is at risk. Ambiguity prevails. No one seems certain about how and when God will be present.

The situation in *Exodus 33* reminded me of the ambiguity in Sean and Sarah's relationship. For months it was unclear whether they had any relationship at all. Finally, those of us surrounding this fractured family began to see signs that their marriage would endure. They were talking more. They made several joint decisions about the children. We all began to hope that the relationship would survive.

Since we know the end of the story of God and Israel, it may be difficult for us to appreciate their uncertainty and concern. I cite the Sean and Sarah parallel, not because it is a perfect match, but because it allows us insight into the ambiguities facing Israel. Would the relationship endure? The next three events in Exodus give striking affirmation about God's presence with the people.

1. God makes a personal appearance with Moses, who stands in the cleft of the rock and sees God's back (*Ex 33:17-23*). Moses gets a front row seat in the presence of God.

2. God offers His self-introduction (*Ex 34:1-7*) affirming that the relationship between God and Israel is still firm. Through Moses all Israel hears the longest and most intimate description of God in the entire Bible.

3. God orders the construction of the tabernacle (*Exodus 35–40*). After the tabernacle is completed, *"the glory of the LORD filled the tabernacle"* (*Ex 40:34*). God keeps His promise! He wants them to build the tabernacle so He can be present among them, and when it is constructed, His glory fills it.

The relationship survives. God is faithful despite their unfaithfulness. God agrees to be present among the people. He reveals Himself to the people. He offers them a look into His heart at the exact moment when they most sense His possible distance.

Scholars have observed that in light of the dominating issue of God's presence, the revelation of His name in *Exodus 34:5-6* takes on a deeper significance. Birch (127) believes God's revelation of His name is God's way of making Himself available. Mettinger (23) calls the divine name a "password." Fretheim (*Suffering,* 100-101) writes,

> *Naming entails a certain kind of relationship. Giving the name opens up the possibility of, indeed, admits a desire for, a certain intimacy in relationship. . . . Naming entails vulnerability. In giving the name, God becomes available to the world and at the disposal of those who can name the name.*

The context of God's self-disclosure indicates that God reveals His name as a means of stating His accessibility and presence. The complex conversation between God and Moses in the tent of meeting in *Exodus 33:12-16* provides the immediate background. Moses repeatedly asks: "How can I know you? How can I be sure you are present?" God responds by telling Moses His name. God, by giving His name, says, "Let me tell you My name so you can know Me and be sure I am with you."

Two earlier passages in Exodus involve God's personal name.

1. *Exodus 3:14-15.*

Moses' first conversation with God occurs at the burning bush. God commissions Moses to deliver His people. One of the issues Moses raises is God's name. Moses does not believe he can carry out the commission unless he knows who it is that sends him. Moses asks God for His name. God replies, *"I AM WHO I AM"* (*Ex 3:14*). God instructs Moses to tell people *"The LORD, the God of your ancestors . . . has sent me"* (*Ex 3:15*).

2. *Exodus 6:2-3*

After Moses fails to bring release for Israel, he speaks again with God. God reveals more about the origin of the name:

> [2]*God also spoke to Moses and said to him: "I am the LORD.* [3]*I appeared to Abraham, Isaac, and Jacob as God Almighty, but by my name 'The LORD' I did not make myself known to them." (Ex 6:2-3)*

God repeats His name, tells Moses that although He spoke to the patriarchs, He never revealed His name, but implies that He first disclosed His name to Moses in *Exodus 3*. The God who had previously been known as "God Almighty" (*'el Shaddai*) now sought to reveal His personal name and to make Himself known. Scholars frequently discuss the difficulties raised by this text: How can the name be revealed first to Moses in *Exodus 3*, but be used by the patriarchs all through Genesis (see Abraham's use of the name in *Gen 12:8*)? Moberly (*Patriarchal Narratives*) devotes a whole book to this issue.

God's revelation of His name points to God's accessibility. The powerful one tells people His name. He takes on a name that describes who He is and what He does and reveals it to us.

God's name gives the people a means of access to Him, just as names continue both in Scripture and in our time to give people access to one another. There are cases in Scripture where people want to know another's name. Abraham's servant inquires about the family name of the woman he meets at the well (*Gen 24:23*) because it is crucial to his mission. Boaz has an obvious interest in the young woman gleaning in his fields (*Ruth 2:5*) and wants to know her name. Jesus asks the name of the demon in the man by Galilee (*Mk 5:9*) as a means of accomplishing His work.

Through a mutual friend I learned about Rusty Jones, who works as a missionary in the nation of Zaire. Local culture holds that a person who knows one's name has control over that person's destiny. Individuals therefore only reveal their names to people they trust. Often the final stage of a person's conversion to Christ is when they go before the church and say, "My name is _____." Such statements affirm that they trust this community. The revelation makes them vulnerable to those in that group. People who live in Zaire would read and appreciate *Exodus 34:6* at a different level because of their culture's use of a person's name.

The God who withdrew from those who made and worshiped the golden calf now opens Himself to those people. As Moses leads the people near to God, God responds by drawing near to them.

God's revelation in *Exodus 34* might be compared to God giving out His Social Security number and Internet passwords. When we draw near to God, He draws near to us by revealing His name. We know His email address and His cell phone number. There is no need for prayers addressed "To whom it may concern" or with an impersonal "Greetings" or to end with a stiff "Regards." God has a name that gives us access. He is not some impersonal force but rather a personal being. He reveals His name to those who seek Him. His willingness to tell us His name indicates He is positively disposed toward us. We can approach Him in confidence.

> In a similar way, *James 4* shows that the Christians who war with each other and with their own passions find themselves far from God. However, those who repent of their sin, submit, and draw near to God find God drawing near to them (*Jas 4:8*). The creator God remains accessible. Call on Him and He answers.

FORGIVENESS IS GRANTED

I remember the first thing Sarah said to me when I dropped by after she learned of Sean's sexual infidelity:

"I can't forgive him. I'll never forgive him! I won't forgive him!"

He had betrayed her in the most intimate of ways. He had violated their marriage. Her anger was justified. Her rage was understandable. For weeks afterwards she would not even talk about forgiveness. She kept replaying images of Sean and the other women. Each rerun reinforced her refusal to forgive. Even when she agreed to keep on talking with Sean and confessed that she hoped their relationship could somehow survive the infidelity, she stood firm in her refusal to forgive.

Then, one day she told me she had changed her mind. With the help of counselors and friends, with considerable prayer and Bible study, she recognized that her unforgiving spirit made her a prisoner of the past, kept her from fully healing, and prevented the full restoration of their relationship.

I was amazed at the power of God working in her life to prompt her to forgive.

The parallels between my two friends and the Exodus story seems to break down at this point. Sarah, like most of us, resisted forgiveness. When we are hurt we withhold reconciliation. God in the Exodus story does the opposite!

Israel betrays and sins against God. God responds with anger that quickly dissipates, with punishment that is far less than what was promised or expected, and with a temporary withdrawal of His presence. Then God explains Himself. God describes Himself as *"a God merciful and gracious, slow to anger, and abounding in steadfast love and faithfulness"* (*Ex 34:6*).

In the hearts of the people, the sin with the golden calf and the aftermath places the promises of God in profound jeopardy. God briefly considers their total annihilation. Some of the people are punished. The people (*Ex 33:4-6*) and Moses (*Ex 33:12-16*) sense God's displeasure and potential absence. As a result the people sense the absence of the mercy, grace, patience, and faithful love of God. But this aspect of God is not at risk. Unlike most of us who resist offering forgiveness and grace, God's revelation affirms these qualities even in the face of the sin with the golden calf and the following punishment.

> **God's most significant self-disclosure comes in a context of question and doubt.**

God's self-disclosure contains good news that God remains a God of mercy and grace throughout this particular sin. The sin with the golden calf did not extinguish or exhaust His mercy and grace. His punishment of that sin did not mean He withdrew compassion and forgiveness. God's most significant self-disclosure in all of Scripture comes in a context of question and doubt, in the midst of sin and punishment.

The timing of this most significant passage is itself an act of mercy and grace. In a low moment for Israel, both in terms of their sin with the golden calf, and with regard to their doubt over His presence, God tells them what they most need to hear. The words are not Moses' statement to the people of how he perceives God, but they are God's words to humanity revealing His essence, stating how He sees His relationship with sinful and doubting humanity. It is a moment of incredible insight into the heart of God.

> God affirms His mercy and grace. In offering this affirmation God draws on His previous assurances of mercy and grace evident in both the Exodus out of Egypt and the offer of the Promised Land. The Bible refers to God bringing the people out of Egypt over 50

times.[1] One of the most critical references to this expression of God's grace comes as a basis of the Ten Commandments: *"I am the LORD your God, who brought you out of the land of Egypt, out of the house of slavery"* (**Ex 20:2**). The Ten Commandments follow. When Moses intercedes for Israel during the golden calf sin, He cites this very act of grace:

> But Moses implored the LORD his God, and said, *"O LORD, why does your wrath burn hot against your people, whom you brought out of the land of Egypt with great power and with a mighty hand?"* (**Ex 32:11**)

Moses argues that the same mercy and grace that gave the people deliverance from Egypt can now forgive the people of the sin with the golden calf. There are five other references to the phrase *"brought the people out of Egypt"* in the golden calf story (**Ex 32:1,4, 8,23; 33:1**).

The second persistent expression of God's grace is His promise of land. The pledge to give Israel the land of Canaan appears in the OT over 70 times.[2] Moses uses God's gracious gift of the land as a reason for God not to abandon Israel after the golden calf sin:

> Remember Abraham, Isaac, and Israel, your servants, how you swore to them by your own self, saying to them, *"I will multiply your descendants like the stars of heaven, and all this land that I have promised I will give to your descendants, and they shall inherit it forever."* (**Ex 32:13**)

Again Moses argues with God that He recall His gracious promise of the land and draw on the same mercy and graciousness to forgive the people of their sin with the golden calf. The incident at the foot of Sinai with the calf (*Exodus 32*) prompts a reaffirmation of God's fundamental graciousness at the top of Sinai (**Ex 34:5-7**).

While the grace of redemption from slavery was a past example

---

[1]*Ex 12:17; 16:3,6,32; 20:2; 29:46; 32:11; Lev 19:36; 22:33; 23:43; 25:38,42, 55; 26:13,45; Num 15:41; Deu 1:27; 5:6,15; 6:12; 8:14; 13:5,10; 20:1; 29:25; Jos 24:17; Jdg 2:1,12; 1Sa 12:6; 1Kgs 8:21; 9:9; 12:28; 2Kgs 17:7,36; 2Chr 6:5; 7:22; Ps 81:10; Jer 2:6; 7:22; 11:4,7; 16:14; 23:7; 32:21; 34:13; Eze 20:10; Dan 9:15; Am 2:10; 3:1; 9:7; Mic 6:4; Acts 7:36,40; 13:17.*

[2]*Gen 12:7; 13:15,17; 15:7; 17:8; 23:13; 24:7; 26:3; 28:4,13; 34:21; 35:12; 45:18; 48:4; Ex 6:4,8; 12:25; 13:5,11; 32:13; 33:1; Lev 14:34; 20:24; 23:10; 25:2,38; Num 13:2; 14:8; 15:2; 32:29; 34:13; 36:2; Deu 1:8,25,35f; 2:31; 4:38; 5:31; 6:10,23; 7:13; 10:11; 11:14,21; 19:8; 28:11f; 30:20; 31:7; 32:49,52; 34:4; Jos 1:2,6; 5:6; 9:24; 21:2,43; 1Chr 16:18; Neh 9:8,15; Pss 85:12; 105:11; Jer 3:19; 11:5; 32:22; Eze 11:17; 20:28,42.*

of grace, the promise of land was a future expectation of grace. The land promise, first given to Abraham over 400 years earlier, figures predominantly in Israelite thinking. When Moses and the people heard God introduce Himself as the merciful and gracious God, it was in the context of their experience and expectation of God's gifts to them.

In *Exodus 34:6*, God's "*faithful* love" reveals that He is reliable and sure. One of the most remarkable aspects of the relationship between God and Israel in the OT is that God remains true to His people even though they fail Him on numerous occasions. Not every individual who promises intimacy and grace delivers on those promises. People who claim to be patient and loyal often erupt in anger and betrayal.

God reveals Himself through His name and opens His heart to show His passion for grace and mercy, to express His longsuffering and love, and now affirms it all with a proclamation of His faithfulness. Just as we say "Amen" to show our support for the prayer, God says "Amen" through His faithful love to affirm His loyalty to Israel. God, in effect says, "I confirm all these qualities. This is how I will act."

I have often pondered over this wonderful passage in *Exodus 34:5-7* about the essence of God. One of my earliest reactions to the text was that it was buried in Exodus where it was difficult to find and even harder to understand. It seemed to me that it might rather have been a good way to begin the Bible. Genesis might have opened with God saying, "Before I give you my Words, let Me tell you about Myself." But God chose to make this grand introduction in a different setting.

Now I am in a position to appreciate God's decision. In the midst of sin, in the aftermath of punishment, in the context of law and calls for obedience, come some of the most hopeful words I have ever read. I am continually amazed that God openly revealed Himself that morning to Moses. God's words continue to speak clearly about His essence. We have in this self-disclosure clear insight into God's heart.

We have in this self-disclosure clear insight into God's heart.

THE BEST IS YET TO COME

Sarah and Sean finally reconciled. They are still husband and wife to this day. But it has not been an easy journey. Sean's season of infidelity took a toll on him and his family. The years of living a double life haunted him. Their subsequent marriage relationship was persistently difficult. Unfortunately their children faced a number of unusual problems in life, and now after a couple decades have passed, I understand that their grandchildren are also encountering some remarkable challenges. Most people can tell similar stories of families devastated for generations by highly problematic and sinful behavior.

Despite the struggles in overcoming Sean's infidelity, I have seen remarkable victories. When Sarah encountered serious health problems, you could not find a more loyal husband than Sean. As they faced issues with their children, they did it with strength and unity. Sean moved into the center of the spiritual community, became a source of strength to other people, and developed a deep sense of spirituality. His business has soared and he has used his leadership skills to help several ministries reach new heights. I never would have expected that from a man who darted around at the edge of our congregation for years.

Sean and Sarah's situation raises a critical question that often comes up in the aftermath of sin and forgiveness: How can God both punish and forgive? Sean and his whole family suffered as the result of his sin. Yet, I also knew the forgiveness of God was at work in his life. Sarah's forgiveness of his infidelity reminded us all of the grace of God.

The last part of God's self-introduction explains that God both forgives and punishes. Raitt (45) makes the point remarkably clear: "The rigor of juxtaposing a forgiving pole with a punishing pole is echoed but never put more strongly elsewhere in the Old Testament." He means that we often read about God's love, forgiveness, and mercy without any indication of His willingness to punish, and we frequently hear about His efforts to punish His people that make no mention of His love, forgiveness, and mercy. In *Exodus 34:7* we get both.

God's self-disclosure in that verse exactly echoes His actions in the aftermath of the golden-calf sin. He punishes and forgives. How can a gracious and forgiving God still punish? How does He decide who to punish? The answer is not revealed. That He does decide is clearly stated just prior to His self-disclosure:

*And he said, "I will make all my goodness pass before you, and will proclaim before you the name, 'The LORD'; and I will be gracious to whom I will be gracious, and will show mercy on whom I will show mercy." (**Ex 33:19**)*

God makes grace dependent on His own will.

This passage uses the verbal form of the same initial two words in God's introduction (merciful and gracious). Here God makes grace dependent on His own will. God's mercy is subject to God's resolve. Grace and mercy are as universal as the heart of God permits. Grace and mercy are not above God, but are within God.

Just after His self-disclosure, God speaks again:

*He said: I hereby make a covenant. Before all your people I will perform marvels, such as have not been performed in all the earth or in any nation; and all the people among whom you live shall see the work of the LORD; for it is an awesome thing that I will do with you. (**Ex 34:10**)*

The OT repeatedly refers to the "marvels" that God performs, including the crossing of the Red Sea and the defeat of Israel's enemies. Is God referring to those "marvels" here? It seems unlikely. Perhaps in mentioning the "marvels" He will do, God is referring back to the actions He promises to take in *Exodus 34:7*. McCann (207) argues that God's forgiveness of sinners must be one of these "marvels." I wonder if the "marvel" in mind is God's heart, which can contain unlimited grace and mercy, motivated by faithful love, and at the same time hold a willingness to punish.

God does give some sense of how His loving forgiveness and punishment as a consequence of sin are actually distributed. He shows His steadfast love for the thousandth generation but visits sin on only a few generations. In effect, He promises to love an *unlimited* number of succeeding generations, but gives ongoing attention to human sin in a *limited* number of generations.

Even in the writings of Jeremiah at the beginning of the sixth century BC, the contrast between a God who loves for many generations and punishes for a few generations is restated:

*You show steadfast love to the thousandth generation, but repay the guilt of parents into the laps of their children after them, O great and mighty God whose name is the LORD of hosts. (**Jer 32:18**)*

Writing in the "the book of hope" (*Jeremiah 30–33*), Jeremiah seeks to comfort those facing the destruction of Jerusalem by keeping God's punishment in perspective. God punishes the guilty. Jeremiah and his contemporaries feel the force of that punishment as Jerusalem falls around them. But Jeremiah points to how God's love abounds and dominates over His punishment. God punishes those who are guilty, but that recompense pales alongside the demonstration of His steadfast love. In the midst of punishment, Jeremiah reminds the people of hope, perhaps just as God in His self-disclosure to Moses after the golden-calf situation seeks to help the people keep perspective on God's actions.

Raitt (56) notes that God's covenant with Israel did not prevent them from being punished, but it did protect them from annihilation. He implies that even in God's punish-

> **Even in God's punishment there is often mercy and grace.**

ment there is often mercy and grace. By God's grace we seldom get the discipline or punishment we deserve. Israel makes a golden calf, bows down before it, and calls it their god. Some of them die as a result. Many survive. God forgives and punishes. He does both.

Sean suffered for his infidelity. One day while we were talking in my study, Sean asked, "If God wants to forgive me, why do I feel like I'm being punished?" Things at that time were not going well with his firm. Sarah, his wife, still reeling from his infidelity, was making his domestic life miserable. Sean felt like he was being punished even though he had repented, put the sin behind him, and wanted forgiveness. What he did not want was the punishment. He faced a God who both forgave and punished.

Exodus 20 discusses this aspect of God in the context of the Ten Commandments. After prohibiting idols, God says:

> ⁵You shall not bow down to them or worship them; for I the LORD your God am a jealous God, punishing children for the iniquity of parents, to the third and the fourth generation of those who reject me, ⁶but showing steadfast love to the thousandth generation of those who love me and keep my commandments. (*Ex 20:5-6*)

The passage contrasts God's punishment with His steadfast love. God's punishment comes at the end of His patience. His punishment continues for up to four generations. His love lasts for a thousand generations. While the writer did not imply a statistic about God, the claim that there are a thousand occasions for God's love for every four appearances of His punishment points to something significant about God's nature and His heart. *Psalm 30:5* states the point poetically: *"For his anger is but for a moment; his favor is for a lifetime."* The best is yet to come!

CONCLUSION

God's self-introduction in *Exodus 34:5-7* gives us considerable insight into the essence of God. That insight is deepened when we consider that passage within the context of Exodus. Israel's sin angers God, prompts Him to punish, and briefly leads Him to withdraw His presence. But God does not permit the relationship He has with Israel to end, but makes Himself available and vulnerable to His people.

> **God makes Himself available and vulnerable to His people.**

Their sin does not drain or douse His remarkable grace and mercy. His faithful love remains true to those who are unfaithful and unloving. Perhaps His greatest marvel is His ability to both forgive and punish. His discipline affects the children and the grandchildren, but His love abounds to multiple generations. God does discipline. He does it even as He forgives. He promises a hopeful future.

Not all of us have sinned as Sean did. Most relationships face some kind of crisis even if it is not of the same intensity as the subsequent marriage of Sean and Sarah. The God who gives us insight into His essence in *Exodus 34:5-7* does not do so in a sterile laboratory, but rather makes this response in the midst of sin and broken relationships. The God who meets Israel at the scene of their idolatry in order to keep the relationship alive, to offer them mercy, and to forge ahead into the future continues to meet us at the place of our sin with the hope of maintaining fellowship with us, promising that the best is yet to come.

God's introduction in *Exodus 34:5-7* takes the form of a theophany. An epiphany refers to God coming *to act*, while a theophany is God coming *to speak*. God visits the earth to introduce Himself. God talks to Moses, tells him His name twice, and then describes Himself and His actions. This appearance is not visual but auditory. Even though

Moses repeatedly seeks visual proof of God's presence (*Ex 33:11-16*), God tells Moses, *"You cannot see my face; for no one shall see me and live"* (*Ex 33:20*). Seeing God is deadly. Instead of showing Himself, God makes Himself accessible through words.

Listening allows us entrance to His heart. God insists that we make no graven images of Him. God provides us a book without pictures, filled only with words. He refuses to let Moses see Him, but He regularly speaks to Moses. Even when He comes in Jesus, He is called the Word of God. We listen in order to see. Rembrandt's painting, in a sense, visually contains the same message. The younger son listens to his father's heartbeat. Moses listens rather than sees. We too join the listening crowd hearing the heartbeat of God.

Although I represent those who often wonder why this significant passage is buried in a complex text in Exodus, there are many others who found this text and used it in their own setting. This passage is widely quoted and alluded to throughout both testaments which continue to give it life and meaning. This outer circle is the subject of the next chapter.

What Do You Say?

1. Consider the context in which God reveals Himself to Moses in *Exodus 34:5-7*. What does this say about God?

2. Why does God need to affirm His mercy, grace, patience, and love to His people?

3. *James 4:8* says, *"Come near to God and he will come near to you."* Look at the context of *verse 8*. What is involved in coming near to God? By implication, what keeps us from being near to God?

4. The author writes, "Listening allows us entrance to His heart." On the bar below, put an "x" indicating how well you are listening to God each day (1–not listening at all, 10–listening and following completely).

1_____10

What keeps us from listening? What is something you can do to listen more fully to God?

5. God's mercy and grace are demonstrated by bringing His people out of Egypt and giving them the land. He redeems them from slavery and gives them the gift of land. Think about God's redemption and gifts in your life. What are they? In what way do they reveal God's heart to you?

CHAPTER TEN

GOD'S SELF-INTRODUCTION: ALWAYS APPROPRIATE

Begin your study of this chapter by reading *Numbers 14:1-45*

I have no hard evidence to back up this statement, except for my own experience, but let me propose that the following lines are some of the most widely known words from the Bible among people of our time:

> *¹ The LORD is my shepherd, I shall not want.*
> *²   He makes me lie down in green pastures;*
> *he leads me beside still waters;*
> *³   he restores my soul.*
> *He leads me in right paths*
> *for his name's sake.*
>
> *⁴ Even though I walk through the darkest valley,*
> *I fear no evil;*
> *for you are with me*
> *your rod and your staff—*
> *they comfort me.*
>
> *⁵ You prepare a table before me*
> *in the presence of my enemies;*
> *you anoint my head with oil;*
> *my cup overflows.*
> *⁶ Surely goodness and mercy shall follow me*
> *all the days of my life,*
> *and I shall dwell in the house of the LORD*
> *my whole life long. (Ps 23:1-6)*

It is the Shepherd Psalm. I did not take a survey and I have not analyzed the literature of our age. I have not even searched the Internet to see how many hits I might get. Based on my experience of talking to people inside and outside the church, *Psalm 23* is one of the best-known biblical texts among my contemporaries.

A few years ago I was called to the bedside of a man dying of a brain tumor. He was in his mid-thirties, under hospice care, and occasionally lucid. We had never met, but I knew him as the editor of an atheistic journal. As he faced his own death, he told his caregiver to find a Christian minister. He wanted to talk.

He was curled up in bed in a back room of the house. No one explained why this promoter of atheism wanted to talk with a preacher. I introduced myself, offered words of comfort, and waited for a response. It was apparent that speaking a single word took great effort on his part. Finally he whispered something. Embarrassed that I had missed what he said, I had to ask him to repeat himself. By the third time, I heard his request.

"Psalm 23."

Once I understood, I knew what to do. I took his hands, looked into his eyes, and began to quote the words of the old psalm. As I worked my way through the simple lines, I heard other voices in the room; Christian family and friends of this dying man joined in reciting the lines about the walk through the darkest valley. When we reached the end of the psalm, the dying man relaxed his grip on my hands, closed his eyes, and fell asleep. As his head turned toward the pillow, I saw a brief smile on his face.

He died a few days later. Yet his request reminded me of how those simple words from antiquity offered him and others such comfort.

Fairy Cunningham was a saint. She was like an angel in our congregation. When she was diagnosed with cancer, we all prayed for her remission. She died some time later. Her funeral was a celebration of a life lived for God. I concluded my remarks by reciting *Psalm 23*. I had misgivings about using such a well-known passage at the funeral of this wonderful woman, because I felt there might be more appropriate words to help the mourners reflect on her life, but when I finished the psalm, I saw people wiping away tears. Afterwards one of our church elders took me aside to tell me that when I launched into *"The LORD is my shepherd"* he too thought it was an inappropriate Scripture to read. Then he said this, "By the time you were done, I realized that it was exactly what we all needed to hear. It fit perfectly."

One day while coaching a young minister about some issues in the new congregation which he had helped launch, I sensed that he was carrying too much of the burden of that ministry. He was despondent and frustrated. In the middle of the conversation, I asked him if I could read him the words of *Psalm 23*. He agreed. I watched his countenance carefully and listened to his response. It was the right medicine for what ailed him. These words reminded him of who really carried the burdens of his life.

Nearly every morning I spend part of an hour in prayer. I read Scripture. I meditate on God's words. I pray through a list. As I think through the events of the day, I raise each one before the Father. About every other day, I recite the words of *Psalm 23*. I am not facing death or mourning over a loss or trying to carry the whole ministry load on my back, but I find those words appropriate for what I face.

Psalm 23 is a remarkable poem. The words clearly speak to a wide variety of circumstances. But I believe the versatility of the psalm is not in the words or the poetry, but in the God that the words and poetry describe. When I witness the influence of this psalm on a dying man or a mourning elder or a troubled young minister or even my own soul, it is not something that I do as the one who recites the poem, nor is it something David did as the author, but it is

> **The versatility of the psalm is in the God that the words and poetry describe.**

of God. The profound effect of this poem is not so much a work of God (which it is), as it is a reflection of who God is.

WORDS THAT LIVED ON—
EXODUS 34:5-7

What *Psalm 23* does for people in our times, *Exodus 34:5-7* did for people in biblical times. Both speak of the deeper realities of life. Both offer comfort and direction. Both reach into the recesses of the human soul. Again, I do not propose that the power is in these words, or in the pens of those who wrote them or on the tongues of those who spoke them, but I propose that people, through these words, gained insight into the heart of God. Once they entered into the heart of God, whatever their circumstance, they found God being with them in a meaningful and helpful way.

Even though I cannot prove that *Psalm 23* is one of the most widely quoted biblical passages among our contemporaries, I can show that *Exodus 34:5-7* is the most widely cited passage about God within the Bible itself. The use of this passage is almost overwhelming. I have

Exodus 34:5-7 is the most widely cited passage about God within the Bible itself.

put the most commonly suggested passages which use *Exodus 34:5-7* in the list below. Look over these passages before going on with the rest of this chapter.

Exodus 34:5-7 ⁵The LORD descended in the cloud and stood with him there, and proclaimed the name, "The Lord." ⁶The LORD passed before him, and proclaimed, "The LORD, the LORD, a God merciful and gracious, slow to anger, and abounding in steadfast love and faithfulness, ⁷keeping steadfast love for the thousandth generation, forgiving iniquity and transgression and sin, yet by no means clearing the guilty, but visiting the iniquity of the parents upon the children and the children's children, to the third and the fourth generation."

Exodus 20:5-6 ⁵You shall not bow down to them or worship them; for I the LORD your God am a jealous God, punishing children for the iniquity of parents, to the third and the fourth generation of those who reject me, ⁶but showing steadfast love to the thousandth generation of those who love me and keep my commandments.

Exodus 22:27 [F]or it may be your neighbor's only clothing to use as cover; in what else shall that person sleep? And if your neighbor cries out to me, I will listen, for I am compassionate.

Exodus 33:19 And he said, "I will make all my goodness pass before you, and will proclaim before you the name, 'The LORD'; and I will be gracious to whom I will be gracious, and will show mercy on whom I will show mercy."

Numbers 14:18 The LORD is slow to anger, and abounding in steadfast love, forgiving iniquity and transgression, but by no means clearing the guilty, visiting the iniquity of the parents upon the children to the third and the fourth generation.

Deuteronomy 4:31 Because the LORD your God is a merciful God, he will neither abandon you nor destroy you; he will not forget the covenant with your ancestors that he swore to them.

Deuteronomy 5:9-10 ⁹You shall not bow down to them or worship them; for I the LORD your God am a jealous God, punishing children for the iniquity of parents, to the third and fourth generation of those who reject me, [10]but showing steadfast love to the thousandth generation of those who love me and keep my commandments.

Deuteronomy 7:9 Know therefore that the LORD your God is God, the faithful God who maintains covenant loyalty with those who love him and keep his commandments, to a thousand generations[.]"

2 Chronicles 30:9 "For as you return to the LORD, your kindred and your children will find compassion with their captors, and return to this land. For the LORD your God is gracious and merciful, and will not turn away his face from you, if you return to him."

Nehemiah 1:5 I said, "O LORD God of heaven, the great and awesome God who keeps covenant and steadfast love with those who love him and keep his commandments[.]"

Nehemiah 9:17 [T]hey refused to obey, and were not mindful of the wonders that you performed among them; but they stiffened their necks and determined to return to their slavery in Egypt. But you are a God ready to forgive, gracious and merciful, slow to anger and abounding in steadfast love, and you did not forsake them.

Nehemiah 9:31 Nevertheless, in your great mercies you did not make an end of them or forsake them, for you are a gracious and merciful God.

Psalm 25:10 All the paths of the LORD are steadfast love and faithfulness, for those who keep his covenant and his decrees.

Psalm 40:10-11 [10]I have not hidden your saving help within my heart, I have spoken of your faithfulness and your salvation; I have not concealed your steadfast love and your faithfulness from the great congregation. [11]Do not, O LORD, withhold your mercy from me; let your steadfast love and your faithfulness keep me safe forever.

Psalm 57:3 He will send from heaven and save me, he will put to shame those who trample on me. Selah. God will send forth his steadfast love and his faithfulness.

Psalm 78:38 Yet he, being compassionate, forgave their iniquity, and did not destroy them; often he restrained his anger, and did not stir up all his wrath.

Psalm 85:10 Steadfast love and faithfulness will meet; righteousness and peace will kiss each other.

Psalm 86:5 For you, O Lord, are good and forgiving, abounding in steadfast love to all who call on you.

Psalm 86:15 But you, O Lord, are a God merciful and gracious, slow to anger and abounding in steadfast love and faithfulness.

Psalm 89:32-33 ³²[T]hen I will punish their transgression with the rod and their iniquity with scourges; ³³but I will not remove from him my steadfast love, or be false to my faithfulness.

Psalm 99:8 O LORD our God, you answered them; you were a forgiving God to them, but an avenger of their wrongdoings.

Psalm 103:8 The LORD is merciful and gracious, slow to anger and abounding in steadfast love.

Psalm 111:4 He has gained renown by his wonderful deeds; the LORD is gracious and merciful.

Psalm 112:4 They rise in the darkness as a light for the upright; they are gracious, merciful, and righteous.

Psalm 116:4-5 ⁴Then I called on the name of the LORD: "O LORD, I pray, save my life!" ⁵Gracious is the LORD, and righteous; our God is merciful.

Psalm 145:8 The LORD is gracious and merciful, slow to anger and abounding in steadfast love.

Isaiah 48:9 For my name's sake I defer my anger, for the sake of my praise I restrain it for you, so that I may not cut you off.

Isaiah 54:7 For a brief moment I abandoned you, but with great compassion I will gather you.

Isaiah 63:7 I will recount the gracious deeds of the LORD, the praiseworthy acts of the LORD, because of all that the LORD has done for us, and the great favor to the house of Israel that he has shown them according to his mercy, according to the abundance of his steadfast love.

Jeremiah 15:15-16 ¹⁵O LORD, you know; remember me and visit me, and bring down retribution for me on my persecutors. In your forbearance do not take me away; know that on your account I suffer insult. ¹⁶Your words were found, and I ate them, and your words became to me a joy and the delight of my heart; for I am called by your name, O LORD, God of hosts.

Jeremiah 30:11 For I am with you, says the LORD, to save you; I will make an end of all the nations among which I scattered you, but of you I will not make an end. I will chastise you in just measure, and I will by no means leave you unpunished.

Jeremiah 32:18 You show steadfast love to the thousandth generation, but repay the guilt of parents into the laps of their children after them, O great and mighty God whose name is the LORD of hosts[.]

Daniel 9:4 I prayed to the LORD my God and made confession, saying, "Ah, Lord, great and awesome God, keeping covenant and steadfast love with those who love you and keep your commandments[.]"

Joel 2:13 Rend your hearts and not your clothing. Return to the LORD, your God, for he is gracious and merciful, slow to anger, and abounding in steadfast love, and relents from punishing.

Jonah 4:2 He prayed to the LORD and said, "O LORD! Is not this what I said while I was still in my own country? That is why I fled to Tarshish at the beginning; for I knew that you are a gracious God and merciful, slow to anger, and abounding in steadfast love, and ready to relent from punishing."

Micah 7:18 Who is a God like you, pardoning iniquity and passing over the transgression of the remnant of your possession? He does not retain his anger forever, because he delights in showing clemency.

Nahum 1:3 The LORD is slow to anger but great in power, and the LORD will by no means clear the guilty. His way is in whirlwind and storm, and the clouds are the dust of his feet.

John 1:14 And the Word became flesh and lived among us, and we have seen his glory, the glory as of a father's only son, full of grace and truth.

Romans 9:15 For he says to Moses, "I will have mercy on whom I have mercy, and I will have compassion on whom I have compassion."

James 5:11 Indeed we call blessed those who showed endurance. You have heard of the endurance of Job, and you have seen the purpose of the Lord, how the Lord is compassionate and merciful.

2 John 1-3 [1]The elder to the elect lady and her children, whom I love in the truth, and not only I but also all who know the truth, [2]because of the truth that abides in us and will be with us forever: [3]Grace, mercy, and peace will be with us from God the Father and from Jesus Christ, the Father's Son, in truth and love.

These 40 passages all in some way reflect *Exodus 34:5-7*. We might debate whether some of them are quotations or allusions to *Exodus 34* at all. I have simply surveyed the secondary literature on *Exodus 34* and included on the list all the passages that commentators and scholars suggest are quoting or alluding to *Exodus 34*.[1] Some of the allusions

[1]To explore these allusions to *Ex 34:5-7* further, note these studies: Trible (2-5)

are clearer in the original Hebrew. A portion of the passages are clearly quoting God's words to Moses on Mount Sinai. In a couple of cases it takes some digging to see the connection between the passage and *Exodus 34*.[2] Three of the texts appear in the biblical story prior to *Exodus 34*, so the question of which one is original must clearly be raised. A full exploration of each of these passages is not attempted here, since, aside from being lengthy, such a study also tends to place the focus on the use of the passages rather than on the heart of God. This survey simply seeks to make us aware of the substantial way in which the rest of the Bible makes significant use of these words of God's introduction.

Clearly, numerous biblical texts recite the qualities of God listed in *Exodus 34:5-7* or allude to its content. In effect, it is an example of another trajectory in Scripture. The accompanying chart lists the most commonly suggested passages which actually quote *Exodus 34:5-7* and indicates which parts of the original introduction are cited. Additionally, the chart indicates other qualities of God that are added in the citations. The columns on the right identify the speaker and a brief summary of the context of each citation.[3] Several general observations about the citations are easily noted.

	The LORD, the LORD	Merciful	Gracious	Slow to anger	Abounding in steadfast love	Faithfulness	Steadfast love for thousands	Forgiving	Visiting the iniquity	Additional qualities	Speaker	Occasion
Ex 20:5-6	X						X		X	Jealous	God	Ten Commandments
Ex 34:5-7	X	X	X	X	X	X	X	X	X		God	Crisis
Num 14:18	X			X	X			X	X		Moses	Crisis
Deu 5:9	X						X		X	Jealous	God	Ten Commandments
Neh 9:17		X	X	X	X			X		No forsake	Ezra	Crisis
Neh 9:31		X	X							No forsake	Ezra	Crisis
2 Chr 30:9	X	X	X							Not turn face away	Hezekiah	Reform

and Bosman (**234**) both cite 20 partial allusions in the OT while Raitt (**44**) notes 23 echoes of this passage. References to *Ex 34:5-7* are found by Denton (**34-51**) in the wisdom literature; Bosman (**233-243**) and Van Leeuwen (**31-49**) in the minor prophets, and Hanson (**90-101**) and McCann (**206-211**) in the NT.

[2]Some scholars see John's *"full of grace and truth"* (*Jn 1:14*) as a *direct quotation* of *"abounding in steadfast love and faithfulness"* from *Exodus 34:6*. Hanson (**90-121**) explains the various positions and arguments.

[3]The chart does not indicate those cases where the citation changes the order of the qualities of God.

Reference									Description	Author	Occasion
Ps 86:15	X	X	X	X	X					David	Crisis
Ps 89:32				X	X		X			God	Covenant
Ps 103:8	X	X	X	X	X					David	Thanksgiving
Ps 111:4	X	X	X							Unknown	Praise
Ps 112:4		X	X						Righteous	Unknown	Blessing
Ps 145:8	X	X	X	X	X				Compassion	David	Praise
Joel 2:13	X	X	X	X	X				Repents of evil	Joel	Crisis
Jonah 4:2	X	X	X	X	X				Repents of evil	Jonah	Crisis
Nah 1:3	X		X				X		Great might	Nahum	Crisis

1. The chart shows that no other biblical passage quotes this text in its entirety, but the table also reveals that it was being quoted in a vast number of situations.

2. *Exodus 34:5-7* is quoted throughout biblical history. The *Numbers 14* citation records events that come shortly after the events of *Exodus 34*, while Nehemiah chronicles a situation nearly a thousand years later.

3. *Exodus 34:5-7* is quoted by a wide variety of people. Prophets including Joel, Jonah, and Nahum cite this text. On three occasions psalmists use the material. Kings David and Hezekiah made use of it, as did Ezra the priest. It also appears in the history books of Israel (*Nehemiah* and *2 Chronicles*).

4. *Exodus 34:5-7* is cited for a variety of audiences. *Joel* writes to Israel while *Jonah* and *Nahum* use the material in addressing Assyria. In *Nehemiah* the citation is reused for a postexilic audience.

5. *Exodus 34:5-7* is reapplied to new circumstances. Part of the language used in *Exodus 34:5-7* also appears in the Ten Commandments (*Exodus 20; Deuteronomy 5*). In times of crisis the words provide comfort. David reused the words as a basis of thanksgiving while other psalmists applied them to situations of praise and blessing. Hezekiah found the passage helpful in the institution of his reform in the eighth century BC.

In addition to the 40 passages that quote or allude to *Exodus 34*, God's self-introduction contains the vocabulary by which the entire Bible speaks about God. No attempt is made here to even list all the uses of

God's self-introduction contains the vocabulary by which the entire Bible speaks about God.

the vocabulary of *Exodus 34*, but my modest goal is simply to show how the description of God in *Exodus 34:5-7* informs the rest of the

Bible. This vocabulary is used by Jesus and often describes Jesus. A sampling of how this vocabulary appears throughout the Bible appears below.

The following passages are among those biblical texts which use the vocabulary of *Exodus 34:5-7* to describe God and Jesus. This survey follows the areas of *Exodus 34:5-7*.

The Lord

Genesis 2:4 These are the generations of the heavens and the earth when they were created. In the day that the LORD God made the earth and the heavens. . . .

John 8:24 "I told you that you would die in your sins, for you will die in your sins unless you believe that I am he."

Revelation 22:20-21 [20]The one who testifies to these things says, "Surely I am coming soon." Amen. Come, Lord Jesus! [21]The grace of the Lord Jesus be with all the saints. Amen.

Gracious and merciful

Genesis 19:16 But he lingered; so the men seized him and his wife and his two daughters by the hand, the LORD being merciful to him, and they brought him out and left him outside the city.

Genesis 43:29 Then he looked up and saw his brother Benjamin, his mother's son, and said, "Is this your youngest brother, of whom you spoke to me? God be gracious to you, my son!"

Luke 6:36 Be merciful, just as your Father is merciful.

Romans 12:1 I appeal to you therefore, brothers and sisters, by the mercies of God, to present your bodies as a living sacrifice, holy and acceptable to God, which is your spiritual worship.

2 Corinthians 4:1 Therefore, since it is by God's mercy that we are engaged in this ministry, we do not lose heart.

Hebrews 2:17 Therefore he had to become like his brothers and sisters in every respect, so that he might be a merciful and faithful high priest in the service of God, to make a sacrifice of atonement for the sins of the people.

1 Peter 1:3 Blessed be the God and Father of our Lord Jesus Christ! By his great mercy he has given us a new birth into a living hope through the resurrection of Jesus Christ from the dead[.]

Slow to anger

Romans 9:22 What if God, desiring to show his wrath and to make known his power, has endured with much patience the objects of wrath that are made for destruction?

1 Peter 3:20 . . . who in former times did not obey, when God waited patiently in the days of Noah, during the building of the ark, in which a few, that is, eight persons, were saved through water.

Abounding in steadfast love and faithfulness

Deuteronomy 7:7-9 ⁷It was not because you were more numerous than any other people that the LORD set his heart on you and chose you—for you were the fewest of all peoples. ⁸It was because the LORD loved you and kept the oath that he swore to your ancestors, that the LORD has brought you out with a mighty hand, and redeemed you from the house of slavery, from the hand of Pharaoh king of Egypt. ⁹Know therefore that the LORD your God is God, the faithful God who maintains covenant loyalty with those who love him and keep his commandments, to a thousand generations.

John 14:6 Jesus said to him, "I am the way, and the truth, and the life. No one comes to the Father except through me."

Romans 5:15 But the free gift is not like the trespass. For if the many died through the one man's trespass, much more surely have the grace of God and the free gift in the grace of the one man, Jesus Christ, abounded for the many.

1 John 4:7-8 ⁷Beloved, let us love one another, because love is from God; everyone who loves is born of God and knows God. ⁸Whoever does not love does not know God, for God is love.

Forgiving sin, iniquity and transgression

Psalm 32:5 Then I acknowledged my sin to you, and I did not hide my iniquity; I said, "I will confess my transgressions to the LORD," and you forgave the guilt of my sin.

Matthew 9:6 "But so that you may know that the Son of Man has authority on earth to forgive sins"—he then said to the paralytic—"Stand up, take your bed and go to your home."

1 John 1:9 If we confess our sins, he who is faithful and just will forgive us our sins and cleanse us from all unrighteousness.

Visiting the iniquity

Psalm 89:29-34 ²⁹I will establish his line forever, and his throne as long as the heavens endure. ³⁰If his children forsake my law and do not walk according to my ordinances, ³¹if they violate my statutes and do not keep my commandments, ³²then I will punish their

> transgression with the rod and their iniquity with scourges; *³³but I
> will not remove from him my steadfast love, or be false to my
> faithfulness. ³⁴I will not violate my covenant, or alter the word that
> went forth from my lips.*
>
> **2 Thessalonians 1:6-10** *⁶For it is indeed just of God to repay with
> affliction those who afflict you, ⁷and to give relief to the afflicted as
> well as to us, when the Lord Jesus is revealed from heaven with his
> mighty angels ⁸in flaming fire, inflicting vengeance on those who
> do not know God and on those who do not obey the gospel of
> our Lord Jesus. ⁹These will suffer the punishment of eternal destruc-
> tion, separated from the presence of the Lord and from the glory of
> his might, ¹⁰when he comes to be glorified by his saints and to be
> marveled at on that day among all who have believed, because
> our testimony to you was believed.*

Let me offer several explanatory notes to the survey of passages
that use the vocabulary of *Exodus 34*.

GOD'S NAMES

Exodus tells of God revealing His name, the LORD, to Moses on
three different occasions (*Exodus 3, 6, 34*). That name becomes the
central nomenclature for the entire Bible. The name is first used in
Genesis and it last occurs in Revelation. The NT renders the Hebrew
"the LORD" (Yahweh) as "Lord" (*kurios*). This rendering follows the
rabbinic practice of substituting the word "Lord" (*adonai* in Hebrew
with no small caps in English) for "LORD."

Jesus frequently makes reference to the divine name in His self-
descriptions. Mettinger (**40-48**) explores how Jesus uses God's name
in the Gospel of John. Jesus says, "I am" as in "I am the good shepherd" (*Jn 10:11*) or "I am the true vine" (*Jn 15:1*). In these passages,
Jesus uses the same Greek words that God uses to describe Himself in
the Greek version of *Exodus 3:14-15*. However, Jesus also repeatedly
declares "I AM" (e.g., *Jn 8:24*), which
draws on God's name "the LORD"
from *Exodus 34:5-7*. Though not
readily apparent in English versions, the connection Jesus makes
with the OT name of God is signifi-

**The God who spoke to
Moses in the desert is
the same God who came
to earth in a manger.**

cant: the God who spoke to Moses in the desert is the same God who came to earth in a manger. All of these statements are linked to the name of God, and by them Jesus claims divine status.

THE DESCRIPTIONS OF GOD

The vocabulary of God as merciful, gracious, slow to anger, and abounding in steadfast love and faithfulness continues throughout the Bible. This same terminology for the most part is used to describe Jesus. Since the OT and NT were originally written in different languages, and since this study translates the ancient languages into English, the matter of "same vocabulary" becomes complex. The Hebrew OT was translated into Greek. Many believe that Jesus and the early Christians made substantial use of the Greek OT. For the sake of simplicity, this study will take the Greek words used to translate the traits of *Exodus 34:5-7* and trace them in the NT.[4] This process sets aside a complex set of issues regarding translation.

The compassion and mercy God reveals to Moses on Mount Sinai in *Exodus 34* reverberates throughout Scripture. In fact, in one version of the Hebrew NT (Salkinson-Ginsburg Hebrew NT) the Hebrew word for "mercy" from *Exodus 34:5* appears in *Luke 15:20* as "compassion." In English we read of the father showing compassion on the prodigal son. Just as a parent motivated by compassion seeks to be with the child, so God motivated by compassion seeks to be with His people.

> **Just as a parent motivated by compassion seeks to be with the child, so God seeks to be with His people.**

Following God's mercy and grace is His slowness to anger. All of the OT references to God's slowness to anger are on the chart of quotations of *Exodus 34:5-7*. The NT continues to celebrate the patient aspect of God.

God also describes himself as *"abounding in steadfast love and faithfulness."* The Hebrew word *chesed*, which the NRSV renders as "steadfast love" in *Exodus 34:6*, is not translated by one English word

---

[4]To add to the complexity, the same English words are not always used to translate each Hebrew or Greek word. For instance, the Hebrew word *channun* (NRSV "gracious" in *Ex 34:6*) is translated by the Greek word *eleemon*, which appears in *Mt 5:7* as the English "merciful." The concepts of "merciful" and "gracious" are so similar that the words are interchanged during translation.

throughout the OT. As mentioned before, the KJV uses ten different English words,[5] while the NRSV employs 23 words.[6] Even the Greek translators chose different Greek words to render this Hebrew term. The Salkinson-Ginsburg Hebrew NT uses the word *chesed* to translate the Greek word *charis* (grace) 81 times (*Jn 1:14; Acts 11:23; Rom 5:15; 6:14-15*). In general, the NT texts that appeal to God's love, grace, kindness, and loyalty tend to have roots in the Hebrew concept of *chesed*.

The Greek translators of the OT used the common Greek word for "truth" to translate the Hebrew word for "faithfulness" (as in *"abounding in steadfast love and faithfulness"*). The same Greek word appears translated as "truth" in the Gospel of John referring to Jesus (*Jn 1:14; 14:6*). In *John 14* Jesus affirms that He is the truth, which in *Exodus 34* was one of the qualities of God. Against the background of God's self-disclosure in *Exodus 34*, Jesus does not simply claim to be presenting true information or conveying true doctrine, but He will be true to the relationships He forms. It is not just that His words are reliable; they certainly are, but *He* is reliable. It is not simply that the Christian faith He founded is sure, but that when He says, *"I will be with you always to the close of the age,"* it is a promise which has surety.

> **Against the background of God's self-disclosure, Jesus will be true to the relationships He forms.**

THE ACTIONS OF GOD

The word "forgiveness," along with the three words for wrongdoing—"iniquity," "transgression," and "sin"—appear together only one other time in the Bible (*Ps 32:5*). Sometimes called the "the penitent's psalm," the text from *Psalm 32* includes all three descriptions of wrongdoing, with iniquity (translated by the NRSV once as "guilt") and sin listed twice. What God promised to do in *Exodus 34*, the psalmist receives in his life in *Psalm 32*.

---

[5]In the KJV this Hebrew word *chesed* appears as "mercy" (149 times), "kindness" (40), "loving kindness" (30), "goodness" (12), "kindly" (5), and a small number of times each as "favor," "good," "goodliness," "merciful," and "pity."

[6]In the NRSV the Hebrew word *chesed* is translated as "steadfast love" (170 times), "kindness" (15), "loyalty" (15), "loyally" (8), "kindly" (6), and a small number of times each as "clemency," "constancy," "devotion," "devout," "faithful," "faithfulness," "faithful deeds," "faithful love," "favor," "godly," "good deeds," "gracious deeds," "love," "loyal," "merciful," "mercy," "righteous," and "rock."

The word for "forgive" is literally "to lift off." The basic function of picking up a burden comes to refer to God or to a priest on God's behalf taking the sin off of the sinner. During the Day of Atonement ritual, the priest symbolically takes the sins off the people and puts them on a live goat. Then the goat is taken to the wilderness:

> The goat shall bear on itself all their iniquities to a barren region; and the goat shall be set free in the wilderness. (*Lev 16:22*)

The phrase "shall bear" is the same Hebrew word as "forgive" in *Exodus 34:7*. In the Day of Atonement ritual, the scapegoat goes into the wilderness with its burden of sin. The goat carries the sins as far away as possible from the tabernacle, the seat of God's presence, signifying that the wrongdoing has been taken out of God's sight.

Isaiah makes an equally familiar use of the term in the suffering servant song in *Isaiah 52–53*:

> Surely he has borne our infirmities and carried our diseases; yet we accounted him stricken, struck down by God, and afflicted. (*Isa 53:4*)

The servant bears the iniquities just as the scapegoat carried the sins. The word "borne" translates the same word as "forgives" in *Exodus 34:7*. Philip explains to the Eunuch in *Acts 8* that Jesus is the suffering servant. While Philip does not go into detail, we are surely correct in suggesting that Philip linked the words of Isaiah's servant bearing our infirmities to Jesus' dying on the cross for human sin. The servant suffered for the sins of others. The servant suffers for what was not his to bear, just as Jesus suffers for sins that were not His own. In Jesus' bearing what was not His to bear, God's offer of forgiveness is complete and universally available.

In *Exodus 34*, God reveals himself as a forgiving God. That trait will echo throughout the Bible, from Jesus' seeking his Father's forgiveness for those who put Him on the cross (*Lk 23:34*) to John's claim that the blood of Jesus cleanses us from all sin (*1Jn 1:9*).

God promises not to *"clear the guilty"* but to *"visit the iniquity"* on succeeding generations. *Psalm 89* rehearses God's covenant with David. Part of that covenant is explained in words that use vocabulary of *Exodus 34:7*. This passage understands that if David's children sin, they will be punished, but God's discipline will not negate His steadfast love.

The NT never uses the language from the end of *Exodus 34:7*. There is no reference to *"by no means clearing the guilty"* or *"visiting the iniquity of the fathers"* upon succeeding generations. However, the NT does speak frequently of the *"wrath of God"* upon disobedient sinners.[7] In fact, the NT becomes more specific about God's future punishment and of the role Jesus himself will play, as explained in *2 Thessalonians 1:6-10*. Although this passage does not use any of the same words as *Exodus 34:7*, there is a clear theological link between the two texts. God's not clearing the guilty and visiting the iniquity of the fathers on succeeding generations can be understood as a function of God's justice just as the eternal destruction of *2 Thessalonians 1* is a function of a "just" God.

Exodus 34:5-7 provides the language and theological concepts around God who forgives and disciplines that echo throughout the Bible. Our attempt here is not to treat that influence in any detail, but simply to show how the language and thinking of God's introduction continues throughout Scripture.

WORDS THAT TAKE US TO GOD'S HEART— EXODUS 34:5-7

Just as a wide spectrum of people in our world draw on *Psalm 23* in a variety of circumstances, so biblical writers applied *Exodus 34* in a wide array of settings. This broad survey shows how *Exodus 34:5-7* is quoted and alluded to in subsequent biblical texts and how the vocabulary and concepts of the passage provide the words by which the Bible describes both God and Jesus.

People in the Bible regularly used the material from *Exodus 34:5-7* because they found it an apt and insightful description of God. *Exodus 34:5-7* is one of the earliest, one of the longest, and clearly one of the most cited descriptions of God in the entire Bible. It has endured. All of that suggests that the passage gets at the core of who God is. What we have in this passage is the essence of God. We have come to a statement of His heart.

We have spent three chapters on this one passage, partly because the issues surrounding it are so complex. We would expect such an

---

[7]*Mt 3:7; Lk 3:7; 21:23; Jn 3:36; Rom 1:18; 2:5,8; 3:5; 5:9; 9:22; 12:19; 13:4f; Eph 5:6; Col 3:6; 1Th 1:10; 2:16; 5:9; Rev 6:16f; 11:18; 12:12; 14:8,10,19; 15:1,7; 16:1,19; 18:3; 19:15.*

insightful look into God's heart to be complex. Like a painter reducing a mix of chemicals to the color "red," the writer John appropriately reduces God's description to *"God is love."* But within the complexity of *Exodus 34:5-7*, its context, and its use in Scripture, there is rich detail of who God is. We may not completely comprehend all of the descriptions and how they functioned. We should not expect to. We cannot completely understand God. However, God's self-introduction provides a clear avenue into the heart of God.

The long survey which we have completed establishes that people from all the historical periods in biblical history found these words

> **The Bible speaks with one voice about one God.**

to be appropriate descriptions of God. There is no indication that the words describing God had to be edited or altered. In fact, we are struck by the continuities. Despite the fact that some, such as Marcion mentioned in the first chapter, have proposed two biblical Gods, one from the OT and the other from the NT, the Bible speaks with one voice about one God.

God introduces Himself to Moses. About 500 years later Hezekiah uses the same words to call for religious reform. A thousand years after Moses, Nehemiah reaches back a millennium to draw on these lines to describe God in the postexilic period. At least 1500 years after Moses, John, an old man, pens his Gospel, and based on the thinking of many scholars, he uses God's words to Moses *"abounding in steadfast love and faithfulness"* to describe Jesus as *"full of grace and truth."*

God's biography maintains its integrity over a long period of time. The simple contrast between God and any of our constantly changing lives reveals His consistency. Our survey is a striking confirmation of the biblical claim that God does not change.

Biblical authors tend to cite the words of God's self-disclosure in the midst of crisis.[8] Consider the context of six of the passages that quote *Exodus 34:5-7*:

> *Numbers 14*: The ten spies' negative scouting report on the Promised Land prompts the people's rebellion and God's anger. In the midst of this crisis, Moses cites *Exodus 34:5-7*.
> *Nehemiah 9*: Ezra's reading of the law reveals how the people have

---

[8]See the discussion in Brueggemann (**"Crisis-evoked,"** 95-105).

failed God, prompting their repentance and cry for renewal. In that crisis context, the words of *Exodus 34* are quoted.

Psalm 86: David seeks help against his enemies. He finds comfort in these ancient words about God in the midst of his crisis.

Joel 2: Joel writes in the middle of a national emergency. Using *Exodus 34*, he calls for national repentance in response to an invasion.

Jonah 4: Jonah is in crisis because God has forgiven the people of Nineveh whom he deems unforgivable. He returns to the words God gave Moses to explain the situation.

Nahum 1: Nahum chronicles a major upheaval and the destruction of Assyria, and justifies God's actions by citing *Exodus 34*.

Each of these authors recalls the words of *Exodus 34:5-7* in the midst of some difficulty. The original context in *Exodus* is also a crisis as the nation deals with the sin and punishment coming from the worship of the golden calf. Although each crisis is different and the citation is applied in different ways, the use of God's self-disclosure in the midst of difficulty indicates that inspired authors found these words to be appropriate in times of trouble.

Exodus 34:5-7 offers key elements of reassurance and comfort. It provides God's name in a context of making Him accessible and approachable. In light of human sin and rebellion, the passage pledges God's loyalty, His practice of grace and mercy, and His patience. The forgiving nature of God offers hope. Even God's promise to discipline those who sin is understood by those being oppressed as a promise that God will right their world's wrongs. It seems the earth is always in crisis somewhere. Biblical history reveals constant difficulties. *Exodus 34* describes a God who reassures and comforts in the midst of those problematic times. We will return to this point in more detail in a later chapter.

Nahum's use of what has previously been identified as the more problematic portions of the *Exodus 34:7* passage illuminates how biblical writers understood the text. The atrocities and wickedness of Assyria are often rehearsed in the Bible (*2Kgs 17:24; Isa 10:5; 14:25; 37:18; 52:4*). Despite the momentary repentance described by Jonah, their violence was unabated until God decides that they had gone on too long with their wicked ways. Few neutral observers in the 7th century BC would have protested the destruction of such violent and unmerciful people. Indeed, many would have decried their lack of punishment. Nahum reaches back to God's disclosure of Himself to quote what by his time is an admirable trait of God. Nahum cites the passage to say God *does* punish. He *does* visit the iniquity of the fathers on succeeding generations. Generations of Assyrian leaders and warriors had wreaked havoc on dozens of nations in the ancient world. Their atrocities remained unaddressed. Their descendants continued the atrocities. Finally, God "visited" the iniquity and destroyed the Assyrians. What is often taken as a tension in *Exodus 34* is now applauded by Nahum's readers as a gracious gift of a merciful God to rid the earth of such a menace. Justice has been done.

In some ways, *Exodus 34:5-7* functioned in Israel much like *Psalm 23* works in our culture. When faced with a life-threatening situation or when confronted with events that are spinning out of control, many in today's society find solace and certainty in the lofty words about God as shepherd. The commonality of the two passages is that they both point to the nature of God whose essence speaks to troubled souls.

I suggest that God is ambidextrous. I do not mean that God can use both hands equally well or that He is somehow deceitful, two definitions associated with that word. Rather, God is versatile. I do not mean that He changes to fit each occasion, but that God is appropriate for each occasion. People of all ages find strength, comfort, direction, insight, explanation, justification, and help in Who He is. He is not just a God of the synagogue or the church. He is God of the world. Ancient peoples had their storm gods and their goddesses of love. They found a god who could fit the occasion. The God of Scripture is ambidextrous. He fits all situations. Students of God describe Him as omnipotent, omnipresent, and omniscient. We must also understand He is omni-appropriate.

> God is "ambidextrous," in the sense of appropriate for each occasion.

CONCLUSION

The words God uses in His self-disclosure in *Exodus 34:5-7* become the vocabulary by which biblical writers describe God and often the words by which Jesus is described. The words are used in new situations for spiritual purposes different than the original context in *Exodus 34*, but meaningful and relevant to their new setting. By the use of the same vocabulary, God's essence remains unchanged. Along with the continued emphasis in the NT on these descriptions of God, it is clear that God's merciful and gracious nature lies deep in His heart, stands behind His relationship with humanity, and prompts the image of the father welcoming home the sinful son. The God who exists within Himself, who seeks to be known, who is present among His people, wants a beneficial relationship with humans that He Himself initiates. God is the final arbitrator in both testaments of who receives His grace and mercy. Throughout the Bible, God takes sin seriously, with the final pages of Scripture revealing the nature of an eternal punishment God has planned for those who resist Him. In the process, it will become clear that God's essence does not change, that people across the centuries found reason to use these words as they sought to understand and know God, and that they found these qualities of God helpful in life's experiences.

> **God's gracious nature lies deep in His heart.**

I have been puzzled by the scant use of *Exodus 34:5-7* in Christian circles. Few people cite this passage as a favorite. I know of no Christian hymn that embodies this significant description of the God we worship. My sense is that the passage is not widely memorized by Sunday school students and seldom engraved on buildings at Christian schools. I find that puzzling in light of the biblical significance of the text. Even scholarship has tended to avoid this passage until the past two decades, when it has attracted more attention. Clearly the perceived tension at the end of the text contributes to this scant usage, but even that did not prevent biblical authors from making substantial use of the passage. Additionally, the complexity of the passage (even its length) discourages some from making wider use of it. I believe we must rediscover this text in our churches and our teaching by imitating the biblical use of the passage.

The investigation of *Exodus 34:5-7* covers three chapters in this study. It is one of the first and clearly one of the longest descriptions of God in Scripture. The investigation focused on an inner context in looking at the words and the process by which the passage unfolds, then on an intermediate context seeking to understand how the passage functions within the book of Exodus, and finally on an outer context exploring the quotations and allusions to the passage in the rest of the Bible.

The significance of this passage points to its importance in understanding the heart of God. No one can completely comprehend the divine essence. No one can fully understand His passions. Yet in these simple words God himself allows us insight into His remarkable nature. We never see the divine being, but listen over the shoulder of Moses to the divine words which allow us to know and understand Him in ways otherwise not possible. My colleague Dr. Kathy Thompson has skillfully put these words to music, allowing us to use them in worship (see overleaf). Singing, reading, reflecting, and pondering over *Exodus 34* may be as close as we can get to our goal which we illustrated by the scene in Rembrandt's painting. As we take the role of the younger son, his left ear pressed into his father's chest, we too, hear the heartbeat of the father, and by listening, learn, and understand what we have never known or comprehended.

> **As we take the role of the younger son, we too, hear the heartbeat of the father.**

Heartbeat of God

Exodus 34:6-7

Kathy Thompson

1. Lord, Lord, com - pas - sion-ate, gra - cious God,___ Slow to
2. Lord, Lord, The Prod - i - gal Son con - fessed___ And was
3. Lord, Lord, we of - fer our thanks and praise,___ For the

an - ger, a - bound - ing in love and faith - ful - ness,___ Main -
wel - comed and pressed to his fa - ther's lov - ing breast.___ Though
breadth of your faith - ful-ness bless - es all our days.___ We

tain - ing love to thou-sands,___ For - giv - ing wick - ed - ness, re - bel - lion, and
wea - ry and un - wor-thy,___ he heard that heart-beat of re - demp - tion and
strive to walk in your ways,___ but when we fall we find the depth of your

sin. Lord, Lord, we hear your heart - beat of love.___
rest. Lord, Lord, we hear your heart - beat of love.___
grace. Lord, Lord, we hear your heart - beat of love.___

WHAT DO YOU SAY?

1. How are each of the following descriptions of God (*Ex 34:5-7*) seen in Jesus? Give a particular situation or event.

   a. Mercy

   b. Patience

   c. Love and faithfulness

2. The words from *Exodus 34:5-7* are often used later on during a time of crisis because they brought comfort. Think of a present crisis, either in your family, church, city, or world. Write a prayer using words from Exodus to address and bring comfort to that situation.

3. Do you feel there is a tension between God being loving and merciful and God being one who disciplines and punishes? How do you explain this tension?

4. Read the "I Am" sayings of Jesus in the Gospel of John. Write a phrase about how each is linked to God.

   8:12

   10:7

   10:11

   11:25

   14:6

   15:1

CHAPTER ELEVEN

BROKENNESS: THE GOD WHO CARES

Begin your study of this chapter by reading *Psalm 34*

oes God care when we hurt? Does He know about our pain? If He knows and if He cares, why does He not act? Is God concerned about the brokenhearted people in our world?

Some conceptions of God place Him so far away from humanity that He cannot hear, so high that He cannot reach us, so distant that He cannot see our predicaments. When God does not respond to our cries for help, we are tempted to conclude that either He cannot hear us or does not want to hear us. We find it difficult to worship a God who seems so cold and unresponsive.

> **We are tempted to conclude that God cannot or does not want to hear us.**

Psalm 34:18 affirms, *"The LORD is near to the brokenhearted."* He does care. He can hear. He does act. This chapter looks closely at the God who stays close to brokenhearted people, examines what that says about God's heart, and explores how it plays out in human lives.

Before turning to several passages that describe God's response to brokenheartedness, let me tell you about a recent experience that helped me appreciate at a deeper level the kind of brokenness the psalmist describes. Anthony, an urban minister in Memphis, Tennessee, took me along on a day of ministry in the American inner city. We visited with a woman I'll call Sandra. For most of her adult life Sandra had a good job and a healthy family, but then her husband mismanaged their finances, resulting in a huge debt. Shortly afterwards she lost her job due to downsizing at her company, and then her husband left her for another woman. With few other options, Sandra and the children took up residence in government housing in a neighborhood filled with crime and in a project riddled with managerial corruption. Unable to pay her bills, Sandra turned to prostitution, only to find herself arrested and imprisoned.

When we visited Sandra she was facing two additional tragedies in her life. Just months before, her mother, one of the only sources of stability in Sandra's life, was diagnosed with terminal cancer. On top of that, Sandra had increasing difficulty with her teenage son, Ricky, who had recently joined a gang. A week before we arrived, Ricky found himself in the middle of a gang war, and was shot to death.

Sandra never planned to be a broken person. A series of events drove her deeper into poverty and powerlessness. Two tragedies sent her into deep mourning.

During the visit, Anthony asked me to step outside, so they could talk. I didn't understand, but I left. Later he told me that he had heard on the street that Sandra had AIDS. He wanted to talk with her privately. She admitted that she was HIV positive. Anthony consoled her, called her to repent, made sure she was getting medical attention, and challenged her not to spread the disease.

I left Sandra's house discouraged and depressed, wondering what could be done in a situation like hers. Prostitution, gangs, cancer, murder, and AIDS on top of welfare survival, government housing, corrupt officials, and unemployment all added up to no hope. If anybody could be called brokenhearted, Sandra was that person.

Her situation raised questions for me. Was God aware of Sandra's agony? What was He doing? What could help me understand God's work in her life? I turned first to the psalms.

THE GOD WHO IS NEAR THE BROKENHEARTED—PSALM 34

Psalm 34 expresses human gratitude for how God has broken into the world of human pain. It opens in the first person, *"I will bless the*

LORD *at all times."* That line reflects the confidence that the writer has in the God who stays nearby when difficulties arise. After blessing God, the writer recalls a time of need and rescue. Then he turns to teaching (*"I will teach you," 34:11*). In the teaching section, the writer offers a remarkable picture of God:

> ¹⁵ *The eyes of the LORD are on the righteous,*
> *and his ears are open to their cry.*
> ¹⁶ *The face of the LORD is against evildoers,*
> *to cut off the remembrance of them from the earth.*
> ¹⁷ *When the righteous cry for help, the LORD hears,*
> *and rescues them from all their troubles.*
> ¹⁸ *The LORD is near to the brokenhearted,*
> *and saves the crushed in spirit.*
> ¹⁹ *Many are the afflictions of the righteous,*
> *but the LORD rescues them from them all.*
> ²⁰ *He keeps all their bones;*
> *not one of them will be broken.* (**Ps 34:15-20**)

The Psalm describes both the brokenhearted person and the God who is nearby. The brokenhearted are called righteous, victims of evildoers, filled with trouble and affliction. God is close at hand, eyes open, ears listening, face turned in the right direction, ready to help, save, and rescue.

As I pondered the Psalm, I could not help but think of people like Sandra. The Psalm offers an apt description of her brokenness. Twice the psalm calls the brokenhearted person "righteous." In the OT the word "righteous" often describes

> **God is close at hand, ready to help, save and rescue.**

people who fall into some crisis through no fault of their own—that is, they are innocent victims. When I read that, I thought of how all Sandra's problems started. While Sandra did not remain completely innocent, her husband's unwise decisions and her job loss were largely beyond her control.

The psalm points out that the innocent people face evildoers, troubles, afflictions, and danger of broken bones. They are broken-hearted and crushed in spirit. That seemed to describe the Memphis inner-city situation perfectly. Evildoers drew Sandra deeper into the pit; sin multiplied her troubles and doubled her afflictions. She was brokenhearted. The day Anthony and I visited Sandra, I saw a woman crushed in spirit.

> While overall *Psalm 34* centers on thanking God, it also provides a clear description of God and His actions toward broken people. This psalm suggests that God's actions point to an important part of God's nature. In this presentation of God, He is active. He watches out for the vulnerable, listens for problems, chases away the mischief-makers, rescues those in trouble, stays near the brokenhearted, mends the crushed spirits, liberates the afflicted, and protects those in danger. From a contemporary human point of view, God appears to be a combination of security guard, physician, and mother.

The point of the psalm is not to describe the Sandras of the world,

God is near to the people with broken hearts.

but to focus on God. The psalm speaks of God's eyes, ears, and face. He sees the hurting. He hears the brokenhearted. He turns toward the afflicted. The psalm describes God listening, rescuing, saving, and protecting. God is near to the people with broken hearts.

Frankly, as I read the psalm in light of the visit with Sandra, I had my doubts. God did not seem at hand. He seemed to be ignoring the world's Sandras. I wished I could ask the psalmist, "How is God nearby Sandra in her brokenness and crushed situation?"

I began to look for the language of *Psalm 34* in other places in both testaments. If I could find out what it meant for God to hear the cries of the crushed and to be near the brokenhearted, perhaps I could see and understand how God was working in Sandra's life. The actions that are described in general terms in *Psalm 34* take on specificity in many texts, three of which are discussed in this chapter.

THE GOD WHO HEARS THE CRIES OF PAIN—EXODUS 3

> *Exodus 1* chronicles the change in Israel's circumstances from the time when one of their sons (Joseph) plays a powerful role in the destiny of Egypt to desperate days when the Egyptians turn Israel into slaves and programmatically destroy their children. Even the one Israelite slave (Moses) fortunate enough to be adopted into the royal household becomes a hunted fugitive. Far from Egypt where he lives in the security of the wilderness, Moses tends sheep that are

not his and encounters a sight that was not within his experience. Confronted by God in *Exodus 3*, Moses recognizes the unusual nature of this encounter. Moses, who has no news from Egypt and no insight into heaven, then receives word about both.

In *Exodus 3* God meets Moses at the burning bush and gives him a mission. The passage is well-known for revealing the meaning of the name of God: I AM WHO I AM. But in this significant narrative, Moses hears God tell him something quite remarkable.

> [7]Then the LORD said, "I have observed the misery of my people who are in Egypt; I have heard their cry on account of their taskmasters. Indeed, I know their sufferings, [8]and I have come down to deliver them from the Egyptians, and to bring them up out of that land to a good and broad land, a land flowing with milk and honey, to the country of the Canaanites, the Hittites, the Amorites, the Perizzites, the Hivites, and the Jebusites. [9]The cry of the Israelites has now come to me; I have also seen how the Egyptians oppress them. [10]So come, I will send you to Pharaoh to bring my people, the Israelites, out of Egypt." *(Ex 3:7-10)*

Moses has not heard about circumstances in Egypt, but God has. The ears and eyes of God for which the psalmist is so thankful work here in a specific way for the slaves under Egyptian bondage. God observes, hears, and knows about all the events in Egypt, not just in the halls of power but also in the fields of torture. The misery and suffering of these people prompt God to action. He promises to deliver them from slavery, take land from six other peoples, and give that territory to Israel. The next step in His plan involves a human representative to talk to Pharaoh.

It is clear that the Israelites in Egypt are a broken people. God listens to the cries of Hebrew slaves with Egyptian mud on their hands, people who live in a slave ghetto where the sanitation is poor and the air is thick. He knows about the new pharaoh who has no regard for the past, who has enslaved the men, abused the mothers, and killed the children.

It is also clear that God hears the ones in deepest pain. God does not see only the significant people, the Egyptian philosophers, mathematicians, physicians, or artists. God has regard for the brick makers, the ghetto dwellers, and those mixing desert dirt with Nile water

God is not only aware, but takes action.

to build structures for Pharaoh. He knows about oppressive Pharaoh who, instead of rewarding the Hebrews' hard work, misuses them all the more.

The passage gives a concrete example of what *Psalm 34* spoke of in general terms. God is not only aware of human brokenness, but is affected by human misery, and takes action in response to their affliction. When these humans experience pain, God sees that pain and then acts to heal that misery.

Moses later reflects on what he witnessed God doing with the brokenness of Israel. On the edge of the Promised Land he tells Israel about their experience with God:

> *⁷It was not because you were more numerous than any other people that the LORD set his heart on you and chose you—for you were the fewest of all peoples ⁸It was because the LORD loved you and kept the oath that he swore to your ancestors, that the LORD has brought you out with a mighty hand, and redeemed you from the house of slavery, from the hand of Pharaoh king of Egypt. (Deu 7:7-8)*

Moses thinks back to the burning bush, his call to lead the slaves out of Egypt, and how against substantial odds God rescued the Israelite people from the crushing experience of bondage. Before God appeared to Moses at the burning bush, He had heard the cries of the slaves in Egypt. It was then that God *"set his heart"* on that group of people. It was not Israel's attractiveness that prompted God to select them, but something of His heart. God chose Israel not because of who Israel was, but because of who He was. He did not choose a populous people, but a small group. They were not free, but slaves, not the victors, but the captives, not the managers, but the workers, not the people on top, but the ones on the bottom. Israel was not mighty, intelligent, courageous, or persistent, but God picked them out of His own heart.

God's attention to the Israelite slaves gives a concrete example of God as One who knows about the broken, understands the pain of their brokenness, and responds to mend their brokenness. In human situations, we understand why people help others when the motivation is payment, acclaim, or potential influence. It is much harder for us to comprehend those who serve others when there is no personal

Chapter 11
The God Who Cares

incentive. Using the historical setting of the Egyptian bondage, we can understand somebody helping a hurting Egyptian because the Egyptian has the potential of rewarding such service, but it is more difficult to comprehend someone helping the slave who has no real likelihood of benefiting his helper.

As I pondered Sandra's situation, I thought there was little motivation for anyone to seek out Sandra. Battered by events beyond her control and then further broken by a series of bad decisions, Sandra was not the most sought-after person in the projects. She was not brimming with potential. She was not among the important, the wise, the brave, or the diligent of our society. Sandra seemed to be the exact kind of person God promises to help.

The exodus out of Egypt offers a clear affirmation that God is near to the brokenhearted. God hears the cries of the slaves in Egypt. God sends a man to rescue them. God appears at the right time at the Red Sea to crush their enemies. God gives them a wonderful new home in Canaan. It's a complete story that starts in pain and ends in joy.

God knows of human misery and He responds to mend it. The redemption of Israel out of Egypt becomes one of the most significant actions of God in the OT. The event contains significant revelation about the inner workings of God, who is shown to be a being who knows and responds to human brokenness.

When I read the story of the exodus in light of the situations of people such as Sandra, I began to wonder if she feels saved in the same way. My first response was, "I don't

Why does God seem to listen to some people in their brokenness and not to others?

think she feels rescued." God does not appear to her out of a burning bush. He does not send her a Moses. She does not get a new house in the suburbs. Why does God seem to listen to some people in their brokenness and not to others? Why does He act so decisively with Israel and apparently not at all with Sandra? Those questions led me to some words from the prophet Isaiah to the people living in post-exilic Jerusalem.

THE GOD WHO REBUILDS—
ISAIAH 61

The setting of *Isaiah 61* is not as well-known as the story of the exodus out of Egypt. But the passage is worth probing for two reasons: First, it addresses the ambiguity surrounding how God sometimes seems to listen to the brokenhearted, and other times appears to turn a deaf ear. Second, it serves as a backdrop for the ministry of Jesus to broken people. We can go deeper in understanding God's heart for the broken by investigating *Isaiah 61*.

> The massive prophecy of Isaiah addresses three different histori-cal periods to show that the Word of God is true and trustworthy. *Isaiah 1–39* addresses the eighth century, *40–55* are written to the exiles, while *56–66* take up conditions in postexilic Jerusalem.
>
> Scholars are divided about the composition of the book of Isaiah. This study joins those who see the book as a unity from the pen of the eighth-century prophet named Isaiah.
>
> The final eleven chapters of Isaiah include God working in three ways: releasing Israel from exile (*Isa 56:8*), bringing them back to Jerusalem (*56:5,7*), and rebuilding the city (*58:12*).

Isaiah 56–66 is set in postexilic Jerusalem. During the late seventh and early sixth century BC, the people of Jerusalem turn away from loyalty to God, fail to care for the vulnerable people in their society, and ignore the prophets God continually sent. God finally decides to destroy Jerusalem. The city falls in 586 BC. The destruction scatters the people in all directions, but many end in Babylonian exile. Prophets such as Isaiah, Jeremiah, and Ezekiel begin to talk about a time when God will bring His people back to a glorious Jerusalem. In exile there is a growing sense of anticipation.

But life in postexilic Jerusalem fell short of expectations. Some Jews are depriving others of food, clothing, and shelter (*Isa 58:7*) while many in the city experience bloody oppression from the ruling powers (*59:3-7*). Jew-on-Jew violence (*60:18*) and robbery and theft (*61:8*) fill the city with victims. The people turn again to idol worship, even sacrificing their children to these false gods (*57:1-10*).

When I read about the crime and violence, the oppression and greed, the faithlessness and abuse of children in fifth-century-BC

Jerusalem, it is hard not to think about my experiences in the inner city of Memphis. Sandra's world was not that different from the one Isaiah describes. I suspect Jerusalem mothers also lost their children to the violence on the streets just like Sandra did. When Isaiah talks about how the Jewish leaders did not seem to care about the plight of the harassed people in their city (**56:9-12**), it does not seem too different from the leaders of many of our communities today.

It is unlikely that the mothers of postexilic Jerusalem faced the same exact circumstances as Sandra, but while the details may vary, the brokenness and misery of their situation is similar, and Sandra's situation puts a human face on the nameless hurting people in the fifth century living in what they hoped would be a glorious age.

In the midst of this broken world, Isaiah reports the words of God. Several passages in Isaiah tell that God knew of their pain, but *Isaiah 61* describes it most fully:

> ¹*The spirit of the Lord GOD is upon me,*
> *because the LORD has anointed me;*
> *he has sent me to bring good news to the oppressed,*
> *to bind up the brokenhearted,*
> *to proclaim liberty to the captives,*
> *and release to the prisoners;*
> ²*to proclaim the year of the LORD's favor,*
> *and the day of vengeance of our God;*
> *to comfort all who mourn.* **(Isa 61:1-2)**

God's spirit sends a messenger to address a community that, according to these verses and the ones that follow, is oppressed, brokenhearted, captive, in prison, in mourning, faint of spirit, living in ruins and devastation, filled with shame, and full of victims of robbery and wrongdoing. The LORD's anointed and God Himself will bring good news, bandages for binding up, liberty, release, the LORD's favor, comfort, provisions, garlands, oil of gladness, and a mantle of praise. When God is finished keeping His promises, the world will stand amazed at the way God has blessed them. The passage reveals a God who knows and understands the human condition and is moved by that condition to action, actions that are appropriate for healing the brokenness.

Isaiah is one of the first in the Bible to raise the issue of good

> **When God is finished keeping His promises, the world will stand amazed.**

news.[1] The messenger announcing the good news of the return from exile in *Isaiah 52* becomes the basis of Paul's comments in **Romans 10**. When the people return to Jerusalem, they find life does not measure up to the prophet's glorious vision. So God sends His messenger to refresh the people about the good news. In *Isaiah 61* the prophet is not telling the exiles that their long-awaited homecoming is near, but the prophet addresses those who now live in Jerusalem. Their "new" Jerusalem is less glorious than they expected, and many find themselves in a miserable state. Isaiah directs that the good news is to be announced to the poor, to the same people described as homeless, poor, naked, and hungry in *Isaiah 58:7*.

The one behind the announcement is God, who understands their need for good news. The multiple descriptions of the people who receive this announcement point not only to people who are without the physical necessities of life, but those who are broken in spirit. Their spirits are crushed, their hearts are smashed under the weight of their misfortune. God finds the most vulnerable, marginalized, and powerless people and, in effect, He says, "I can help these people." Not only rejected by society, but rejected by themselves, these are people who often do not believe they deserve any better, who are convinced they are unacceptable. God instructs His servant, "Tell them good news." A more complete understanding of the nature of the good news comes in the next verse. To the brokenhearted God makes this promise: *"They will be called oaks of righteousness, the planting of the LORD, to display his glory"* (*Isa 61:3c*). God is willing to transform the brokenhearted into people of stability and substance. God does not want to grow weeds in the new Jerusalem, but oaks. He does not want a city of wickedness, but of righteousness. God's mending of the people, God's repair of their broken hearts, will be so impressive that these renewed people will tower above the community as evidence of the good and right way in which God responds to broken people. God's righteousness and just treatment (*Isa 61:8*) of the broken and faint will testify to God's reputation and identity among all who watch, including the broader world (*Isa 61:9,11*).

> **God will transform the brokenhearted into people of stability and substance.**

[1]Isaiah mentions good news in *Isa 40:9; 41:27; 52:7; 60:6; 61:1*.

To extend the passage's metaphor, the people who were once treated as broken twigs, who were as easily broken as rotten branches, who were considered kindling for the fires of the rich have now been transformed into towering oaks, symbols of strength, signs of permanence, oaks that point to what is right, good, and equitable. The God responsible for such transformation delights in taking the broken and making them whole.

As Anthony and I sat with Sandra, I thought about the congregation down the street where Anthony preached. It was filled with people who had been brokenhearted, but were now oaks of righteousness. I thought of Herman, who had been in and out of prison and was now writing hymns that this inner-city church used to praise God. Women who once walked the streets now served in the church nursery. Men who had carried knives and dealt in drugs now prayed over the bread and fruit of the vine at the Lord's Supper. God was doing on the streets of Memphis exactly what he promised to do on the streets of Jerusalem in *Isaiah 61*. I learned that God did hear the cry of the brokenhearted and He did act on their behalf. Though the words of *Isaiah 61* are nearly 3,000 years old, they are as crisp and true in our time as the day they were written, and they describe accurately the heart of God who is near the brokenhearted. But we have not exhausted what *Isaiah 61* says about God's heart for the broken.

> **These nearly 3,000-year-old words are as crisp and true as the day they were written.**

The down and out of *Isaiah 61* would not only be turned into "oaks of righteousness," but through Isaiah God tells the same group, *"You shall be called priests of the LORD, you shall be named ministers of our God"* (*Isa 61:6*). God promises that the people who were oppressed, brokenhearted, and faint of heart will be transformed by God into priests. Those who need help will become those who help others.

God appointed priests to mediate between the divine and human worlds, to represent the people before God and to represent God to the people. God dreamed that all Israel would be priests to the world (*Ex 19:6*) and that every Christian would play that role (*1Pet 2:5,9*). The good news to the devastated people of Jerusalem included being made into oaks of righteousness, and then, incredibly, being made into priests of God. Those who needed help can now help others.

Those who were brokenhearted now mend hearts on behalf of God. The receivers now become givers.

God's enabling of the people reveals the full nature of His heart for the brokenhearted. He finds people whose hearts are crushed and does heart surgery which not only restores them to health, but makes them the health-givers to others.

God enables the receivers to become givers and mend hearts on His behalf.

God is a full-service God. He detects what is wrong and, being fully aware of the depth of the pain associated with that wrong, He determines a course of action. His plan not only mends the wrong, but raises those who had been broken to unexpected levels of service to others. They then become part of the desired change. God has passion for the brokenhearted.

My experiences in the inner city affirmed that God continues to work in this way. God often uses the formerly broken to minister to the currently broken. It reminded me of a prostitute named Sheila who turned to Christ. She then reached out to a former street woman named Claudia and taught her about Jesus. Claudia then guided Christina, who often worked the same street with her, into a saving relationship with Christ.

At one point we hired a formerly homeless man, Donald, to work as a custodian at our church building. He carried out my trash and vacuumed my study. But Donald also ministered to me by teaching me about faith. His simple trust in a God who provided for him in plain ways helped me to see how God often worked in my life. I was the minister of that 1400 member congregation, but the "minister of God" who helped me was a formerly homeless man that God used as a priest in my life.

Yet I realized that for every Donald and Sheila there were hundreds of people such as Sandra whose lives were still broken, whose cries still seemed unheard by God, who awaited His rescue. I wondered why God was so selective.

God sends His prophet in *Isaiah 61* to announce God's great hopes and dreams for postexilic Jerusalem. In the midst of crime, oppression, and faithfulness, God paints a picture of a substantially different kind of society. He expresses His willingness to rescue, restore, and rebuild. Sadly, many of the people were not willing to let God do

His work. Their unwillingness to allow God to bind up the broken-hearted leaves God brokenhearted. A few chapters later, God speaks out of His disappointment and frustration:

> ¹ I was ready to be sought out by those who did not ask,
> to be found by those who did not seek me.
> I said, "Here I am, here I am,"
> to a nation that did not call on my name.
> ² I held out my hands all day long
> to a rebellious people,
> who walk in a way that is not good,
> following their own devices;
> ³ a people who provoke me
> to my face continually,
> sacrificing in gardens
> and offering incense on bricks;
> ⁴ who sit inside tombs,
> and spend the night in secret places;
> who eat swine's flesh,
> with broth of abominable things in their vessels. (Isa 65:1-4)

God's ears are listening for the people to cry out. They do not ask. God's face looks eagerly to Jerusalem, but few turn in His direction. God holds out His hands for hours on end, but

Unwillingness to let God bind up the brokenhearted leaves Him brokenhearted.

nobody grabs hold to be rescued, restored, or rebuilt. God shows His face, but they only provoke His divine spirit. The passage imagines God crying out to Jerusalem, "Here I am. Here I am. I come to help. I come to bind up the brokenhearted." But few in Jerusalem listen.

The narratives of Ezra and Nehemiah, along with the prophecies of Haggai, Zechariah, and Malachi detail the ongoing gloom and disappointment of postexilic Jerusalem. There are some who respond. Ezra, Nehemiah, Haggai, Zechariah, and Malachi are among those through whom God works to restore Jerusalem to the promised glory. No doubt there are some brokenhearted people bound up by the marvelous work of God. No doubt there are days and events through which God sets captives free, turns twigs into oaks, and commissions those who had been oppressed into priests for the community. But those moments are the exception. Postexilic Jerusalem turns a deaf ear to God.

Part of God's work to bind up the brokenhearted takes an unexpected turn in **Isaiah 61:2**: *"proclaim the year of the LORD's favor, and the day of vengeance of our God; to comfort all who mourn."* The God who has passion for the brokenhearted also turns to those who are the heartbreakers. Vengeance is clearly a part of God's activity and is more fully probed in another chapter. Offering comfort to the brokenhearted, however, cannot be complete as long as those who violate steadfast love, justice, and righteousness in the community continue undisciplined and unrestrained. Part of the good news is the vengeance of God.

The text contrasts God's grace of binding the brokenhearted and God's vengeance on the heart breakers. The work of vengeance takes a day. The work of grace (favor) takes a year. Though the text does not does not mean it in this way, our analytical society can appreciate a 365 to 1 ratio of grace to vengeance. Home remodelers must destroy the rotten before they can rebuild. God too must destroy the rotten before He can rebuild.

Despite the lack of human cooperation, Isaiah makes it clear that God still heard and saw the oppression and brokenness. Isaiah affirms for those of us who encounter people like Sandra that God knows about the brokenness. God stands calling out to the brokenhearted people of the inner city and the suburbs, "Here I am! Here I am!" Postexilic Jerusalem may anticipate a post-Christian America where God calls and few respond.

What happened in postexilic Jerusalem did not have the same spectacular results as the exodus from Egypt. Yet Isaiah confirms that God is *"near to the brokenhearted"* even when the outcome seems to suggest otherwise. In fact, Isaiah powerfully reminds us that in the midst of communities of despair and hopelessness, the spoken Word of God paints a picture of what *might* be and what *can* be and, in the case of those who respond, a picture of what *will* be. That future is real based on a God who is near the brokenhearted and acts on their behalf.

The spoken Word of God paints a picture of what *might* be and what *can* be.

Does God care when we hurt? *Yes.* Does He know about our pain? *Yes.* If He knows and if He cares, why does He sometimes seem not to act? Isaiah reveals the painful truth that people often turn a deaf ear to God's offer to help and that we often have to look closely in the lives of people like Haggai or Donald or Sheila to see God at work. God does care about the brokenhearted people in our world.

As I pondered Sandra's situation, I turned my attention to Anthony. He lived in the inner city, but was not an inner-city person. He was there for Sandra even though he was not a relative and not paid by the government. Socially, he had little in common with Sandra. What made their paths cross? Why do people like Anthony seek to be God's ears, hands, and face to the brokenhearted of this world? Isaiah's passage about the God of the brokenhearted takes on second life in the days of Jesus, and it was there that I found the reason Anthony went.

THE GOD WHO SENDS— LUKE 4

In Luke's Gospel, after Jesus faces Satan in the three temptations and after a preaching tour through Galilee, Jesus returns to an assembly at His hometown synagogue in Nazareth. Someone hands Him the Isaiah scroll. The text He reads was a combination of **Isaiah 61:1-2** noted above and **Isaiah 35:3-6**:

> He unrolled the scroll and found the place where it was written:
> [18] "The Spirit of the Lord is upon me,
>> because he has anointed me
>>> to bring good news to the poor.
>> He has sent me to proclaim release to the captives
>>> and recovery of sight to the blind,
>>>> to let the oppressed go free,
> [19] to proclaim the year of the Lord's favor."
> [20]And he rolled up the scroll, gave it back to the attendant, and sat down. The eyes of all in the synagogue were fixed on him. (**Lk 4:17-20**).

Jesus notes four of the six items mentioned in **Isa 61:1-2**, including bringing good news to the poor, release to the captives, letting the oppressed go free, and proclaiming the year of the Lord's favor. In reading this text, in addition to combining the readings from two passages in Isaiah,[2] Jesus makes these words the purpose of His min-

---

[2]See the commentaries for theories on the reason Jesus quotes two texts from Isaiah in such unique fashion. Regardless of the process, Jesus cites the material that gives Him a foundation for His work.

Chapter 1

Jesus states the purpose of His ministry and immediately begins to do what the passage proclaims. istry, and He immediately begins to do what the passage proclaims. This passage becomes significant for all who follow Jesus, who want to walk in His steps, who want His purpose to be their purpose. In effect, this passage is what prompts people like Anthony to get to know women like Sandra.

After reading the Isaiah scroll and returning it to its proper place, Jesus announces, *"Today this scripture has been fulfilled in your hearing"* (*Lk 4:21*). The synagogue event thus becomes a self-revelatory event for Jesus who announces who He is, what He stands for, and what is in His heart by identifying Himself with the God and His anointed One who speak so clearly in the Isaiah texts. It is a way of Jesus revealing His heart: "This is who I am. This gives insight into my inner being." Jesus advances this idea by making the *Isaiah 61* mission the agenda for His ministry. Jesus claimed that He was the one the Spirit had anointed for this work. The work outlined in the passage was to be His work. Thus, in a profound way, Jesus aligns Himself with the quality of God that is aware of and tends to the miseries of the downtrodden.

Immediately following the events in the Nazareth synagogue, there are six stories of Jesus' ministering to the downtrodden:

Casting out the unclean spirit (*Lk 4:31-37*)
Healing Peter's mother-in-law (*Lk 4:38-39*)
Healing the sick (*Lk 4:40-44*)
Casting out demons (*Lk 4:40-44*)
Cleansing a leper (*Lk 5:12-16*)
Healing and forgiving the paralytic (*Lk 5:17-26*)

Jesus immediately begins to do what the Isaiah passage outlines. Jesus' teaching includes reflections on this same ministry:

The Sermon on the Plain (*Lk 6:17-36*) focuses on the poor and vulnerable.
His report to John the Baptist (*Lk 7:18-23*) includes information about His Isaiah-like ministry.
His parable about the Samaritan (*Lk 10:25-37*) illustrates the kind of ministry Jesus maintained.
Jesus' parables of the banquet and great dinner (*Lk 14:7-24*)

show His concern for the poor, crippled, lame, blind, and rejected.

Twice Jesus alludes to the God of mercy. In the Sermon on the Plain, Jesus summarizes what He was about and the nature of His ministry with the line, *"Be merciful, just as your Father is merciful"* (*Lk 6:36*). Similar statements come both before and after the parable about the Samaritan. Prior to the parable Jesus quotes the two great commandments (*Lk 10:25-28*) in which He makes love a priority. After the parable (*Lk 10:37*) He reissues the call to be merciful.

We cannot find a better model of one who is *"near to the brokenhearted"* than Jesus. We cannot see a better picture of how the world is changed when God's hands, face, and ears turn to the crushed in spirit. We cannot find a better agenda for how God acts to bind the brokenhearted than the ministry of Jesus. In Jesus we see the perfect example of God who is near to the brokenhearted sending a real flesh-and-blood person to represent Him in the lives of the downcast and broken.

> **We cannot find a better model of one who is "near to the brokenhearted" than Jesus.**

Men like Anthony remind us that walking with Jesus leads us to people like Sandra. The God who heard the cries of the brokenhearted in postexilic Jerusalem and sent His workers, and who listened to the poor and needy suffer in first-century Jerusalem and sent Jesus, is the same God who continues to hear the cries today and sends workers like Anthony. For a brief moment that hot afternoon in Memphis, Sandra felt the comfort of God through His worker Anthony. He offered consolation. He called her to change from her wicked ways. He pointed the way to medical help. Rather than continue to spread her disease, he called her to rise above her situation much like Isaiah called the brokenhearted to be priests to their own city. Anthony urged Sandra to join with others in the local Christian community.

Anthony's experience in being a Jesus follower stresses that when the psalmist describes the eyes, ears, and face of God, that He may well be using humanlike language to show us that Sandra's experience of God's binding her broken heart may come in a human vessel. God may send me. He may send you.

CONCLUSION

If it had not been for God, I would not have known of Sandra's brokenness. I could easily live my whole life without interacting with those who face the tragedies and inequities of life. But God has ears that hear what I do not hear and eyes that see what I do not see. He has ways of using each of us to do as Jesus did in binding up the brokenhearted and as Anthony did in tending to the wounds of Sandra.

God has ways of using each of us to do as Jesus did. It all goes back to the essence of God, to His heart which has a place for those who cry out from bondage, to those who are unfairly afflicted, to people who experience life at its worse.

I do not know what became of Sandra. At first, I thought that is a poor way to end this chapter. We all want closure, to read the "happily ever after" part of the story. But after many rewrites and a lot of pondering, I now believe it may be the best way to end the chapter. Sandra, and other people in her situation, are still out there. They await the arrival of the people God sends. People with names such as Isaiah and Haggai and Jesus. Servants such as Sheila, Donald, or Anthony. Sandra's situation reminds us that brokenness is a never-ending part of the human experience. Wherever she is, God hears her heart. Wherever she is, I hope God is sending an Anthony into her life. It's just like God to do just that. I may be far away from Sandra now, but when she and others like her are broken, I know that God is nearby.

WHAT DO YOU SAY?

1. In your community or city, who are the brokenhearted? Is there evidence that God is near them?

2. Reread *Psalm 34*. How does the Psalmist show that God is close to the brokenhearted?

3. Jesus aligns himself with God and states His mission in *Luke 4:17-20*. How can you be involved in His mission of

   a. bringing Good News to the poor

   b. proclaiming release to the captives

c. giving sight to the blind

d. freeing the oppressed

4. God's closeness to the brokenhearted helps us understand His heart. How does your congregation minister to the hurting and brokenhearted? How do you personally help those who are broken?

5. God can transform the brokenhearted into oaks of righteousness. Share with the group how you have seen God do that.

CHAPTER TWELVE

DELIGHT: WHAT MAKES GOD SMILE

Begin your study of this chapter by reading *Jeremiah 9*.

R aymond taught me what it meant to delight in something. He and his wife, Tiny Grace, joined Sally and me, along with another couple, to start a new congregation on the north side of Milwaukee, Wisconsin. I have known few men as kind, gracious, and empathetic as Raymond.

Each spring he would ask Tiny Grace what she wanted for Mother's Day. Every year she would say, "I want us to take Harold and Sally, and the other couple on the church planting team, out to the finest restaurant in southeastern Wisconsin." Every year after church on Mother's Day, we would climb into Raymond's Oldsmobile to drive to some five-star restaurant nestled next to a lake or housed in a pioneer log cabin. That's where I learned about delight.

Imagine being at the finest restaurant in the whole area. Raymond had called ahead to alert the wait staff to our coming and to insist on a certain table by the window or a particular appetizer that had to be prepared in advance. Once seated, Raymond would gently guide us to select whatever we wanted from the menu, with options about what to expect next and clues about a special treat for dessert. After the meal Raymond would have some unique outing planned. Sally and I felt like a queen and king after a day with Raymond and Grace. Years later I still remember my personal delight in looking forward to, experiencing, and then recalling those Mother's Day outings with this wonderful couple.

But the best treat of all was watching Raymond. He loved to please Tiny Grace. He was like a child on Christmas morning when we got into the car after services. He would describe our destination with great satisfaction. But his greatest joy came when he saw how his plans pleased Tiny Grace. At the restaurant when she would react with surprise to some special secret he had planned or when she watched approvingly as he gave us instructions on picking the best item on the menu, Raymond would beam with delight.

During the years I worked in ministry, I encountered many godly husbands. There was the elderly man who used a cane, but still opened the car door for his wife of 52 years. Another husband became the primary caregiver for his new bride after she unexpectedly suffered a stroke. For the next 30 years he pushed her wheelchair, cooked her meals, and even interpreted her unintelligible speech when people came to visit. I remember another husband who discovered his wife having an affair. He urged her to give it up, and when she did, he moved the whole family across the country to begin life again. It worked. Thirty-five years later they are happily married.

Then there was Raymond, the devoted husband, the generous friend, the kindhearted man. I remember Raymond for the look of delight on his face. Nobody I have known has taught me more about delight than Raymond. I can still see him beaming with joy and pleasure in one of those many special moments when he demonstrated his love to Tiny Grace.

THE SMILE OF DELIGHT

Just as I have told you what delighted Raymond, the prophet Jeremiah tells us what delights God. We might turn to many different biblical passages to explore the things that please God's heart, but none are as clear and powerful as the words of Jeremiah to the people of Jerusalem in the late seventh century BC.

Jeremiah is the longest book in the Bible, that is, it has more words than any other biblical book. Much of this long volume is given over to a critique of Judean society, the complaints of the prophet, and the oracles against the nations. Jeremiah writes in the last days of the kingdom of Judah (late seventh and early sixth century BC), warning of the coming destruction of Jeru-

Jeremiah tells us what delights God.

salem, and then continues to speak during and after the fall of the capital city, offering words of hope. Jeremiah is often known as the "weeping prophet." The book records that both God and Jeremiah weep over the coming fate of Jerusalem. At times it is difficult to determine whether it is God or Jeremiah that is so moved. Much of that weeping occurs in **Jeremiah 9**.

At the end of that chapter the prophet speaks directly to the core of what he knows about God. By telling the people about what delights God, he hopes to bring about reform among those oppressing their fellow Judeans, those worshiping Baal, those leaders forming foreign alliances, and those opponents persecuting him. He believes that if they understand and know what delights God, it will begin to delight them. In that context, Jeremiah writes theses lines:

> [23]*Thus says the LORD: Do not let the wise boast in their wisdom, do not let the mighty boast in their might, do not let the wealthy boast in their wealth;* [24]*but let those who boast boast in this, that they understand and know me, that I am the LORD; I act with steadfast love, justice, and righteousness in the earth, for in these things I delight, says the LORD.* (**Jer 9:23-24**)

wealth

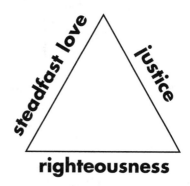

righteousness

Jeremiah uses what scholars call the messenger formula, *"thus says the LORD,"* to cite the words of God. Jeremiah instructs the people on how to "know" God and then points to three qualities that delight God. Brueggemann (**Israelite Wisdom, 93-97**) notes the existence of a double triad in this passage. The first triad is wisdom, might, and wealth. The second triad is steadfast love, justice, and righteousness. The first triad reflects the *status quo* in Jerusalem while the second represents a call for how the people should live, which is based on the character and delight of God.

Jeremiah uses the word "delight" or "desire" (*chaphets* in Hebrew) which means to choose or to will, but also to take pleasure in. The Bible uses this word to describe what God does *not* delight in:

Fools (*Ecc 5:4*)

The death of the wicked (*Eze 18:23; 33:11*)

Horses (*Ps 147:10*, perhaps a reference to military units)

The blood of bulls and goats (*1Sa 15:22-23; Ps 51:16; Isa 1:11*)

Wickedness (*Ps 5:4; Isa 65:12; 66:4; Mal 1:10*)

On the other hand, the Bible tells about other matters that *do* delight God:

People (*Num 14:8; 2Sa 22:20; Ps 18:19; 1Kgs 10:9; 2Chr 9:8; Job 22:3; Pss 16:3; 22:8; 35:23; 41:11; Isa 44:28; 56:4; 62:4; Mal 2:17*)

His own freedom to act as He wants (*Pss 115:3; 135:6; Prov 21:1; Jonah 1:14*)

God's sovereignty over humans (*Jdg 13:23; 1Sa 2:24-25; Eze 18:23*)

God's wishes to make His will known (*Isa 42:21; 46:10; 48:14; 55:11*)

Interestingly, the same word (*chaphets*, bolded in the following citations) is used twice in *Isaiah 53:10* of the Suffering Servant: *"It was the*

God makes clear what does and does not delight Him.

will of the LORD *to crush him"* and *"through him the **will** of the* LORD *shall prosper."* God makes clear what delights Him and what does not delight Him.[1] But few texts rise to the power of *Jeremiah 9*.

In Jeremiah's day, the people of Jerusalem boast about the elements of the first triad. These are not necessarily bad qualities, but they become empty when those possessing them believe they achieve them on their own:

"Wisdom" may refer to the wisdom teachers and priests in Jerusalem who rely on themselves and urge the people of Jerusalem to worship the Baals and ignore Jeremiah. As a result of their teaching, the orphans and needy suffer, according to *Jeremiah 5:19-31*. They have wisdom but no righteousness.

"Might" could point to the Davidic kings, who after Josiah all consider Jeremiah an enemy of the state because he opposes their self-serving policies. One king adds a wing to his palace using the

[1]There are numerous other Hebrew and Greek words associated with desire and delight that might be investigated for further insight into the heart of God.

labor of the poor, according to *Jeremiah 22:13-16*. That monarch has power but no justice.

"**Wealth**" might refer to the wealthy in Jerusalem who oppress the poor, widows, orphans, and aliens in *Jeremiah 7:6*. They have wealth but no kindness. Whether Jeremiah has his opponents in mind or just the general populace of the city in view, Jeremiah is calling for a change in character.[2]

The elements of the second triad—steadfast love, justice, and righteousness—aim to alter the first triad. Jeremiah links the two triads to show that those who seek the second triad will find the proper place for the qualities of the first triad. Jeremiah also reveals that the three qualities of the second triad are not only traits the people in Jerusalem should seek. They are also qualities deeply desired by God, values that are part of His heart.

Jeremiah calls the Judeans to adopt the second triad of steadfast love, justice, and righteousness over the first triad of wisdom, might, and wealth because the second makes up core attributes of God. If they know and understand God, they would know what delights God. As they know what pleases God, these traits would increasingly characterize their own lives. In *Jeremiah 9:23-24*, Jeremiah tells the people of Jerusalem that the way to know God is to practice steadfast love, justice, and righteousness and to allow those godly qualities to characterize their wisdom, might, and wealth.

> **As they learned what pleases God, this would increasingly characterize their own lives.**

Jeremiah describes the heart of God. These are the values in which God delights. He takes great pleasure in steadfast love. He is pleased with justice. He desires and longs for righteousness. These are not simply qualities God wishes the people would adopt, or the basic elements of what it means to know Him, but these words describe the inner nature of God.

---

[2]See the confessions of Jeremiah in *Jer 11:21–12:1; 17; 18; 20:10*, where he laments the moral and physical opposition he encounters.

THE DELIGHT IN
STEADFAST LOVE

God delights in *steadfast love*. We encountered this term in earlier chapters. "Steadfast love" is one translation of the Hebrew *chesed*. God takes pleasure in doing the best for another regardless of circumstances. He loves to be in a relationship that is not forced, needs no reciprocation, does not rely on the qualities of the receiver, and is not based on feeling or emotion. God's steadfast love is not demanded but freely given. He does not love because He has to, but because He wants to. There is no coercion in this kind of love. God shows people steadfast love even when they do not respond with love for Him. It is the universal love of *John 3:16* and eternal love of *Romans 5:8*. God shows people steadfast love regardless of their qualities. God did not choose Israel because it was an attractive nation. Many kinds of contemporary love are based on external attractiveness or the nature of one's possessions. This *chesed* kind of love does not use any of those criteria to determine who is loved.

He does not love because He has to, but because He wants to.

Being able to express steadfast love puts a smile on God's face. Receiving steadfast love from His people gives Him delight. Seeing people live by steadfast love rather than wisdom, might, and wealth fills Him with pleasure.

THE DELIGHT OF
RIGHTEOUSNESS
AND JUSTICE

Jeremiah then indicates that God delights in righteousness and justice. Both testaments cite the righteous and just nature of God. In His unity prayer, Jesus calls out, *"O righteous Father"* (*Jn 17:25*) just as David pleads, *"O righteous God"* in his complaint psalm (*Ps 7:9,11*). In the NT, Jesus concludes His parable about the persistent widow by affirming, *"Will not God grant justice?"* (*Lk 18:7*), while in his discussion of sin, Paul cites the *"justice of God"* (*Rom 3:5*). In the OT, Isaiah writes that *"the LORD is a God of justice"* (*30:18*). Scripture affirms the righteousness and justice of God.

Yet righteousness and justice can be difficult concepts to understand. The words have different meanings in Scripture. Since they are difficult concepts and have different meanings, people often reduce them to ideas that do not reflect the original intent. Without their original meaning, we fail to understand significant aspects of our righteous and just God.

Righteousness (*tsedaqah* in Hebrew) in its various forms appears over 600 times in the Bible. It may be that many who encounter the concept in the Bible tend to read over it, or reduce it to an inappropriate meaning. The word "righteousness" means different things in different contexts: It comes to be associated with salvation, both with regard to Abraham (*Gen 15:6*) and in the teachings of Paul (*Rom 5:17, dikaiosune* in Greek). Other times righteousness connotes the opposite of a wicked life, in other words a life that reflects God (cf. *Ps 1:1; Mt 5:20*). In Amos righteousness describes the innocent (*Am 2:6*). Often in the Bible the word "righteousness" refers to a kind of conduct and character. A righteous individual treats another with the best intent. Von Rad (*Theology*, I:370-82) notes that God's righteousness means He treats people fairly, delivers them from problematic circumstances, guides them in difficult times, and lifts them out of the mire. It is in this element of righteousness that God delights.

The following passages all use righteousness to speak of the quality of God's character when He relates to others. God's righteous relationships are mentioned frequently in Psalms:

> For the LORD is righteous; he loves righteous deeds; the upright shall behold his face. (*Ps 11:7*)

> My mouth will tell of your righteous acts. (*Ps 71:15*)

> My tongue will talk of your righteous help. (*Ps 71:24*)

God is a being who, in His interactions with others, acts in the most truthful and beneficial way and who calls others to act in honest and good ways because righteousness is part of His being.

The word *justice* (*mishpat* in Hebrew) also occurs about 600 times in the Bible in a variety of forms. Readers of the NT often encounter this legal term as a synonym for salvation (*Rom 4:25, dikaiosis* in Greek) and another form for God as the final judge (*Rev 6:10, krino* in Greek). In the OT the Hebrew word is variously translated as judgment (*Ex 23:6*) and justice (*Gen 18:25*). Justice

God calls others to act in honest and good ways because righteousness is part of His being.

is a legal metaphor that speaks of a fundamental fairness and up-
rightness of character. This aspect of the word "justice" is often applied to God. **Deuteronomy 32:4** describes Him as *"a faithful God, without deceit, just and upright is he"* while **Isaiah 5:16** adds, *"But the LORD
of hosts is exalted by justice."*

The two words "justice" and "righteous" appear together almost
100 times in the OT, calling for good relationships built on fairness
and equity. The two words work together to serve the people like a
mother and father raising a child. Like faithful love, they form a hendiadys. To discuss them separately ignores the interrelatedness of the
two words. They speak of treating another person not simply in a way
that seems good to the first person, but in a manner that is judged fair
by an outside standard. They speak of regarding another person with
fairness and equity, but doing so in a way that builds and enhances
the relationship, not merely a cold, legal justice.

God takes great delight in these matters. He delights in treating His
people fairly and within a relationship. He takes great pleasure when
He witnesses His people rising to these
standards in their relationships by
prizing equity and community above
what seems wise to them, what they
can enforce by their own power or
what profits them financially.

> **God's desire for these
> qualities is not in the
> abstract, but in the
> lives of real people.**

Jeremiah raises the issues of justice and righteousness throughout
his book. In doing so he gives these two words content. By giving
them practical substance, Jeremiah reveals what God's desire for justice and righteousness is all about. God's desire for these qualities is
not just in the abstract, but it exists in the lives of real people.
According to Jeremiah, this is the justice and righteousness that God
so desires:

> Creating a society of justice and righteousness which other
> nations admire (**4:2**).
> Treating the oppressed, the alien, orphan, and widow with jus-
> tice and righteousness (**5:28; 22:3**).
> Acting justly with each other (**7:5**).
> Expecting God to treat them with the same justice and right-
> eousness they use to treat others (**11:20; 30:11; 46:28**).
> Not oppressing the vulnerable in order to maintain an affluent
> way of life (**22:13**).

Kings ensuring that the weak and unprotected are supported and given security (*21:12; 22:15 23:5; 33:15*).

Building a just and righteous society because it is God's dream for their future (*31:23*).

God tells Jeremiah to run through Jerusalem's streets looking for a just person (*5:1*). It seems the prophet found no one who met the requirements.

> More than a century after Hosea, Jeremiah used the thoughts of Hosea to restate the heart of God for steadfast love, righteousness, and justice, and also announces the destruction of Jerusalem. In the early chapters of Jeremiah, God remains hopeful that the people of Jerusalem will repent. *Chapters 3–4* repeatedly announce that God will accept His people back. After the temple speech in *Jeremiah 7*, there are increasingly intense announcements of the coming destruction which is finally described twice, once in *Jeremiah 39* and again in *Jeremiah 52*. The prophet goes through an anguished time of ministry during which he, too, calls for punishment on Jerusalem:
>
> *But you, O LORD of hosts, who **judge righteously**, who try the heart and the mind, let me see your retribution upon them, for to you I have committed my cause. (**Jer 11:20**)*
>
> *O LORD of hosts, you test the **righteous**, you see the heart and the mind; let me see your retribution upon them, for to you I have committed my cause. (**Jer 20:12**)*
>
> The prophet's comments come in his first and sixth confessions. He recognizes that the coming judgment will be executed by a God of righteousness, that as such a God He evaluates His people based on His righteous nature, and when His people are found wanting, it is out of His righteous nature that He expresses retribution.

THE SMILE OF KNOWING GOD

Together the three qualities of *Jeremiah 9:24*—steadfast love, justice, and righteousness—describe God and His desires. God reflects these not as three separate qualities, but as a unified whole. These are not pieces of demographic information such as God is six feet tall, lives in the 74034 zip code, and likes vanilla ice cream. Those three items are basically unrelated to each other. Steadfast love, justice, and

Steadfast love, justice, and righteousness combine to describe God.

righteousness combine to describe God. He seeks the best and the equitable and the good. He wants to be in relationships that excel in loyalty, fairness, and empathy. His love will not allow Him to fathom doing anything that is not fair and good. He cannot do something fair in a disengaged way. He cannot do something good without it also being balanced and relationship building.

Jeremiah wants the people to know what delights God. He uses two verbs ("understand and know") to underscore their lack of understanding and their refusal to know God. Jeremiah's words introduce the people of Jerusalem to their God. To understand God, one must dwell on the qualities of steadfast love, justice, and righteousness. To know God is to understand His basic nature. This call to know God does not come in a vacuum.

A century earlier Hosea wrote extensively about knowing God. From what we read in the book of Jeremiah, he appears to have been heavily influenced by his predecessor. Jeremiah adapts Hosea's illustrations and reuses his words and theological concepts. To properly understand Jeremiah, we also need to know Hosea.

The story of Hosea and Gomer is told in *Hosea 1–3* and *11*, which I take as one continuous story of a real man and his unfaithful wife (Shank, *Minor Prophets*, 40-41). God calls Hosea to marry a prostitute (*Hos 1:2*). Many commentaries on Hosea do not think this marriage was appropriate, and they struggle to explain it away. But God had a bigger purpose in mind than just a domestic situation in the eighth century BC. Soon Jezreel is born, followed by Lo-ruhamah and Lo-ammi (*Hos 1:4-9*). I understand *Hosea 2:1-4* to imply that the second two children were not Hosea's. He puts up a thorn hedge fence and tries to keep her home by locking her behind a wall (*Hos 2:6*), but Gomer is intent on being with her lovers (*Hos 2:10*). Gomer finally leaves home. The book of Hosea does not say how long she is gone, but *Hosea 11* suggests that the prophet was a single parent of children old enough to runaway (teenagers?) and able to make his life miserable. In *Hosea 3*, God tells His prophet to find Gomer and love her again. That meant buying her out of a difficult situation. Hosea pays the money and brings her home.

Hosea illustrates the point about knowing God with his own marriage. To begin with, he marries a woman named Gomer who has "street experience." Things go well for a while as the two of them seem to come together when their oldest son is born. But soon Hosea realizes she has been sneaking out in the middle of the night to go to a neighbor's house. Hosea puts up a fence across the back yard, but she goes around it. He locks the bedroom door, but she slips out another way. She has a girl and then another boy in quick succession. Hosea apparently realizes they do not look like him.

Sometime later Gomer quits the marriage altogether, leaving her husband to raise the children alone. She is gone long enough that Hosea becomes a single parent of teenagers. Not unexpectedly, they rebel and cause Hosea a great deal of heartache. One runs away, but Hosea manages to bring him home. He agonizes over those children.

Then Hosea does what nobody could imagine anybody doing. He learns his ex-wife is in an awful condition. After the way she treated him, few would have thought that Hosea would want anything to do with her. But he defies common expectations, goes to bail her out of the situation, and brings her back home. They even marry again.

Gomer's unfaithfulness to Hosea allows Hosea to draw the dramatic parallel between his own marriage and the marriage of unfaithful North Israel and God. A century later Jeremiah draws on the same metaphor to describe how Judah forsakes God. Although North Israel, which Hosea addresses, has now fallen, Jeremiah makes the same accusation against Judah in hopes that their future will take a different course. *Jeremiah 2–4* borrows heavily from Hosea's allegory of a marriage relationship between God and Israel:

> **A century after Hosea, Jeremiah uses the same metaphor to describe Judah.**

> Go and proclaim in the hearing of Jerusalem, Thus says the LORD:
> "I remember the devotion of your youth,
>   your love as a bride,
> how you followed me in the wilderness,
>   in a land not sown." (**Jer 2:2**)

Jeremiah alludes to Hosea's marriage metaphor. Both prophets cite the wilderness as a courtship time between God and His people. But the marriage does not last. Israel does not know or understand what delights God.

After setting up the marriage image in **Jeremiah 2:1-3**, Jeremiah presents a complex set of four poems filled with multiple images. It is not easy material to read and understand. Diamond and O'Connor (123-145) help us sort out the intricate thinking: Two of the poems reverse the image. Israel is an unfaithful husband in the passages in **Jeremiah 2:4-16** and **2:26-32**. In the other two poems Jeremiah continues Hosea's metaphor: Israel is an unfaithful wife in **Jeremiah 2:17-25** and **2:33–3:5**.

In the first poem (**Jer 2:4-16**), masculine Israel is accused of unfaithfulness:

> *for my people have committed two evils:*
> > *they have forsaken me,*
> *the fountain of living water,*
> > *and dug out cisterns for themselves [masculine],*
> *cracked cisterns*
> > *that can hold no water.* (**Jer 2:13**)

The second poem (**Jer 2:17-25**) switches to an unfaithful feminine Israel:

> *Have you not brought this upon yourself [feminine]*
> > *by forsaking the* LORD *your God,*
> > *while he led you in the way?* (**Jer 2:17**)

Jeremiah's third poem (**Jer 2:26-32**) returns to a masculine Israel:

> *But in the time of their [masculine] trouble they say,*
> > *"Come and save us!"* (**Jer 2:27b**)

The fourth poem (**Jer 2:33–3:5**) describes Israel in feminine terms again:

> *If a man divorces his wife*
> > *and she goes from him*
> *and becomes another man's wife,*
> > *will he return to her?*
> *Would not such a land be greatly polluted?*
> *You [feminine] have played the whore with many lovers;*
> > *and would you return to me?*
> > > *says the* LORD. (**Jer 3:1**)

The word *know* (*yaw-dah'* in Hebrew) expresses a wide variety of meanings in the Bible, from sexual intimacy to a devoted mutual and committed understanding. Gomer knows a variety of men sexually. Hosea desires that he and Gomer have a mutual commitment to each other. The people of Israel often participate in the sexual rites of the

Baal fertility religion (*Hos 4:12-16*), but God wants to know the people and the people to know Him in a deeper way. *He expects a deep relationship of mutual commitment.* Hosea is a critical book about knowing God. In Hosea's words there is a lack of knowledge about God in the land (*4:1*), among the priests (*4:6*), and among the people (*4:12,14; 5:3,9; 6:1,3,6*).

> **Hosea is a critical book about knowing God.**

Just as Gomer does not know Hosea, so Israel does not know God, and at some points the Israelites do not even know that they do not know and slip into disloyal unawareness. Just as Gomer is unfaithful to Hosea, so Israel is unfaithful to God.

Jeremiah joins Hosea by repeatedly stating that Judah no longer knows God.[3] The intense words and weeping of *Jeremiah 9* are twice directly linked to Israel's lack of a committed relationship with God, described below by the bolded word "know." Speaking of the people in Jerusalem, Jeremiah writes,

> *They bend their tongues like bows;*
> > *they have grown strong in the land for falsehood, and*
> > *not for truth;*
> *for they proceed from evil to evil,*
> > *and they do not **know** me, says the LORD. (Jer 9:3)*
>
> *Oppression upon oppression, deceit upon deceit!*
> > *They refuse to **know** me, says the LORD. (Jer 9:6)*

Jeremiah's statement about what delights God comes in the context of a people who do not know and understand what pleases God. They do not have a deep relationship of mutual commitment to God. Jeremiah explains that not only do they not know God, they refuse to know Him. As a result of not knowing God, deception and oppression rule in Judean society. The basic components of a civilized world—steadfast love, justice, and righteousness—are missing among people who have no recollection of their LORD and benefactor.

When I read of these prophets building on the metaphor of a bad marriage, I cannot help but think of Sean and Sarah's relationship and other couples I have known where unfaithfulness has caused

[3]The word "know" in the context of knowing God appears in *Jer 2:8; 4:22; 5:4f,15; 8:7; 9:3,6,24; 10:25; 12:3; 15:14f; 16:21; 17:4,16; 22:16; 24:7; 31:34; 44:28f; 48:17.*

pain. Just as the prophets understood God's desires by means of the marriage illustration, so can we. I am often surprised at how little a husband and wife know about each other and how they are not committed to finding out what delights the other. But then, I think of Raymond and Tiny Grace as examples of what happens when couples are faithful to each other. I can still see both them of them beaming with delight: Grace delighted with Raymond's special acts of kindness and Raymond's pleasure that Grace was delighted. On those Mother's Day outings, I was always struck by how well Raymond and Tiny Grace knew each other. He had a knack for doing the exact things that pleased her. She reacted in a way that delighted him.

One day, Raymond called me from the airport. While Raymond was gone, Tiny had dented the Oldsmobile while backing it out of the garage. When Raymond telephoned her about his travel plans, she told him about the accident. He consoled her, but could not alter his agenda to do what he knew had to be done. So he called me. He gave me complete instructions about driving over to the house, visiting with Grace about some church matter, and letting her bring up the mishap. He told me to inspect the car, and no matter what the damage, I was to minimize it and reassure Grace that all would be well. When I announced that the dent was nothing to worry about, Grace beamed. Raymond knew exactly what to do to make his wife smile.

Jeremiah's invitation to understand and know God also reveals that God *can* be understood and known. Not only can He be known, but they can understand what fills His heart with delight. Both Hosea and Jeremiah complain that the people do not know God at this level. Their complaint is not that the people do not know *about* God or that they are ignorant of His history with their people or that they are unaware of His temple in Jerusalem. Cerebral knowledge is not at stake. What concerns both prophets is that the people do not *know God spiritually*, that they do not understand what is significant to Him, what delights Him, that they do not know and understand what God desires and what is in His heart. In essence, they do not know how to listen to His heart. By the double invitation to understand and know, Jeremiah reveals that something of God's inner self can be known,

> **Jeremiah's invitation reveals that God *can* be understood and known.**

and that He is about to reveal what one finds when God's desires are revealed.

We have seen how Jeremiah relies on the eighth-century prophet Hosea. *Jeremiah 2–4* uses the same marriage metaphor as *Hosea 1–3*, and Jeremiah stresses the issues of knowing and being faithful to God just as Hosea did. Jeremiah's triad echoes God's marriage vow in *Hosea 2:19-20*.

The Wedding Vows of the Ideal Husband

As the first three chapters transition from Hosea's troubled marriage with Gomer into God's attempt to win Israel's heart, God commits Himself to court Israel and win her heart (*Hos 2:14*). God says, *"I will take you for my wife forever"* (*Hos 2:19*). God goes on to rehearse the vows He will make when He takes Israel as His wife. The vows are, in effect, an attempt to describe the kind of husband God wants to be and the kind of husband Hosea is.

In Hosea, God speaks through the marriage metaphor. He cites His courtship of Israel (*Hos 2:14*) and His gifts to her (*v. 15*). Then comes the wedding ceremony (*vv. 16-20*). God makes His vow:

> ¹⁹And I will take you for my wife forever; I will take you for my wife in righteousness and in justice, in steadfast love, and in mercy. ²⁰I will take you for my wife in faithfulness; and you shall know the LORD. (*Hos 2:19-20*)

To an Israel that repeatedly does not *know* Him, God offers a means for Israel to know who He is. Against a backdrop of Israel's unfaithfulness, God offers His own *faithfulness*. God offers Himself as a partner for Israel by describing the kind of relationship He desires based on four values: *righteousness, justice, steadfast love, mercy.*

Jeremiah also follows Hosea in discussing what *delights* God. In one of the highpoints of his prophecy, Hosea writes,

> For I desire steadfast love and not sacrifice,
> the knowledge of God rather than burnt offerings. (*Hos 6:6*)

Both prophets write about what God desires.

Not only does Jeremiah rely on Hosea, but so does Jesus, who cites Hosea on two occasions:

> "Go and learn what this means, 'I desire mercy, not sacrifice.' For I have come to call not the righteous but sinners." (*Mt 9:13*)

*"But if you had known what this means, 'I desire mercy and not sacrifice,' you would not have condemned the guiltless." (**Mt 12:7**)*

Jesus used Hosea to correct misunderstandings about God. God's heart is filled with concerns about mercy, justice, and righteousness.

CONCLUSION

Raymond and Tiny Grace spent a lifetime together living in faithfulness learning to know each other in remarkable ways. About three weeks after we started the new congregation, Sunday fell on Valentine's Day so Raymond urged us to have a church potluck meal cooked by the men. When the men met to plan the menu, Raymond insisted on a special beef brisket recipe. Most of us had no idea how to make it or how to afford it, but we willingly followed Raymond's lead. Naturally he knew where to get the best cuts of meat and how to cook it. He also paid for it.

That Sunday in the small rented room where our congregation met, we pushed back the chairs, set up tables, and served the finest meal of beef brisket, baked potatoes and green beans I've ever eaten. All of the women were impressed with the menu. For years they talked about the Sunday the Northtown Church men served beef brisket at a potluck. Raymond beamed. He loved to make people happy. Only later did I discover, not unexpectedly, that it was Tiny Grace's favorite meal.

They were a couple that delighted in each other. Nothing brought a smile to Raymond's face like a smile on Grace's. They enjoyed each other. They delighted in pleasing each other. Those of us who knew them were delighted just to be with them.

Jeremiah serves us well. In a moment of utter clarity, he tells us what puts a smile on God's face. When we know God's heart for steadfast love, justice, and righteousness, we understand what delights and pleases him. It is not just that those are qualities of God; they are, but they are standards that delight God wherever He finds them. He takes pleasure in expressing that love, fairness, and community with His people. He delights when His people treat Him with the same qualities. He is pleased when He views the human community making decisions and living not just based on their own wisdom, strength, or wealth, but when they dwell in steadfast love, justice, and righteousness.

These three values are crucial to God. God makes them central to both the eighth-century prophecy of Hosea and the seventh-century prophecy of Jeremiah, uses them as a key to understanding and knowing Him, and designates them as what He desires. In the next chapter we will explore one more way God expresses two of these three qualities.

On our journey into the heart of God, we pass many points of interest. On this trip, we might come close to the place where God is most at home, where His true nature and passions lie. As we come upon steadfast love, justice, and righteousness we have come somewhere close to that inner sanctum.

We expect that just as any three human qualities are intermingled in one's personality, so these three aspects of God take on wholeness in the divine being. His steadfast love is directed by His righteous nature and His just ways. His righteousness is affected by His steadfast love and balanced by His justice. His justice is built on His steadfast love and righteousness.

Here we have drawn close to the heart of God. We have listened to the divine heartbeat, and whatever else we learn and sense about Him, we must not forget that He delights in steadfast love, justice, and righteousness.

Raymond always beamed when he had pleased Tiny Grace. We knew what was on his heart. God allows us the same access to His heart. When He sees steadfast love, justice, and righteousness in the human community, I often imagine that He must beam just like Raymond did. I believe that nothing can give us greater fulfillment in life than knowing we reflect the qualities that delight God. It just makes you want to smile.

> **Nothing can give us greater fulfillment than knowing we reflect the qualities that delight God.**

WHAT DO YOU SAY?

1. Tell about a man you know who is an outstanding husband. What motivates him to be that kind of husband?

2. Look up the following verses. What do you discover about knowing God?

   a. *Exodus 33:13*

   b. *Psalm 9:10*

   c. *Psalm 46:10*

   d. *Jeremiah 24:7*

   e. *John 6:69*

   f. *1 John 4:8*

   g. *1 John 5:20*

3. God desires steadfast love, justice, and righteousness. What changes need to take place for these three interrelated qualities to be evident in your community?

4. In the first triad, "wisdom, wealth, and might" reflects the status quo of Jerusalem. What words would you use to describe the status quo of your city?

CHAPTER THIRTEEN

RIGHTEOUSNESS AND JUSTICE: WHAT MAKES GOD ACT

Begin your study of this chapter by reading *Isaiah 1*

James calls them *"doers of the word."* I have known many people who fit that description. There was Sherrill who taught the Sunday morning women's Bible class. She not only talked about Christianity, but she walked it. If a disadvantaged woman in her class needed a new refrigerator, Sherrill knew how to get ahold of one. She provided cars and furniture right along with teaching God's word. I was with David, another doer, at a children's hospital in Ukraine when we learned that due to funding problems during the last days of the Communistic era, the children would not have any lunch. I can still see him walking up to the hospital director with his open wallet. The children ate well that day. My wife, Sally, is another doer. For 16 years she drove downtown once a week to be a Christian sponsor in the HopeWorks Life Skills Lab.

But nobody outdid Don. He generally blended in with the Sunday morning crowd. Soft-spoken (you had to get up close to hear him sometimes) and unassuming, Don lived out all the Christian virtues. He was kind, patient, loving, fair, joyful, loyal, and compassionate. All those qualities were important to him. They were his passion.

But kind, gentle, quiet Don could explode into activity. Since I need to protect the identity of some of those involved, let me tell the story this way. A drunken father stopped his car on a busy city street to toss out some things he did not want. Among the stuff he jettisoned was his nine-month-old daughter. A passerby found the child and took her to the police, who put her in the hands of the state agency for abandoned children. When Don heard about the brutal abandonment of this little girl, he sprang into action and soon he and his wife were fostering the infant in their home.

Then Don learned that it was not the first time the child had been abandoned or mistreated. She had suffered a long list of injustices in her short months of life. Don set his mind to ensure that nothing like that would happen again.

That's when the child's father went to court to get her back. The case went to trial, but it was often delayed because the father showed up drunk or high on drugs. Social workers repeatedly urged that the little girl not be returned to his care, but the legal maneuvering went on for months. Such situations are far too common in contemporary America. It soon became apparent that it would take time and money to guarantee that this child was not mistreated again.

I was one of many people sitting on the sidelines cheering for Don. He hired lawyers. He took off work to attend hearings. He read up on the laws. He sought out counsel. He spent money. Even though I cheered him on, I wondered how far he would go, how long he could endure, how much he would spend. As the months turned into years, I realized, he would go to the end, he would stay until it was done, and he would spend whatever it took.

He did. Today that little girl is his adopted daughter. The child that was dumped out of a car onto the asphalt of an inner-city street has a father who loves her. Don is a doer of the word.

God is also a doer. He delights in steadfast love, justice, and righteousness. But He does not just *delight* in these qualities, He *acts* on them. He advocates for them. He enters our world to insist on them. When they are lacking, when justice and righteousness get abandoned by a society, God explodes into action. Insisting on a just and righteous human community is the way of God. It is His passion.

When justice and righteousness get abandoned by a society, God explodes into action.

THE GOD WHO ACTS WITH JUSTICE AND RIGHTEOUSNESS

WITH ABRAHAM

Before the Bible mentions anything about God's steadfast love, mercy, or truthfulness, *Genesis* raises the issue of His righteousness and justice. Genesis calls righteousness and justice the *"way of the LORD."* It comes in the narrative about Abraham.

After God promises Abraham the blessing of a great nation, Genesis follows a series of roadblocks to that promise. Abraham's wife, Sarah, is taken into Pharaoh's household before she can have a child. Lot becomes a possible heir, but there is conflict in the relationship. Hagar provides Abraham with a son, but she and Sarah do not get along. Then Eliezer of Damascus—a mere servant—is suggested as a successor to Abraham. Finally, God acts. We are told in *Genesis 18* that He visits Abraham and Sarah at their desert home to announce the birth of a rightful heir. Sarah will conceive and soon have their child. After the meal and the birth announcement, God and Abraham make their way toward Sodom. As they walk, God's inner thoughts are revealed. He has plans for Sodom which He has not shared with Abraham. Rather than keep His plans from Abraham, God decides to share His thoughts about His intentions.

> **The way of the Lord is to do righteousness and justice.**

> *17 The LORD said, "Shall I hide from Abraham what I am about to do, 18seeing that Abraham shall become a great and mighty nation, and all the nations of the earth shall be blessed in him? 19No, for I have chosen him, that he may charge his children and his household after him to keep the way of the LORD by doing righteousness and justice; so that the LORD may bring about for Abraham what he has promised him." (**Gen 18:17-19**)*

After God recalls His promise to Abraham in *Genesis 12:1*, God explains *"the way of the LORD."* God wants Abraham to charge his children to keep that way. *The way of the Lord is to do righteousness and justice.* Through those activities God would fulfill His promise to Abraham.

God uses the word "righteousness" earlier with Abraham. When Abraham believes the promises of God, God responds and *"reckoned it to him as righteousness"* (**Gen 15:6**). The word *chashab*, translated "reckoned," also appears twice in **Genesis 50:20** as the word "intended." Joseph's brothers intended evil but God intended good. In these two passages it means to give something to somebody that they did not have on their own. God made Abraham a righteous man out of God's own righteousness in **Genesis 15** and now asks Abraham to charge his children to practice that righteousness which originated with God.

IN SODOM

God hears the outcry against Sodom and Gomorrah. Now He tells Abraham His plan to destroy the cities. Abraham bargains with God over the fate of Sodom, perhaps in part, because it was the home of his nephew, Lot (**Gen 19:29**), whose family is eventually spared. Abraham questions whether the wicked and the righteous should both be destroyed. God finally agrees that the presence of even ten righteous people would allow Him to spare the city. Apparently, just as Jeremiah could find no just person in Jerusalem over a thousand years later (**Jer 5:1**), the ten righteous people of Sodom were not forthcoming.

At first, God's conversation with Abraham about charging his children to follow the *"way of the LORD"* by practicing righteousness and justice seems at odds with the general direction of the passage. If God is on a mission to destroy these cities, why is He suddenly concerned with Abraham's parenting tasks? As God reveals His inner thoughts to Abraham, is He also saying something about what is important to Him?

Ezekiel tells us what is on God's mind when God talks to Abraham about Sodom. Ezekiel comes at least 1500 years after Abraham, but the prophet to the exiles in Babylonian captivity provides an inspired commentary on events in **Genesis 18–19**. Ezekiel is explaining to the exiles why God destroyed their homeland. Ezekiel often uses comparisons and stories to convey his message. In this instance, he treats North Israel and Judah as if they were two sisters. Then he compares the two sisters to a third sister, Sodom:

> ⁴⁶*Your elder sister is Samaria, who lived with her daughters to the north of you; and your younger sister, who lived to the south of*

*you, is **Sodom** with her daughters. ⁴⁷You not only followed their
ways, and acted according to their abominations; within a very little time you were more corrupt than they in all your ways. ⁴⁸As I
live, says the Lord GOD, your sister **Sodom** and her daughters have
not done as you and your daughters have done. ⁴⁹This was the
guilt of your sister **Sodom**: she and her daughters had pride,
excess of food, and prosperous ease, but did not aid the poor and
needy. (**Eze 16:46-49**)*

Ezekiel accuses Samaria and Judah of being like Sodom. What was
Sodom like? Sodom was filled with pride. They had plenty of food
and an affluent life, but they shared none of that prosperity with the
have-nots.

God visits Sodom because the people are so selfish and focused
on themselves that they do not treat others in a fair and kind way. In
short, they lack justice and righteousness. When the just and righteous God sees that the people in Sodom lack what He prizes, He
comes to visit. When He verifies that he cannot find even ten righteous people in these cities, He explodes into action.

Sodom and Gomorrah have jettisoned righteousness. They are so
into themselves that they toss out justice onto the streets of their city.
They trash what God treasures. They ignore what God pursues. They
treat lightly what God takes seriously. How far will God go? How
much will God risk? What action
will God take? God is not willing to
simply value justice and righteousness. He wants it practiced in the
human community. He wants it carried out in Sodom and Gomorrah.
So He comes to act.

> **God is not willing to simply value justice and righteousness. He wants it practiced.**

God debates within Himself about whether He should share His
agenda with Abraham. He decides to tell Abraham about His plans
because Abraham's task involves the same mission. The *"way of the
LORD"* on a mission is to ensure that justice and righteousness are
practiced in places like Sodom and Gomorrah. Abraham is to charge
his children with practicing those exact traits. God's visit does double
duty. He keeps Abraham at his task of raising up a great nation that
will be tutored in justice and righteousness, and He visits Sodom and
Gomorrah to do whatever it takes to establish justice and righteousness there.

God acts. God is a doer. God comes with a mission in mind. His delight in steadfast love, justice, and righteousness makes Him explode at what He sees and hears. Soon the cities lie in ruins. Justice and righteousness must prevail.

God is just and righteous. That is His way. He gives Abraham the task of charging his children and household with living in justice and righteousness. The outcry of the oppressed people in this unjust and unrighteous city prompts God to act. He and Abraham discuss how God could respond toward Sodom in a just and righteous way. God finally destroys Sodom and Gomorrah because they lack justice and righteousness.

Sodom becomes a symbol of wickedness in Scripture and even into contemporary western society. Of the 51 times the city is mentioned in the Bible, 21 occur in *Genesis*. Another concentration of references to Sodom comes in the prophets. They join Ezekiel to comment on the story in Genesis and see relevance for his own time.

In Jerusalem

Isaiah speaks on behalf of God to Jerusalem. The opening five chapters of this long prophetic book reflect the eighth century BC when God is unhappy with Jerusalem. Isaiah makes it clear why God is displeased and outlines the action God plans to take.

Isaiah uses language we have already encountered in our study of Hosea and Jeremiah: The people do not know God. They are less aware than animals. An ox knows its owner and a donkey finds its master's crib, but Israel does not know God (*Isa 1:3*). Because they do not know God, their community lacks justice and righteousness (note the bolded words):

> "How the faithful city has become a whore! She that was full of **justice, righteousness** lodged in her— but now murderers!" (*Isa 1:21*)

One might wonder if God in heaven is even aware of the injustice and lack of righteousness on the earth. *Psalm 82* describes God in heaven looking down at the earth. Often called an imprecatory psalm, this short poem records events that take place in the divine council where God holds court over those He charges with not taking care of the weak, fatherless, afflicted, destitute, and needy. God accuses them of dealing unjustly and without righteousness toward these people. The psalm indicates that those who are in charge of the poor are "gods." Jesus quotes this text in *John 10:34* to establish that men have been called gods before Him, and in the process, He argues that Scripture cannot be broken. The point of *Psalm 82* is that these gods who are charged with doing righteousness and justice have failed.

God announces their punishment. What is particularly striking about the text is that the concern for the poor is known and discussed in the divine council. God himself is so concerned with the vulnerable that He maintains surveillance on those charged with their care and personally addresses the issues when they fail. The reason God calls the heavenly council and disciplines those who failed the weak is because He is a God of justice and righteousness. The question rings true especially today: "Are we showing righteousness and justice to the marginalized of society?"

Isaiah opens the chapter by accusing the people of not knowing God. Like Hosea and Jeremiah, Isaiah again uses marital imagery to charge them with unfaithfulness. The city of Jerusalem is personified as an unfaithful woman. Once full of justice, the city is now empty of justice. Once a place where righteousness made its home, it is now the haunt of murderers. They do not practice justice and righteousness. Isaiah details how they lack justice and righteousness:

They oppress the people and do not take care of the orphan or widow (*1:17*).

They take bribes (*1:23*).

They abuse the vulnerable in court (*1:23*).

In their greed they accumulate houses and land (*5:8*).

While others suffer, they spend their time in self-indulgence (*5:11*).

They turn morality upside down, calling good "evil" and evil "good" (*5:20*).

They rob defenseless people of their rights (*5:23*).

Isaiah calls for righteousness and justice to be restored: *"Cease to do evil, learn to do good; seek justice, rescue the oppressed, defend the orphan, plead for the widow"* (*Isa 1:16b-17*). He demands the return of justice and righteousness (*Isa 1:27*). The people of Jerusalem must restore righteousness and justice because God desires those qualities:

*"But the L<small>ORD</small> of hosts is exalted by **justice**, and the Holy God shows himself holy by **righteousness**" (Isa 5:16).*

About the same time that Isaiah preached in Jerusalem, his contemporary Amos spoke to North Israel about the kind of nation God demanded. His book is filled with accusations of unrighteous behavior and unjust acts (cf. *Am 2:6-8; 4:1; 5:11-12; 8:4-6*) by the citizens and merchants of the community. Amos makes the nature of God's ideal community clear in the conclusion to His comments about their worship (note the bolded words):

> *²¹I hate, I despise your festivals, and I take no delight in your solemn assemblies. ²²Even though you offer me your burnt offerings and grain offerings, I will not accept them; and the offerings of well-being of your fatted animals I will not look upon. ²³Take away from me the noise of your songs; I will not listen to the melody of your harps. ²⁴But let **justice** roll down like waters, and **righteousness** like an ever-flowing stream. (Am 5:21-24)*

Many contemporary readers wonder why God rejects their offerings and songs and seek some methodological flaw in Israelite worship. Many a "worship war" among the Israelites would have been resolved if they had asked themselves about the heart God values rather than the songs they sang.

While there were clearly problems with their worship, the more fundamental issue was their lack of righteousness in the way they related to each other and their lack of justice in the courts and in their financial dealings. Amos knew, as Jeremiah would later verbalize, that God delights in righteousness and justice. When they are not practiced, no amount of worship can overshadow the inequities of society (**Shank, "Six Other Days," 95-117**).

In the midst of the detailed accusations of what is wrong in Jerusalem, Isaiah decides to use an example of other cities in the same situation. He reaches back nearly a thousand years with this parallel:

> *⁹If the L<small>ORD</small> of hosts had not left us a few survivors, we would have been like Sodom, and become like Gomorrah. ¹⁰Hear the word of the L<small>ORD</small>, you rulers of Sodom! Listen to the teaching of our God, you people of Gomorrah! (Isa 1:9-10)*

Isaiah compares Jerusalem to Sodom and Gomorrah! Not only will Jerusalem be destroyed like the two other cities, but the leaders lack justice and righteousness just as Sodom and Gomorrah did!

God finds the situation unacceptable. *He moves to action.* He refuses to accept their worship (*Isa 1:12-15*). God enters into judgment with the people and their leaders (*Isa 3:14*). He plans to strip the women of their extravagant clothes (*Isa 3:18-22*) and empty the store shelves of the luxury goods (*3:24*). Then, in dramatic language, God reveals His plan. Note the words I have bolded:

> ²⁵*I will turn my hand against you; I will smelt away your dross as with lye and remove all your alloy.* ²⁶*And I will restore your judges as at the first, and your counselors as at the beginning. Afterward you shall be called the city of **righteousness**, the faithful city.* ²⁷*Zion shall be redeemed by **justice**, and those in her who repent, by **righteousness**.* (*Isa 1:25-27*)

God intends for Jerusalem to be a place of righteousness and justice. He moves to ensure that reality. He turns against the people who walk its streets without righteousness and who treat their neighbors with injustice. He will purify the people who live there so that it will again be known as a place where righteousness is practiced and where people live with justice.

In the book of Hosea, God reveals His interior struggle with bringing such destruction. God struggles within Himself, almost at times deciding not to punish the people because of His compassion (*Hos 11:8-9*). Finally, Hosea describes the destruction in all its horror (*13:14-16*). The prophet roots the destruction in God's righteousness and justice:

> *Therefore I have hewn them by the prophets, I have killed them by the words of my mouth, and my **judgment** goes forth as the light.* (*Hos 6:5*)

> *Those who are wise understand these things; those who are discerning know them. For the ways of the LORD are **right**, and the upright walk in them, but transgressors stumble in them.* (*Hos 14:9*)

In *Hosea 6*, the word for justice is translated as "judgment." Just as light travels unhindered, so his judgment will be carried out on Samaria. The book concludes in *chapter 14* with the affirmation of God's righteousness. Those who seek God's way enjoy that righteousness, but those who do not—and clearly North Israel is in mind here—will stumble. The Israelites have not lived in righteousness. That caused them to stumble. God caused them to fall. God acts because of His justice and righteousness.

Isaiah's prophecy explains the role of a just and righteousness God. He zealously wants His people to be just and righteous. He

God zealously wants His people to be just and righteous.

sends His prophets to judge the people based on their practice of justice and righteousness. God finally acts to destroy Jerusalem because they lack those qualities. He destroys them because it is the just and righteous thing to do.

The God who delights in steadfast love, justice, and righteousness (*Jer 9:24*) seeks those qualities in His people because they are qualities of His own nature. Because they are such a deeply seated part of His divine being, His righteousness also prompts His acting out in justice or judgment on the people who rebel against His call for a righteous and just community. Because of God's concern for the vulnerable and brokenhearted, God acts, often in discipline and punishment of His own people.

God told Abraham about the *"way of the LORD,"* which was to practice justice and righteousness. God desires justice and righteousness, but also demands it on earth. When His sense of justice and righteousness is violated, God springs into action. He destroyed Sodom and Gomorrah. He refined the Judeans of Jerusalem. Unjust and unrighteous communities are those where the wealthy, powerful, and wise oppress the poor, take advantage of the orphan and widow, and live self-centered, self-sufficient, self-serving lives. God desires righteousness and justice. It is who He is. It is what He expects. It is how He evaluates. It is what He does. It is why He judges and punishes.

THE GOD WHO CALLS OTHERS TO JOIN HIM IN UPHOLDING RIGHTEOUSNESS AND JUSTICE

My friend Don exploded into action when he learned the whole story of that abandoned baby girl. He took her into his home. He hired lawyers. He went to court. He wrote checks. He pursued every means he could to see that she was treated kindly and fairly. Don became a champion for justice and righteousness for that little girl.

One day at lunch he told me what he had spent. I was dumbfounded. We did not know it at the time, but he was only halfway through the process of advocating for that child. I was amazed by his devotion and the avenues he pursued on her behalf. As we ate our lunch that day, I began to realize exactly how deeply this matter was rooted in his heart.

God desires justice and righteousness, but beyond that He has it in His heart to instill these qualities in the human community. As I reflect on Scripture, I see that He does that in at least three ways:

GOD UPHOLDS RIGHTEOUSNESS AND JUSTICE THROUGH THE KING

God instructs the monarchs in Israel to lead the nation in practicing righteousness and justice.[1] Two clear examples of this instruction come from two different times, the tenth and eighth centuries BC. The first passage is directed to Solomon while the second is an eighth-century prediction of a coming king.

Solomon's reign is taken up in *1 Kings*. After his coronation he receives a special blessing from God. Solomon makes this response (note the bolded words in these citations):

> And Solomon said, "You have shown great and steadfast love to your servant my father David, because he walked before you in faithfulness, in **righteousness**, and in uprightness of heart toward you; and you have kept for him this great and steadfast love, and have given him a son to sit on his throne today." (*1Kgs 3:6*)

This passage gathers up many of the qualities that we have studied. Solomon recognizes them as traits of his father, David. Apparently Solomon learned the lesson well. An outsider, the Queen of Sheba, visited Jerusalem and offered her analysis of Solomon's reign and the community he governed:

> Blessed be the LORD your God, who has delighted in you and set you on the throne of Israel! Because the LORD loved Israel forever, he has made you king to execute **justice** and **righteousness**. (*1Kgs 10:9*)

In the midst of the narrative about Solomon, this visiting dignitary uses some of the most significant theological words mentioned in the OT. She knows about blessing, the personal name of God, His love for Israel, and the task of kings to do justice and righteousness. God repeatedly called the kings to practice justice and righteousness. They

---

[1]Texts in the OT which call the kings to the practice of righteousness and justice include *Isa 32:1; Jer 22:3; Pss 72:1-2; 89:14; 97:2.*

were extensions of His desire that justice and righteousness be part of the human community. Kings were not merely to rule, but to make sure the community practiced righteousness. Kings not only oversaw government, but they were to oversee justice among their subjects.

> **Kings were not merely to rule, but to make sure the community practiced righteousness.**

One of the best known passages about monarchy from the entire OT comes from Isaiah (note the bolded words):

> ⁶*For a child has been born for us, a son given to us; authority rests upon his shoulders; and he is named Wonderful Counselor, Mighty God, Everlasting Father, Prince of Peace. ⁷His authority shall grow continually, and there shall be endless peace for the throne of David and his kingdom. He will establish and uphold it with **justice** and with **righteousness** from this time onward and forevermore. The zeal of the LORD of hosts will do this. (**Isa 9:6-7**)*

This text is one of the great Messianic passages in which Isaiah promises that a future king in Israel will uphold righteousness and justice in ways not previously done. The discussion earlier in this chapter about the lack of righteousness and justice in eighth-century Jerusalem suggests that the current kings had not been successful in establishing righteousness and justice. Now through Isaiah, God promises to send a king who will ensure that such standards are maintained.

God sees that His passion for just and right communities is taken up by kings. But they are not the only ones God assigns to that task.

GOD UPHOLDS RIGHTEOUSNESS AND JUSTICE THROUGH JESUS

The ideal king anticipated by Isaiah is ultimately Jesus, whose ministry was characterized by the practice of righteousness and justice. When Jesus begins His ministry, He cites *Isaiah 61* to describe His work:

> ¹⁶*When he came to Nazareth, where he had been brought up, he went to the synagogue on the sabbath day, as was his custom. He stood up to read, ¹⁷and the scroll of the prophet Isaiah was given to him. He unrolled the scroll and found the place where it was written:*
> ¹⁸ *"The Spirit of the Lord is upon me, because he has anointed me*

> *to bring good news to the poor.*
> *He has sent me to proclaim release to the captives*
> *and recovery of sight to the blind,*
> *to let the oppressed go free,*
> ¹⁹ *to proclaim the year of the Lord's favor." (Lk 4:16-19)*

This "job description" reflects the concerns of righteousness and justice which guide Jesus' ministry. He treats people with goodness and fairness, focusing especially on the vulnerable. Later John the Baptist sought verification that the predicted Messiah had come. Hearing about the work of Jesus, John sent two of his disciples to ask Jesus about His efforts:

> ²⁰*When the men had come to him, they said, "John the Baptist has sent us to you to ask, 'Are you the one who is to come, or are we to wait for another?'" ²¹Jesus had just then cured many people of diseases, plagues, and evil spirits, and had given sight to many who were blind. ²²And he answered them, "Go and tell John what you have seen and heard: the blind receive their sight, the lame walk, the lepers are cleansed, the deaf hear, the dead are raised, the poor have good news brought to them." (Lk 7:20-22)*

Jesus sent back the evidence, including a brief citation of the fulfillment of the call in *Isaiah 61* to *"preach good news to the poor,"* that His ministry to the poor showed He was the one John was expecting. The nature of Jesus' ministry was a clear fulfillment of the messianic promise in *Isaiah 9* of a king doing justice and rightness.

Jesus not only did justice and righteousness in His own ministry, but He called for His followers to take up the mission. Jesus' clearest teaching about justice and righteousness comes in his description of the Judgment Day (*Mt 25:31-46*). Humanity is divided into the sheep and goats based on their attention to the hungry, thirsty, stranger, naked, sick, and imprisoned. Those accepted into heaven were those who provided for these various vulnerable people, and the ones assigned to eternal punishment had neglected the needy. However, when both groups call for further explanation, Jesus claims close connection to the vulnerable people. When they served the vulnerable and needy, they served Jesus. Jesus concludes His teaching with a critical statement (note the bold):

> ⁴⁵*"Then he will answer them, 'Truly I tell you, just as you did not do it to one of the least of these, you did not do it to me.' ⁴⁶And these will go away into eternal punishment, but the **righteous** into eternal life." (Mt 25:45-46)*

Those who followed Jesus understood that He stood for righteousness. Those who cared for the hungry, thirsty, stranger, naked, sick, and imprisoned are called righteous. Jesus did not originate this teaching. He understood that God was a righteous God who called His people to live in righteous ways and to do righteous things. The kinds of activities discussed in this Judgment Day scene were the exact items ignored in Sodom, cast aside in Isaiah's Jerusalem, and absent in Ezekiel's audience. However, they are also characteristic of the coming King and ever-present in the ministry of Jesus Christ. Those who followed Jesus understood that He stood for righteousness, and they became advocates for the same concerns in the human community.

GOD UPHOLDS RIGHTEOUSNESS AND JUSTICE THROUGH THE CHURCH

The early Christians imitated Jesus' practice of justice and righteousness (**Shank, "Justice and Righteousness," 44-51**). When Jewish people from distant lands (see the list of home nations in *Acts 2:5-11*) came to Jerusalem for the Pentecost celebration, many became Christians and stayed on in Jerusalem to learn more about the faith (*Acts 2:41-47*). The longer they stayed, the greater their physical needs. The early church responded to the extent that *"there was not a needy person among them"* (*Acts 4:34*), and when some were overlooked the leaders quickly closed the gap (*Acts 6:1-7*). The practice of the early church rises to God's desire for justice and righteousness. The early Christians behave in a just and righteous manner because they understand what righteous and just people did and likely knew that it was all rooted in a God who delights in justice and righteousness.

About 15 years after the establishment of the church, James calls for the early congregations to take care of the needy and the poor (*Jas 1:26–2:7; 5:1-5*). James describes people acting in a righteous and just way.

Another 15 years or so after James, Paul takes up a special contribution for the Christians suffering from famine (*Rom 15:22-29; 1Cor 16:1-3; 2Cor 8:1–9:15*). These cases of the early Christians taking care of the poor and vulnerable are examples of Christians doing what Jesus did. They were practicing righteousness and justice in their congregations, in their communities, and among the brotherhood just as Jesus had practiced righteousness and justice. They were living out in their lives the very qualities rooted in the heart of God. Just as God had revealed to Abraham and just as Jeremiah had told the people of seventh-century Jerusalem, God was a God of righteousness and justice.

> **The early Christians were living out in their lives the very qualities rooted in the heart of God.**

Job was among those who understood the need to practice righteousness and justice in life. In one of the speeches in which Job defends his life and outlines his practices, Job claims (note the bolded words):

> [14]*I put **on righteousness**, and it clothed me; my **justice** was like a robe and a turban. [15]I was eyes to the blind, and feet to the lame. (**Job 29:14-15**)*

Job claims to practice righteousness and justice by citing specific situations that he addressed. In **Job 31**, he offers a description of what a righteous man does, just as **Proverbs 31** describes the life of a righteous woman. In Job's self-description he tells of his care for the poor and the vulnerable around him.

CONCLUSION

For two chapters we have dwelt on what delights the heart of God. *Jeremiah 9* shows that steadfast love, justice, and righteousness are at the core of God's heart. It is who He is, what He delights in, what we encounter when we know Him, and what we experience when we understand Him.

In this chapter we explored how God acts with justice and righteousness. The two qualities are paired throughout the Bible. Because God is just and right, He acts with those qualities. He acts by setting justice and righteousness as standards for His followers. He acts by hearing the cries of those lacking justice and righteousness. When those unjust and unrighteous communities fail to make corrections, God acts. Out of His own justice and righteousness, He moves to discipline and punish. God advocates for justice and righteousness not just by coming Himself, but also by charging the kings, the Messiah, and the church to join Him in the cause. All of the implications of justice and righteousness are rooted in one place, come from one source, derive from one holy fire: God is a just and righteous God. It is His delight.

I remember the Sunday our congregation celebrated with Don and his family. The adoption was final. The long struggle was over. A child abandoned on a piece of asphalt now had a loving home. As we praised God for all the good He and His people had done, I could not help but think that I was seeing the *"way of the LORD."* I witnessed the practice of justice. What had been terribly unfair and wrong was now corrected. This young girl was testimony to the righteousness of God. I was thankful not only that I served a just and righteous God, but that in His heart He had a passion for sending people to right the world's wrongs.

I remember thinking, God must be smiling.

WHAT DO YOU SAY?

1. Who stands out as a "doer of the word" in your life?

2. What causes God to act:

   a. in Sodom and Gomorrah?

   b. in Jerusalem?

3. The author says "unjust and unrighteous communities are those where the wealthy, powerful, and wise oppress the poor, take advantage of the orphan and widow, and live self-centered, self-sufficient, and self-serving lives." Would the community you live in be considered unjust and unrighteous? Why or why not?

4. In His teaching about justice and righteousness, Jesus gives criteria that will be used on the Judgment Day. On a scale of 1-10 (1 being not doing at all and 10 being fully responding) put an "x" where you believe your church is responding in each area. Put an "o" on how you are doing personally in each area.

   Feeding the hungry 1 10

   Water to thirsty   1 10

   Taking in stranger   1 10

   Clothing the naked 1 10

   Looking after sick   1 10

   Visiting prisoner   1 10

5. God desires for Christians to respond to people when there are tragedies, accidents, illness, and financial problems. Think of that kind of recent event in your sphere of influence. How can you act to respond to those problems? Write a prayer asking God to help you know how to respond with righteousness and justice.

CHAPTER FOURTEEN

VIOLENCE:
GOD AND THE SWORD

Begin your study of this chapter by reading *1 Samuel 15*.

One day between classes at the University of Wisconsin at Milwaukee I talked with another student about God. Despite a religious childhood, he was no longer a believer. He had one simple reason: He could not serve a God who wielded a sword. He pointed to the God who prompted violence in Scripture as the crucial evidence that God was not good. He concluded, "I can't serve a God who kills people."

That was my first real encounter with the common reaction to God and the sword. Our conversation in the student union at UWM drove me back into a deeper study of Scripture. What I found helped me to understand more clearly the nature of our complex God. First, I learned that we cannot say God is not violent. He is. But, secondly, I discovered how His use of the sword grows out of who He is.

THE GOD OF THE SWORD

The Bible associates God with punishment and discipline. In the OT, one of God's first statements to Adam and Eve is the warning that the day they eat of the tree of the knowledge of good and evil they will die. Barely six chapters into the Bible, God orders and carries out the near annihilation of humankind in the flood. By *Genesis 18*, He

God's use of the sword grows out of who He is.

personally visits earth to arrange for the utter destruction of two cities, Sodom and Gomorrah. After the Israelites cross the Red Sea, in their victory song they sing, *"the LORD is a warrior"* (*Ex 15:3*). According to Joshua, God tears the land of Palestine away from its inhabitants and aids Israel in a violent conquest of the territory. Beginning in *1 Samuel 1:3* God is often called the LORD of Hosts, which means "one who leads an army." Throughout the reigns of the kings of Israel God regularly orders and assists with violent wars (e.g., *2Chr 17–18*). The prophets make it clear that God uses the wicked Assyrians to obliterate North Israel, that God calls the Babylonians to destroy Jerusalem, and that God raises up the Persians to annihilate the Babylonians. In the prophetic oracles against the nations, including *Amos 1–2* and *Jeremiah 46–51*, God regularly orchestrates war.

Additionally, the OT frequently associates God's heart with anger and vengeance:

> *For the day of vengeance was in my heart,*
>   *and the year for my redeeming work had come.*
> *(Isa 63:4)*

> *The anger of the LORD will not turn back*
>   *until he has executed and accomplished*
>   *the intents of his mind.*
> *In the latter days you will understand it clearly.*
> *(Jer 23:20)*

> *How can I give you up, Ephraim?*
>   *How can I hand you over, O Israel?*
> *How can I make you like Admah?*
>   *How can I treat you like Zeboiim?*
> *My heart recoils within me;*
>   *my compassion grows warm and tender. (Hos 11:8)*

In the first text Isaiah attributes vengeance to God's heart. The word for heart is translated as "mind" in Jeremiah, where it is associated with anger. In Hosea, as God weighs the potential destruction of North Israel, His heart fills with compassion, but it is not enough to prevent Him from allowing the city to be destroyed (*Hosea 13*).

References to the wrath and punishment of God continue unabated into the NT. Jesus speaks frequently and vividly about the coming punishment of God in a place called hell. According to Jesus' own words, the Son of man will send angels to collect the evildoers to send them to the *"furnace of fire, where there will be weeping and gnashing of teeth"* (*Mt 13:42*).[1] Jesus

Jesus speaks frequently and vividly about the coming punishment of God.

also makes it clear that it was the will of God, His Father, that He suffer brutal death by crucifixion (*Mt 26:36-46*). Although generally understood metaphorically, Jesus gives the violent instruction, *"If*

> Jesus engages in violence in the temple though He does not harm any people. At the same time, He tells us to love our enemies. How do we harmonize these two views of Jesus? This chapter takes up that kind of question.

your right eye causes you to sin, tear it out and throw it away" (*Mt 5:29*). The cleansing of the temple is the only act of personal violence associated with Jesus, though nobody gets hurt (*Mt 21:12*). Great fear seizes the early church when Ananias and Sapphira fall down dead during a ministry project. Peter says the couple *"put the Spirit of the Lord to the test"* (*Acts 5:9*).

Colossians 3:6 is one of several NT texts that refer to the wrath of God. Revelation reports that God's plan for the end times includes massive violence (*Rev 18:21; 20:7-10*). God and violence cannot be easily separated in Scripture.

The punishment and violence of God seem at odds with the love of God. For example, these two texts seem to go in opposite directions:

> For God so loved the world that he gave his only Son, so that everyone who believes in him may not perish but may have eternal life. (*Jn 3:16*)

> Beloved, never avenge yourselves, but leave room for the wrath of God; for it is written, "Vengeance is mine, I will repay, says the Lord." (*Rom 12:19*)[2]

Both NT passages refer to God. One cites His love for all the world. The other refers to His wrath. Earlier chapters explore how God's love

---

[1] All seven biblical occurrences of *"weeping and gnashing of teeth"* are associated with Jesus: *Mt 8:12; 13:42,50; 22:13; 24:51; 25:30; Lk 13:28*.
[2] God claims the sole right to vengeance. Although we do well to imitate many qualities of God, there are some that we cannot imitate (we cannot forgive sins or raise the dead) and others that we are forbidden to imitate (such as vengeance).

for the whole world lies at the core of His being. On the surface, love seems inconsistent with wrath and vengeance, yet three times in Scripture (*Deu 32:35; Rom 12:19; Heb 10:30*), God claims the right to vengeance. Many people sense a logical inconsistency in a being who

God and violence cannot be easily separated in Scripture.

can on one hand claim to love all the world, to the point of sacrificing His Son, yet still insist on His right to take vengeance. One of God's Ten Commandments is *"You shall not kill"* (*Ex 20:13*).[3] Yet the God who gives that command not to kill is praised with the line *"The LORD is a warrior"* after killing an Egyptian army (*Ex 15:3*). God prohibits humans from killing each other, but God kills humans Himself. The two texts raise the question of why God is permitted to kill and humans are not.

Many Christians follow a "just war" theology, arguing that in certain circumstances it is the obligation of civilized people to use violence to stop violence. Other Christians take a "pacifist" position, making a case against the state use of violence. Camp (**95-127**) and Hays (**317-346**) provide helpful discussions of this issue.

The biblical material clearly associates God with punishment and violence. Rather than seeking to explain away this link, I propose that the violence of God arises out of His inner character and that it is the logical end of His patience, justice, and steadfast love. To establish this case, the chapter will take up one of the most violent actions ever commanded by God in order to make sense of why God is associated with punishment, vengeance, and violence. Although the chapter will concentrate on only this one case, it will suggest that the explanations that apply here are also valid at other times when God calls for punishment and violence. We look at the attempt to annihilate the Amalekites, one of the most violent God-inspired scenes in the Bible, to show that more than violence is at work. The violence results from God's character and in the end assures us of the patience, justice, and love of God.

---

[3]The quotation from *Ex 20:13* is from the RSV. More recent translations including the NIV and NRSV render, *"You shall not murder."*

THE BIBLE'S MOST VIOLENT EVENT

First Samuel 15 may be the most violent and gruesome chapter in the entire Bible. It opens with the prophet Samuel giving Saul directions from God to *"punish the Amalekites"* in a military attack in which God commands, *"Utterly destroy all that they have; do not spare them, but kill both man and woman, child and infant, ox and sheep, camel and donkey"* (*1Sa 15:3*). The Hebrew word for "utterly destroy" is *cherem*, used 52 times in the OT for the "ban," or the complete destruction of a people.[4] The instructions to Saul are clear: The ban includes not just the Amalekite army but the civilians, and not just the adults but the children, and not just the people but all their livestock. By the end of the chapter, Saul has only partially carried out the command, and among those he excluded from the ban is the Amalekite king, Agag. Since Saul has not completed God's instruction, Samuel moves to carry out God's command. When Agag is brought before Samuel, the prophet *"hewed Agag to pieces before the LORD in Gilgal"* (*1Sa 15:33*). Few chapters in the Bible contain as much violence as this one, from the opening prospect of God ordering the death of men, women, and babies to the closing scene of Samuel brutally killing Agag where he stood.

Reading only *1 Samuel 15* in isolation from the rest of the Bible raises questions about the justice and appropriateness of God's violent and destructive behavior, but when the larger biblical picture is considered,

> **When the larger picture is considered, events can be understood in a completely different way.**

the events of *1 Samuel 15* can be understood in a completely different way. The broader context—first the role of Saul and then the history of the Amalekite people—allows a fuller theological understanding of these events.

---

[4]*Cherem* appears in verbal form in *Ex 22:20; Lev 21:18; 27:28f; Num 21:2f.; Deu 2:34; 3:6; 7:2; 13:15; 20:17; Josh 2:10; 6:18,21; 8:26; 10:1,28,35,37,39f.; 11:11f.,20f.; Jdg 1:17; 21:11; 1Sa 15:3,8f,15,18,20; 1Kgs 9:21; 2Kgs 19:11; 1Chr 4:41; 2Chr 20:23; 32:14; Ezra 10:8; Isa 11:15; 34:2; 37:11; Jer 25:9; 50:21,26; 51:3; Dan 11:44; Mic 4:13*. A noun form of the word appears another 38 times.

Kill Them All!

Events in this section of *1 Samuel* are arranged around the obedience and disobedience of Saul. *First Samuel 11–13* chronicles the obedience of Saul. In *1 Samuel 13*, however, his character changes. Instead of being obedient to God, he becomes disobedient. Saul, unwilling to obey Samuel's command to wait, intrudes into the priestly office (*1 Samuel 13*), and then commits *"a very rash act"* (*1Sa 14:24*) with a selfish vow. The next test of Saul's willingness to obey comes with the command to *"utterly destroy"* the Amalekites. Saul assembles an army of 210,000 soldiers, sends word to the innocent Kenites to leave the Amalekite city (the Kenites joined the Amalekites in *Jdg 1:16*), and then attacks, putting everyone to the sword except King Agag and the prize livestock. When Samuel hears that Saul only partially obeyed, he cries out all night to God before meeting Saul the next day. Saul believes he has obeyed and even bettered God's command by bringing back animals to offer as sacrifices. Samuel announces that since Saul has not obeyed God, he has lost the crown.

Most contemporary readers of the text likely agree with Saul, not with Samuel. Saul's actions seem to improve on God's extreme command. Saul kept the spirit of God's command and additionally sought the means to offer worship to God. When Samuel presses Saul to see his sin, the king repents, but Samuel will not permit Saul to continue to rule. The chapter ends with Saul worshiping and Samuel cutting up Agag. Often readers of this text do not advance beyond the stage of disagreeing with it.

Samuel states the case against Saul:

> ²²And Samuel said,
>> "Has the LORD as great delight in burnt offerings and
>>> sacrifices,
>>>> as in obeying the voice of the LORD?
>> Surely, to obey is better than sacrifice,
>>> and to heed than the fat of rams.
> ²³ For rebellion is no less a sin than divination,
>> and stubbornness is like iniquity and idolatry.
> Because you have rejected the word of the LORD,
> he has also rejected you from being king." (*1Sa 15:22-23*)

Samuel does not reject the sacrificial system of worship, but stresses obedience. He judges Saul's actions as rebellious and stubborn. He concludes with the surprising accusation that Saul has *"rejected the word of the LORD."* Such severe accusations against Saul suggest that this text cannot be easily dismissed and that there is more happening in these events than

The events of this chapter carry considerable theological weight.

commonly thought. The essence of the case, according to *1 Samuel 15*, goes back to the initial command that Saul attack the Amalekites. Samuel tells Saul that the reason for the punishment of the Amalekites is *"for what they did in opposing the Israelites, when they came out of Egypt" (1Sa 15:2)*. Samuel points to an historical event that we shall return to shortly.

The events of this chapter carry considerable theological weight. Saul, whose intentions are to offer sacrifice to God, is accused of disobedience. That disobedience costs him his kingship. Together these events underline that God's plan to utterly destroy the Amalekites cannot be minimized. God wanted it done by His representative— the king—and when it was not done according to His directions, the repercussions for Saul were severe. We must not diminish the significance of these events.

While the events during Saul's reign might be dated about 1020 BC,[5] the larger context for what unfolds in *1 Samuel 15* begins in the events of *Exodus 17* with the role of the Amalekites.

CENTURIES OF VIOLENCE

The story of the Amalekite people can be divided into two historical periods: Amalekite history prior to the events in *1 Samuel 15* and their history after *1 Samuel 15*.

The Amalekites appear in the Bible long before Saul meets Agag. They emerge as a warlike people during Abraham's time in *Genesis 14:7*, even though in other passages they appear to be descendants of Esau (*Gen 36:12,16; 1Chr 1:36*).

Their first connection with Israel comes in the events of *Exodus 17*. After over 400 years of slavery, Moses leads Israel out of bondage by crossing the Red Sea (*Exodus 14–15*) and moving into the wilderness, where they face food and water shortages as well as enemies (*Exodus 16–17*). At Rephidim, Amalek attacks Israel and prevails until Moses

Chapter 14
God and the Sword

---

[5]This study uses the dates of Bright (**487-495**).

stands on top of the hill with his hands raised. The battle advantage changes based on whether Moses' hands are still raised. The final victory goes to Israel (*Ex 17:8-13*). These events might be dated to about 1280 BC.[6]

After the battle report, an unexpected passage appears:

> [14]Then the LORD said to Moses, "Write this as a reminder in a book and recite it in the hearing of Joshua: I will utterly blot out the remembrance of Amalek from under heaven." [15]And Moses built an altar and called it, The LORD is my banner. [16]He said, "A hand upon the banner of the LORD. The LORD will have war with Amalek from generation to generation." (*Ex 17:14-16*)

God tells Moses to record these events along with God's plans to annihilate the Amalekite people at some point in the future. The passage preserves one of the earliest references to writing, especially the writing of Scripture. Interestingly, one of the first references to Scripture entails the removal of the Amalekites.[7] God instructs Moses to build and name an altar. The reference to the banner suggests that when Moses' arms were held up, it was a signal (in the sense of a banner announcing something) of God's work in the battle. When Moses lifted his hands, it meant that the battle outcome depended on God. The passage also points to multigenerational struggles between God and the Amalekites.

Something is going on between God and the Amalekites that bears further investigation.

This passage, like the one in *1 Samuel 15*, suggests that something is going on between God and the Amalekites that bears further investigation both in terms of the nature of the Amalekite people and their history.

Violence in the Past

A study of the biblical references to the Amalekites suggests these three qualities:

First, the Amalekites *infiltrate* the land of Israel. In *Exodus 17:8* they live in the desert, but by *Numbers 13:29* they dwell in the Negev that God gave to Israel. By *Numbers 14:25* they reside in the rich valleys

---

[6]The chronology of the Exodus is one of the most difficult of dating issues in the entire Bible. For this date, see Bright (**490-491**).

[7]The word *machah* (to blot out) is used here instead of *cherem* (to ban or utterly destroy).

from which they attack Israel (*Num 14:43-45*), and by *Judges 12:15* they migrate to the hill country, the traditional stronghold of Israel in the land of Canaan. In all the subsequent references to Amalek, its people live in Israel proper.

Second, the Amalekites are *marauders*. They raid and plunder. *Genesis 14:7* notes they were people of war in the time of Abraham. According to *Judges 3:13* they form a coalition with the Moabites and Ammonites to raid Israel, resulting in the capture of Jericho. In *Judges 6–7* they join the Midianites in attacking farmers seeding the fields. The Israelites flee to the hills and hide in caves. The Amalekites destroy the Israelite crops, kill their livestock, and lay waste to the land. *Judges 10:12* reports on another Amalekite attack on Israel. Most of these events took place after the battle in *Exodus 17* and before the command to Saul in *1 Samuel 15*, and perhaps characterize the generations of war between God and the Amalekites.

Third, the Amalekites *prey on the weak*. Forty years after the Battle of Rephidim in *Exodus 17*, Moses recalls the earlier events in fuller detail:

> Remember what Amalek did to you on your journey out of Egypt, [18]how he attacked you on the way, when you were faint and weary, and struck down all who lagged behind you; he did not fear God. [19]Therefore when the LORD your God has given you rest from all your enemies on every hand, in the land that the LORD your God is giving you as an inheritance to possess, you shall blot out the remembrance of Amalek from under heaven; do not forget. (*Deu 25:17-19*)

Moses points to three crucial qualities of the Amalekites.

a. *They attack others at their point of weakness*. Moses led a group of exslaves out of Egypt, not an army. They were refugees fleeing oppression, not an army equipped for war.

b. *They also attack the defenseless*. Moses knew that the first Amalekite attacks on Israel were not on the available Israelite military forces but on those Israelites who lagged behind. Moses does not indicate who lagged behind, but generally those who fall behind in such refugee movements are the sick, infirm, elderly, and those who care for such people. The nation's animals may also have followed the main body of refugees. Amalek attacks Israel when they are fleeing the slavery of Egypt. All of this was also apparent to Samuel, who, just before hewing Agag, tells the doomed king: *"As your sword has made women childless, so your mother shall be childless among women"* (**1 Sam 15:33**). Agag, Saul's contemporary, had continued the Amalekite trait of preying on the weak.

c. Finally, *Amalek does not fear God*. Other nations in the time of Moses feared God. Rahab tells how the report of God's work among the Israelites put fear in the hearts of the people of Jericho (**Josh 2:8-11**), but either Amalek had not heard these events or had a different response. Another wilderness tribe, the Midianites, know of God's work in bringing Israel out of Egypt and cast their lot with Israel (**Ex 18:1-12**). Amalek did not fear God like the Midianites.

The character of the Amalekites from the time of Abraham in **Genesis 14** until the days of Saul in **1 Samuel 15** was well-established. They raided what was not theirs, infiltrated the lands of others, and victimized the weak. God's command for Saul to utterly destroy the Amalekites was not made in a vacuum, but was the result of generations of war between these people and God. It was not only the long years of struggle that prompted God's action, but the ignoble nature of the Amalekite people that called for the end of their preying on other peoples.

> **God's command to destroy the Amalekites was not made in a vacuum.**

God finally took action against the Amalekites. The events at Rephidim took place around 1280 BC. God ordered their destruction in about 1020 BC. Based on these dates, the Amalekite scourge had lasted about 260 years after the events at Rephidim. The Amalekites repeatedly showed themselves to be a nation that had no desire to follow God. God waited those 260 years perhaps hoping the people would change, but by the time of Saul God apparently was willing to wait no longer.

First Samuel 15:9 reports that Saul did not utterly destroy the Amalekites. Even though a reading of this passage suggests that all the Amalekites were dead by the end of the chapter, they were not. Subsequent history indicates that Saul failed to eradicate the Amalekite scourge.

Violence in the Future

The Amalekites show remarkable tenacity throughout history. They are destroyed in **Genesis 14:7**, but reappear in **Exodus 17**. In **Exodus 17:13** they are defeated, but are back in *Numbers 14:25*. The Ephraimite army fights Amalek in *Judges 5:14* (KJV), but the Amalekites return in *Judges 6:3*. Gideon destroys them in *Judges 7:12-25*, but they resurface in *1 Samuel 14:48*.

Saul's ill-fated attack on Amalek appears to end their existence, but in *1 Samuel 27:8-9* David raided Amalekite settlements, indicating that the nation survives the purge of Saul. Later, while David's army is away, the Amalekites invade David's adopted hometown of Ziklag, loot it, burn the town, and take the women and children captive (*1Sa 30:1-6*). David pursues the Amalekites, who are eating, drinking, and dancing with their loot until David attacks. Yet even then 400 Amalekite warriors escape (*1Sa 30:17*).

In the days after Saul's failure in *1 Samuel 15* with the Amalekites, he continues to struggle as king, finally losing a crucial battle against the Philistines on Mount Gilboa. In *2 Samuel 1:1-16*, an Amalekite warrior confesses to David that he had killed Saul.[8] God intends to use Saul to eradicate the Amalekite scourge from the earth, but the king does not follow orders. Saul dies by an Amalekite sword.

Late in his reign, David continues to fight the Amalekites in *2 Samuel 8:12* (paralleled in *1Chr 18:11*). The Amalekites persist in marauding even in the time of Hezekiah, according to *1 Chronicles 4:41-43*.

Some of the last recorded events in the OT occur in the book of *Esther* during the Persian period in about 455 BC. The book of *Esther* tells of the conflict between the Jewish people and a Persian leader "Haman son of Hammedatha the Agagite" (*Est 3:1,10; 8:3,5; 9:24*). Assuming, as many scholars do, that Haman is a distant descendant of Agag of the Amalekites God intended to destroy in *1 Samuel 15*, then the final story in the OT about the Jews concerns yet another cowardly, aggressive act by this violent group of people.[9]

From Saul's failure to deal with the Amalekites in about 1020 BC, the Amalekites continue their marauding ways until the late eighth-century days of Hezekiah (715–686/87 BC) and perhaps even into the Persian times of Esther (455 BC). No wonder *Psalm 83:7* lists the Amalekites as one of the persistent enemies of God and His people.

---

[8]See the latest commentaries for a discussion of the report of Saul's suicide attempt in *1 Samuel 31* and the Amalekite confession of Saul's murder in *2 Samuel 1*.

[9]Not all Bible scholars connect this Agag with the Amalekites. See the latest commentaries.

From the time of their first attack on Israel at Rephidim (1280 BC) until the days of Esther (455 BC), the Amalekites terrorized their world for over 800 years. Even if the years are calculated only to the time of Hezekiah, the Amalekites clearly intimidated innocent peoples for around 600 years.

God's call for the utter destruction of the Amalekites and His willingness to command, or at least permit, His prophet Samuel to brutally hew Agag to pieces must be understood against the role the Amalekites played in biblical history. We can now reflect theologically on God's seriousness about their extermination expressed in the *1 Samuel 15* passage and God's response to the character and history of the Amalekite people.

THE SWORD OF GOD

I propose that the punishment and violence of God arise out of His inner character and that it is associated with His patience, justice, and steadfast love. No biblical passage reflects on the theology behind God's actions toward the Amalekites. In laying the qualities identified in this book as part of God's inner being alongside His actions with regard to the Amalekites, we can at least show that His call for their violent destruction is consistent with and the natural implication of who He is.

GOD'S PUNISHMENT
IS SLOW IN COMING

In God's self-disclosure in *Exodus 34*, God reveals that He is slow to anger. That revelation clarified two cases of God's anger in the story of the golden calf. God does get angry, but either His anger is slow in coming or, once it arrives, it does not last long. God's anger is only mentioned once in connection with the Amalekites when Samuel speaks to Saul after being conjured up by the medium of Endor (*1Sa 28:18*).

However, God's dealing with the Amalekites is consistent with His claim to be slow to anger. As mentioned earlier, from God's initial decision to punish the Amalekites in 1280 BC until the command is given to Saul in about 1020 BC, about 260 years pass. Despite the call for *"utter destruction"* and the savage treatment of Agag, God did not act quickly or rashly, and in no sense was He quick to be angry. Nor did God's anger burn long against the Amalekites. After commanding Saul to exterminate this group of people, God never repeats the command. Indeed, it comes as a surprise that the Amal-

> **God did not act quickly or rashly, nor was He quick to be angry.**

ekites persistently reappear in the OT, continuing their marauding ways. The reason God did not repeat the extermination command is not given, but God's actions toward the Amalekites are consistent with this self-disclosed trait of being slow to anger.

Although God is slow to anger, He eventually becomes angry and takes action. God's willingness to visit the iniquity of the fathers on succeeding generations, which appears as the final aspect of God in *Exodus 34*, allows God to vent His anger at wickedness. The comment at the end of the Rephidim passage that notes, *"The LORD will have war with Amalek from generation to generation"* (*Ex 17:16*), is consistent with this concluding action of God. Whether *"visiting the iniquity"* is paralleled by *"have war with"* might be debated, but clearly God takes a multiyear approach in dealing with those who oppose Him.

The reason for God's slowness of anger and His multiyear attention to those who oppose Him is not stated either in *Exodus 34* or in the Amalekite passages. However, a parallel case provides some insight into why God takes so many years to deal with wickedness.

This case involves the nations that God dispossesses from the land of Canaan in the book of *Joshua*. The violence God commands and permits against the people who occupied Canaan often raises questions about the nature of God. How could God take the land from the peoples who lived there and give it to another group of people? Why does God plan and permit the violent takeover of the land? Why does God call for the utter destruction (*cherem*) of cities such as Jericho?

God first speaks of giving the land of Canaan to other people when He makes His promises to Abraham in *Genesis 12:1-7*. That promise is repeated throughout the book. In one of those repetitions, God explains the reason behind His willingness to take the land from its occupants and give it to Israel:

> [13]Then the LORD said to Abram, "Know this for certain, that your offspring shall be aliens in a land that is not theirs, and shall be slaves there, and they shall be oppressed for four hundred years; [14]but I will bring judgment on the nation that they serve, and after-

> ward they shall come out with great possessions. ¹⁵As for yourself, you shall go to your ancestors in peace; you shall be buried in a good old age. ¹⁶And they shall come back here in the fourth generation; for the iniquity of the Amorites is not yet complete."
>
> *(Gen 15:13-16)*

The passage refers first to the years of Egyptian bondage, then to Abram's death, and finally to the conquest of the land chronicled in **Joshua**. This passage in Genesis calls the current owners of the land by the generic term "Amorites." They will be dispossessed. By that time *"the iniquity of the Amorites"* will be complete, meaning in Abram's time God was not yet willing to act against their iniquity.

There is no reference in this **Genesis 15** passage to the "slow to anger" nature of God or to His nature of visiting the iniquity of the fathers to the third or fourth generation, but the current text is consistent with God's self-revelation in **Exodus 34**. God is willing to wait four generations before addressing the iniquity of the Amorite people. In the time of Joshua, God directs and aids His people in the Amorites' destruction. That destruction is the long-delayed response to the growing iniquity of the Amorite people in Abram's time.

God's slowness to anger implies that He eventually becomes angry and takes action. God's intent to visit the iniquity of the fathers to succeeding generations, which appears as an action of God in **Exodus 34**, implies that He will eventually punish. The call for the utter destruction of the Amorite citizens of Jericho often appalls the reader; in the bigger picture of God's history with these people and in light of God's self-disclosure in **Exodus 34**, such a call is exactly what we would expect.

> **God's slowness to anger implies that He eventually becomes angry and takes action.**

GOD'S PUNISHMENT RESPONDS TO INJUSTICE

God delights in justice (*Jer 9:24*) and treats Israel with justice (*Hos 2:19-20*). Justice calls for the righting of wrongs, for addressing evil, for treating people with fairness and equity. Linked with righteousness, it describes the kind of holistic relationships God seeks between Himself and the people and among the people themselves. None of the texts associated with the Amalekites raise the issue of justice and righteousness.

However, God's just nature is consistent with His actions toward the Amalekites, and His call for their utter destruction is the logical implication of His justice. The Amalekites are marauders who prey on weak people. They persistently play this role throughout the OT. Fifteen OT passages speak of their warlike nature, their attacks on the defenseless, their raiding villages, and their plots to take innocent lives.

God's call for the utter destruction of the Amalekite people is consistent with His just nature. God's response to the Amalekites is announced after the first offense but is not carried out until after multiple such offenses. God's justice works in league with His slowness to anger and His willingness to visit the iniquity upon the third and fourth generation.

God's call for the destruction of the Amalekite people included women and children. As mentioned earlier, the word used to describe this demand is *cherem*. No passage about *cherem* mentions the

> **God's justice works in league with His slowness to anger.**

justice of God, but the process of *cherem* is consistent with God's justice. He seeks a world of equity and fairness. He will take measures necessary to create that kind of world. The Amalekite people consistently create the opposite kind of world. The taking of their lives serves the sacred purpose of creating a fairer and more equitable world. God sees fit to visit the iniquity of the Amalekite fathers on the succeeding generations. In the case of the Amalekites, He called for the extermination of the people in order to create a more fair and just society for other peoples. Wickedness grows like a cancer, which means that at some point the cancer and the healthy tissue around it must be removed for the health of the whole person. In the same way, the Amalekites, including the malignant adults and the healthy children, had to be removed for the well being of the larger human society. Niditch (**50**), in a study on war in the OT, argues that *cherem* underscores the value of the lives lost in the ban. The innocent ones die to allow a better world for those who follow.

A God of justice would be expected to execute actions such as the one against the Amalekites. God could not be a just God and at the same time ignore the issue of Amalek's injustice. Humans typically

> **God could not be a just God if He ignored Amalek's injustice.**

demand immediate justice. God's slowness to anger and intent to visit iniquity on the third and fourth generation set a different timetable. One of the most common human cries against God is the perception that He is too tolerant of injustices. It may be the ultimate human inconsistency to criticize God for not acting justly with regard to an injustice *we* have received and then criticize God for acting justly in the case of the people oppressed by the Amalekites.

God calls for the utter destruction of the Amalekites. As noted earlier, when it is not completed, God never calls for the utter destruction of the Amalekites again. No passage gives theological explanation for this occurrence. It might imply that the destruction Saul and Samuel accomplished satisfied God's justice. It could also imply that God's justice can be satisfied short of utter destruction. Perhaps Saul's removal as king of Israel helped satisfy the justice of God in this case.

God's justice and righteousness are not mentioned in the Amalekite passages, but God's actions toward this marauding people are consistent with a just God, and the call for their utter destruction is a clear implication of how a just God might act.

GOD'S PUNISHMENT
DISCIPLINES OUT OF LOVE

God's self-disclosure in *Exodus 34* twice reveals His steadfast love, both in terms of its depth toward any one person and its availability to many people. *Hosea 6:6, Micah 7:18, Jeremiah 9:24,* and *Matthew 9:13 and 12:7* all claim that God desires or delights in steadfast love. God's steadfast love is not mentioned in any of the texts about the Amalekites, but God's response to the Amalekites is consistent with His steadfast love, and His *chesed* toward them can explain some aspects of His response to their marauding.

Micah 7:18 raises an important issue with regard to God's response to the Amalekites. Micah writes that God *"delights in showing clemency [chesed]."* Micah is not referring specifically to the Amalekites, but God's actions toward them are consistent with Micah's description of God. Indeed, many of the times when God's steadfast love is considered, the context is one of openness to and a call for repentance. God sends Hosea to North Israel with a view toward winning them back. God commissions Jeremiah, who includes two chapters of explicit calls to repentance (see *Jeremiah 3–4*). Even Jesus' citation of

> **God waits out of His desire for people to return to Him.**

Hosea 6:6 comes in the general context of His call for people to give up their self-serving ways and to follow Him.

No text explains why God waits about 260 years to issue the command to exterminate the Amalekites. None of these passages, including *Exodus 34*, explain why God is slow to anger or why He might wait three or four generations to visit iniquity. However, it is consistent with the steadfast love of God to argue that God waits out of His desire for people to return to Him. God's patience is prompted by His steadfast love. God's willingness to delay punishment for 400 years is rooted in His steadfast love. His steadfast love stubbornly delays punishment, giving the people in question adequate time to hear about His ways, witness His actions, and to give up their wicked ways.

> God sent Jonah to warn the inhabitants of Nineveh that He planned to destroy the city. They were given forty days to repent. It turned out to be ample time as the king led the people in turning back to God.

God's steadfast love makes quick and immediate retribution questionable. The Genesis account of the Flood only speaks about the depth of human sin and the violent and complete punishment of the human race. However, the NT texts point out the time delay between the announcement of the Flood and its coming, even calling Noah a preacher in addition to a boat builder.[10] The one hundred years it takes for Noah to build the ark provide sufficient time for the people to repent. The preaching of Noah is an expression of God's offer of clemency. In a similar fashion, God's steadfast love delays the command to utterly destroy the Amalekites.

None of the passages about the Amalekites point to any effort on God's part to urge change in their behavior. We simply know that God delays their violent discipline for 260 years. One might argue that during those years God orchestrates other nonviolent attempts

[10]See *Mt 24:37f.; Lk 3:36; 17:26f.; Heb 11:7; 1Pet 3:20; 2Pet 2:5*

to prompt repentance. Such conclusions would be consistent with God's steadfast love.

God's steadfast love in *Hosea* and *Jeremiah*, to cite just two cases highlighted in this book, result in the destruction of the people God loves. In both books God's compassionate nature delays the time of final discipline, but God ultimately punishes out of His loyalty to His people and His desire for them to fully know His mercy. In contemporary language, God's steadfast love was the original "tough love." The popular "tough love" concept acknowledges that discipline is a logical and consistent response of love toward people whose behavior endangers their own well-being. God's discipline of the Amalekites might be conceived as among the most radical form of tough love acts in human history.

God's steadfast love was the original "tough love."

God's steadfast love is not associated with any of the texts regarding the Amalekites, but a God of steadfast love would act toward rebellious people such as the Amalekites in the way presented in Scripture, delaying punishment, seeking during that delay their change of heart, and using that threatened discipline as the ultimate expression of loyalty and hope of granting mercy.

CONCLUSION

That visit with a fellow student in the campus center at the University of Wisconsin, Milwaukee, ended without resolution for him or me, but it started me on a journey to explain to myself what I could not clarify for him. I went to the most violent sections of the Bible. Few people in the ancient world were as violent as the Amalekites. Their aggression was rooted in personal gain. They wanted the fields of other people. They stole the goods of neighboring peoples. They used cruelty to enrich themselves. I cannot justify their self-centered use of violence.

The material about the Amalekites also reflects some of God's most violent moments. When I began, I too was appalled at the thought of God telling His prophet, Samuel, to hew Agag into pieces. If I had stopped there, I would never have discovered the bigger picture.

The series of events surrounding the Amalekites suggest that God was acting in a way that was consistent with and implied by what He revealed about His inner character. The example of the Amalekites permits us to see how a God who loves the entire world can also call for vengeance, how a God who forbids killing can use death as the ultimate expression of His inner person. It is not inconsistent for God to use violence.

God's use of violence is selective. The world could not endure many floods like Noah faced or exterminations like the one faced by the Amalekites. In light of God's nature, our experience of the world is surprising.

> It is not inconsistent for God to use violence, though He is slower to anger than we could imagine.

We would expect more floodlike experiences and more commands such as the one given to Saul. God may be slower to anger than we can possibly imagine. His sense of justice may be beyond our comprehension. His expression of steadfast love undergirds the continuation of the human race.

God uses violence to discipline, punish, and threaten in both testaments. These actions are closely associated with His heart for patience, mercy, and justice. His consistent use of violence prompts us to think that somewhere in His heart there exists a willingness to use violence to accomplish His righteousness and justice. It is not what we expect to hear when we put our ears next to His chest, but after sober reflection, it is a message we want to hear.

WHAT DO YOU SAY?

1. Before reading this chapter, what were your thoughts about a God who destroys cities and people?

2. Review some of the history of the Amalekites: *Gen 14:7; Ex 17:8; Num 13:29; 14:25; 14:43-45; Deu 25:17-19; Jdg 6–7, 10:12.* What is their relationship to God? To Israel?

3. God delays in destroying the Amalekites, the people in Noah's time, and Sodom and Gomorrah. These delays point to His patience. Read *2 Peter 3:1-10.* What is being delayed in this passage? What is the purpose of the delay? How does this relate to God's inner character?

4. Three qualities of God are slowness to anger, justice, and steadfast love. Explain how these qualities are part of God's nature when He calls for utter destruction of the Amalekites and allows His prophet to brutally kill King Agag.

5. Perhaps even today God is being patient with us or other nations in the world, waiting for people to change their hearts and follow Him. We can view God's patience as our opportunity. How can you respond to this opportunity?

CHAPTER FIFTEEN

CARE FOR THE FATHERLESS: RUNNING HOME TO GOD

Begin your study of this chapter by reading *Psalm 68*.

The investigation into the heart of God is never finished. We cannot wrap up our study with the satisfaction that we have explored every issue that is important to God or conclude that we now understand His heart. Although I follow my methodology to its logical conclusion, there may be another proposal that would reveal additional features of the heart of God. This study may prompt other investigations that will help us to understand and know God.

The Bible testifies to God's willingness to be known. A divine being presents us with images and words that give us insight into His being. He speaks in our language about concepts that are beyond our language. He tells us what He wants us to know, what we are able to know, and to some degree, what we want to know. We could not investigate the heart of God if He were unwilling for us to probe who He is.

One of the terms used to describe God is Father. Both testaments call God "Father," but the NT develops the father-child relationship to a deeper degree. Christopher J.H. Wright provides a helpful introduction to this material in his *Knowing God the Father*, and his efforts inform our reflections in this chapter. Wright argues that through understanding God as Father we can more easily identify with the tender, accessible side of God.

One of God's passions that we can hear is His concern for the orphan.

One use of God as Father that probes more deeply into His heart than the others is God's concern for the orphaned child. God's relationship to these children is not gathered together in any one place in Scripture, but scattered in both testaments, yet the language used of God's concern for the orphaned child points to how significant this relationship is to God. This language suggests that if we pressed our ears to hear His heartbeat, one of the passions we would hear about is God's concern for the orphan. We begin with a general reflection on God as Father, then proceed to texts that characterize God's concern for the orphan, and conclude with implications of the investigation for understanding the heart of God.

GOD AS FATHER

God is often called Father. In the NT, God is called *Father* of our Lord Jesus Christ (*Rom 15:6*), *father* of mercies and all comfort (*2Cor 1:3*), and *father* of glory (*Eph 1:17*). God is also *father* of spirits (*Heb 12:9*), of lights (*Jas 1:17*), and *father* of us all (*Eph 4:6*). In the OT, God is *father* of Israel (*Isa 64:8*), of Abraham (*Isa 63:16*), and of the king (*Ps 2:6-7*).

The word "father" appears in the Bible over 1,500 times. Most Christians could name dozens of biblical fathers and sons, from Adam and his sons, Cain and Abel, to Zebedee and his sons, James and John. We could cite several father and daughter relationships, including the elusive "daughters of men" in *Genesis 6:1-4*, Terah and his daughter, Sarah (*Gen 20:12*), and Philip and his four unmarried daughters (*Acts 21:9*).

Indeed, some of our favorite lines of Scripture call God our Father. The line *"Our **Father** in heaven, hallowed be your name"* begins the Lord's Prayer. We baptize in the *"name of the **Father** and of the Son and of the Holy Spirit,"* according to Jesus' Great Commission. In His Sermon on the Mount, Jesus said, *"In the same way, let your light shine before others, so that they may see your good works and give glory to your **Father** in heaven"* (*Mt 5:16*).

God's desire to be called *Father* initially seems at odds with the disparate legacy of human *fathers* in the Bible, some of which are described in the box below. We understand Him as lord, creator, the holy one of Israel, and redeemer, but in light of the experiences that so many inside and outside the Bible have with their parents, why would God seek to be our *father*? The Bible *never* uses a human example to explain God as Father. God does not say "I want to be your father like Abraham was Isaac's father" or "Let me be to you as David was to Solomon" or "You can see me as James and John looked at Zebedee." God as father is not based on a specific human father and his children.

Many biblical sons and daughters did not have good fathers. We can only guess at what kind of a father Cain (*Gen 4:17*) or Eli (*1Sa 2:12; 4:17*) might have been. Even the most famous father-son relationships have huge questions around them. How did Isaac raise a deceitful Jacob and vengeful Esau? The haunting failure of David with his sons Amnon and Absalom (*2Sa 13–18*) alarms every generation who hears those stories.

Yet, despite the failure of many biblical and contemporary fathers, good examples also abound. Abraham seeks to be a good father. When Ishmael and Isaac are born, he exhibits behavior that we both shun and approve. We wince at his sending Ishmael away (*Gen 21:8f.*) and agonize with his desperate decision to sacrifice Isaac (*Gen 22:1*). His obvious concern for both sons and his efforts to *"charge his children . . . to keep the way of the LORD by doing righteousness and justice"* (*Gen 18:19*) attract our admiration and attention.

The entire book of Job revolves around Job's care for his sons and daughters, his grief over their loss, and the birth of a second family. His interest in their spiritual lives stands as a high point in biblical fatherhood (*Job 1:5*). His self-described lifestyle makes him a desirable man to call "dad" (*Job 31*).

Joseph's loving response to Mary's pregnancy seems consistent with the kind of father he becomes for Jesus in the all-too-brief glimpses provided in the Gospels. The image of distraught Mary and Joseph searching Jerusalem for their twelve-year-old illustrates his concern.

Jesus paints a portrait of a wonderful father in the *Luke 15* parable of the prodigal son. The father's faithful waiting for the younger boy's return, his warm welcome to the prodigal, and his kind conversation with his now-alienated older son offer another significant example of what a good father should do.

God as our father *is* based on the relationship Jesus had with God. At age 12, when Joseph and Mary found Him in the temple, Jesus asked, *"Did you not know that I must be in my Father's house?"* (**Lk 2:48**). In **John 10:15**, Jesus said, *"just as the Father knows me . . . I know the Father."* Later, He claims to be one with the Father (**Jn 10:30**), and no one comes to the Father except through Him (**Jn 14:6**). In **John 15:1**, He says His Father is the gardener, and in His prayers near the end of His earthly life, He addresses God as Father (**Jn 17:1; Mt 26:39**). On the cross, Jesus cries, *"Father, into your hands I commend my spirit!"* (**Lk 23:46**).

The perfect, healthy, mutually beneficial father-son relationship which existed between God and Jesus becomes the model for our relationship with God and for our roles as earthly fathers. Whatever our relationship with our own biological father, we rest our lives in the way God the Father cared for Jesus the Son. Although we may experience anguish or regret in our own relationships with our earthly fathers, we can find satisfaction and joy in developing the kind of loving relationship that God modeled with Jesus.

> **The perfect father-son relationship of God and Jesus becomes our model.**

GOD AS FATHER
TO A SPECIAL GROUP

One aspect of the role God plays as Father comes in the unique relationship God has with orphans. God's concern for this group of people sheds significant light on one of God's passions. To fully understand this relationship, we begin by exploring the nature of being an orphan and then turn to God's concern for them.

CHILDREN ALONE

The OT describes orphaned children as fatherless. The word usually translated as "fatherless" is the Hebrew word *yathom* (which appears 42 times in the OT). It comes from a root that means to be alone or sad. It is often thought that these children lost a father to war. Imagine, for example, the number of eighth-century Jerusalem children left fatherless after the North Israelite king Pekah killed 120,000 Judeans in battle (**2Chr 28:6**). Children who lost their fathers in the present war, whose mothers were then solely responsible for their upbringing, are called by this term. There is no case in the OT where a child clearly loses both parents.

The contemporary words used to describe at-risk children provide an insight into the different cultures of our time.[1] In an earlier generation, Americans often spoke of "orphans." That word is used less often in contemporary society, but has been replaced by phrases such as "parentless children" or "children left alone," or children who are "wards of the state." Perhaps we have dropped our use of the word "orphan" because to most English speakers it connotes the loss of both mother and father, which does not fit the description of the majority of at-risk children today. It is difficult to use the word "orphan" to describe a child whose mother and father are still living, but simply do not want or cannot care for the child.

The English word "orphan" comes from the Greek word *orphanos* (used twice in the NT) which means to be deprived of one's parents. Jesus used the word to assure His followers that Christians would not be left alone, that is, they would not be deprived of their Father's care (*Jn 14:18*). James links such children with widows as the objects of true religious practice (*Jas 1:27*). Widows are deprived of a husband just as children are deprived of parents. The use of the word suggests that such children are vulnerable economically and socially.

God's concern for orphans runs throughout the Bible.

God's concern for orphans runs throughout the Bible. That concern can be taken up in three ways: First, God takes on the role as father to the fatherless as in *Psalm 68*. Secondly, God regularly calls His people to take care of orphans. Third, God makes the care of orphans the object of *"religion that is pure and undefiled before God, the Father."*

CHILDREN NOT ALONE

The Father of Psalm 68

Psalm 68 takes up significant language to describe God's relationship to orphaned children. It begins with a call for God to rise up and be worshiped (*vv. 1-4*), followed by a long description of God's acts or

---

[1]Jackson (**128-187**) assembles authors who offer historical perspectives on how different cultures perceive fatherless children.

attributes (*vv. 5-31*) and a closing renewed call to praise (*vv. 32-35*). The psalm takes a historical approach to describing God by mentioning God's work in the wilderness, the conquest, and at the temple. Most of the psalm depicts God's power and transcendence except for two verses near the beginning:

> ⁵ Father of orphans and protector of widows
>   is God in his holy habitation.
> ⁶ God gives the desolate a home to live in;
>   he leads out the prisoners to prosperity,
>   but the rebellious live in a parched land. (**Ps 68:5-6**)

All four of the groups that God helps in this passage are people outside normal relationship networks: The orphan lacks at least one parent, the widow is without a husband, the desolate is literally one who

Among God's mighty works, the psalmist does not ignore those that are so often overlooked.

is alone, and the prisoner—in this case probably an unjustly detained political prisoner—is walled off from the people he knows on the outside. The psalmist recognizes some of the mighty works God does from how the earth quakes when He walks to how He defeats His enemies, but does not ignore the events that are less known and easily overlooked such as providing solace for the isolated. Although, as we shall see below, God calls for people to tend to the orphans and widows, here it is God Himself who provides the comfort. Throughout Scripture both the widow and the orphan fall under His special care. Our focus is on the orphan.

To fully understand how God is father to the fatherless, it is helpful to explore some other uses of the familial relationships connected with the term "father." Believers in God are often called sons and daughters of God, which does not mean any kind of biological relationship but rather uses the intimacy of the human father-child relationship to express some of the intimacy of the God-believer relationship. Similarly, God does not adopt an orphan child in that He goes before a human court that assigns Him parental rights. Rather, the compassion, empathy, and love that an adoptive parent brings to an adopted child characterize God's concern for the orphan. What is significant in *Psalm 68* is that the orphan is a real orphan. When Christians are called sons of God, they are actual humans who are spiritual children of God. In this passage orphan and widow are not symbolic roles, but they are real people. The God who willingly depicts Himself as Father to His spiritual offspring now goes beyond that willingness to depict Himself as the Father to those who have no caring parent. The significance of God being Father to the fatherless is best understood by looking at the image from below and above.

From below (i.e., from the point of view of the orphan), we understand that while most children identify a certain male figure as their biological father, a smaller group of children whose biological father is dead or absent have a surrogate Father in God. While God does not parent in the same way as a present biological father does, such as providing food, clothing, and shelter, God as adoptive father to these unfortunate children can do much that a biological father cannot do. If this view from the bottom were properly understood among those who believe in God, the orphaned children of the world might have more "aunts and uncles" helping the Father of the fatherless.

> **Orphaned children should have countless "aunts and uncles" helping the Father of the fatherless.**

From above (i.e., from God's perspective), we understand that God, who knows every hair on every human scalp, has a special knowledge of a group of children who lack present parents. If this passage about orphans is taken seriously, then God's heart has special concern for these children. God clearly loves the entire world, but this text, when viewed from above, suggests that those qualities of God that humans find so attractive are expressed in a unique way by God to His adopted children who have no caring earthly parents. If this theological perspective were clearly understood by children without caring parents, their view of life might be substantially different.

Given that God takes the role of surrogate father for orphaned children, two other pieces of biblical material find theological explanation: The regular refrain of concern for orphans and widows found throughout the Bible and the *"pure religion"* text in **James**.

The Father of the Orphan Refrain

The OT deals with orphans in different ways, which are outlined in the box overleaf. Beyond these ways are two other uses of orphans in the OT that are intimately tied to God: One expresses God's personal concern for the orphan, and a second describes God's call for the care of orphans.

Ways in which the OT deals with orphans:

1 — laws and commands protecting orphans (*Ex 22:22; Deu 24:17, 19-21; 27:19; Pss 10:18; 82:3*)
2 — curses in which the offender's children will be orphaned (*Ex 22:24; Ps 109:9,12; Isa 9:17*)
3 — means to provide for orphans (*Deu 14:29; 16:11,14; 26:12-13*)
4 — ill treatment of orphans used as examples of wickedness (*Job 6:27; 22:9; 24:3,9; Ps 94:6; Isa 1:23; 10:2; Jer 5:28*)
5 — examples of people who care for orphans (*Job 29:12; 31:17,21; Ps 10:14-18*)
6 — the plight of orphans used to describe the misery of others (*Lam 5:3*)

There is a small group of texts represented by *Psalm 68:5*, mentioned above, that show God's direct concern with the orphan. One such passage links God's concern for orphans with His grandeur:

> ¹⁷*For the LORD your God is God of gods and Lord of lords, the great God, mighty and awesome, who is not partial and takes no bribe,* ¹⁸*who executes justice for the orphan and the widow, and who loves the strangers, providing them food and clothing.* ¹⁹*You shall also love the stranger, for you were strangers in the land of Egypt.* (**Deu 10:17-19**)

As in many of these texts, the orphan is linked with the widow and stranger. The passage points out that the lofty, transcendent God knows of and is concerned about the weakest members of society. Strikingly, this passage which begins with lines that have inspired poems and music about God concludes with reference to God's concern for the isolated. The text anticipates *Psalm 68*'s claim that God is the Father of the orphans. It explains that God uses His justice for their benefit. Another passage reflects the same general concern: *"The LORD watches over the strangers; he upholds the orphan and the widow, but the way of the*

The transcendent God knows of and is concerned about the weakest members of society.

wicked he brings to ruin" (**Ps 146:9**). The word "uphold" has the idea of surrounding or restoring the orphan and widow, suggesting God as the protector of these vulnerable classes of people.

In *Hosea 14:3* North Israel learns that God will be merciful to their orphans, apparently a reference to those who survive the fall of Samaria, while in *Jeremiah 49:10* God promises the Edomites that after their destruction He will care for their orphans. God's punishment often creates orphans. God knows about those vulnerable children and promises to provide for them.

The Father of the Prophetic Call

A series of five prophetic texts show the ongoing concern for orphans in the latter part of OT history. In the eighth century, Isaiah critiques Jerusalem for their lack of proper care for the orphans (*Isa 1:17*).

According to the book of *Isaiah*, there are four positions one can take with regard to children who do not have fathers.

First, some intentionally *defend* the fatherless. Isaiah wrote his first chapter to the religious people of Jerusalem. In order for their worship to be acceptable to God, defending orphans was a priority (*Isa 1:16-17*).

Second, some intentionally *oppress* orphans. In meetings they make laws that hurt fatherless children or they write documents that urge others to take advantage of them. The Israelites in Samaria oppressed the orphans in their community (*Isa 10:1-2*).

Third, some intentionally *despise* orphans because of what their fathers did. Perhaps there is no more severe curse in the OT than the promise to ignore the children of those who are about to die. Few take this role in Scripture. One who does is God. He tells the Israelites in Samaria that they have crossed the line and that He will have no compassion on their orphaned children (*Isa 9:17*).

Fourth, some do *nothing* with regard to the fatherless. They do not take any of the other three positions. They do not hurt orphans or defend them or turn away from them. They just do nothing (*Isa 1:23*). *Isaiah 1–5* reflects on the people who take this stance. They do not appear to intend to hurt orphans, but are just preoccupied with other things. They are busy shopping (*3:18-23*), building houses in the suburbs (*5:8*), and attending parties (*5:11-12*)—not evil activities in themselves, but wrong when it made them forget what they should be doing.

Chapter 15 Running Home to God

305

Over a century later, in the late seventh and the beginning of the sixth century BC, the same assessment is repeated in the same city by Jeremiah (*Jer 7:6; 22:3*). In exile during the middle of the sixth century, Ezekiel again draws attention to society's duties to the orphan (*Eze 22:7*). After the return from Babylonian captivity, Zechariah is called by the elders to address a question about fasting. Before he gives a response, he tells the people about their priorities, including care for the orphans of the late sixth century (*Zec 7:10*). Finally, *Malachi 3:5* raises the same concern in the middle of the fifth century. The chart below shows the regular historical concern in Israel for orphans.

Century	Location	Prophet	Passage
8th	Jerusalem	Isaiah	"defend the orphan, plead for the widow" (*Isa 1:17*)
7th	Jerusalem	Jeremiah	"do not oppress the alien, the orphan, and the widow" (*Jer 7:6*)
6th	Babylon	Ezekiel	"the orphan and the widow are wronged in you" (*Eze 22:7*).
6th	Jerusalem	Zechariah	"do not oppress the widow, the orphan, the alien, or the poor" (*Zec 7:10*).
5th	Jerusalem	Malachi	"I will . . . bear witness against . . . those who oppress . . . the orphan" (*Mal 3:5*)

There is a constant concern for orphans in the Mosaic Law, *Psalms, Proverbs, Job*, and the prophets. This regular refrain reflects God's personal concern for these vulnerable children in His self-appointed role as Father of the fatherless.

The Father of Pure Religion

James takes up Christian conduct, explaining the many ways that Christian behavior makes them either friends or enemies of God (*4:4*). The book stresses concern for the weak and vulnerable (*1:27; 2:1-10; 5:1-6*). The latter part of *James 1* calls for conduct that reflects "*God's righteousness*" (*1:20*) and the ways to live that are "*blessed in their doing*" (*1:25*). In effect, James's prescription for Christian living is a reflection of God's own passions. Given that James wants to help his readers in their friendship with God by leading lives that are a reflection of the divine, the striking language of the conclusion of *James 1* comes as no surprise: *"Religion that is pure and undefiled before God, the Father, is this: to care for orphans and widows in their distress, and to keep oneself unstained by the world"* (*Jas 1:27*). The discussion of the external traits of one's religion stated negatively in *James 1:26* (those who *"think they are religious"*) is now stated positively and defined in its *"pure and undefiled"* state. This state is not defined by humans but by God. James suggests, to use the Rembrandt-inspired metaphor, that when one listens to the heartbeat of God for what external practice is closest to God's heart, what one hears is a concern for the orphan and widow.

> **James's prescription for Christian living is a reflection of God's own passions.**

Although the father image appears frequently in the NT describing God as Father, Christians as His children, and people of faith as adopted sons and daughters,[2] the description of God as Father here suggests some allusion to *Psalm 68:5*. It is consistent that the God who proclaims Himself Father of the fatherless would make caring for the fatherless a *"religion that is pure and undefiled."* When Christians care for orphans, they are being big brothers and sisters for God's own children.

James's unique reference to orphans puts his book in the mainstream of biblical thinking. James mentions the care of orphans only once. There is no other NT reference to the care of fatherless children, nor does anything in the first chapter of James necessarily anticipate the mention of orphans and widows. It is understandable to see how readers might sense some dissonance in this text. James seems to suddenly and unexpectedly raise the care of orphans to the top of the list of Christian living. However, when viewed in light of the theology of the whole Bible, James's statement continues the concern that God made so clear in the OT. James does not invent care of orphans and widows; he inherits this view from God's prior revelation. Readers of all the inspired words of Scripture will find James's line a capstone—or grand finale—to a long trajectory through the Bible that puts the concern for the orphan at the core of God's heart.

[2]This symbolic use of adoption appears in *Rom 8:15,23; 9:4; Gal 4:5; Eph 1:5*.

A WAY INTO HIS HEART

Showing how God's concern for children gives insight into God's heart might be illustrated by an experience I had as the former Soviet Union stood on the verge of collapse. I was part of a preaching team that traveled to the Ukrainian capital of Kiev. We prepared to speak to a large crowd gathered in the auditorium of the Kiev Medical College. We did not know a single person among the hundreds who gathered. Nor did they know us. We had come to speak about Jesus. They had come to hear. After the opening statements, one preacher rose to speak, but before he uttered two or three sentences of his sermon, he stopped. He noticed that many Ukrainian families filled the auditorium. Nobody prepared child care or age-appropriate classes. Instead of launching into his sermon, the preacher asked the parents if they would allow their children to come to the front to join the American preachers for a group photo. The mothers nodded approvingly, the children started toward the front, the preachers picked up the youngest ones in their arms, and for a few chaotic moments we did our best to assemble the group for the photograph. Within ten minutes, the children were back with their parents and the preacher was back into his text.

The preacher, however, had already made a significant point: "We care about your children." The parents sensed that concern and through it understood the hearts of those who came. The Ukrainians were more open to listening to what was said because they knew they were listening to caring hearts.

A discussion about orphans may seem to be an odd place to end a book on the heart of God, but knowing God's deep concern for fatherless children may make two significant points: 1) Just as the Ukrainians gained insight into the foreign American preachers when they showed interest in the Ukrainian children, so we gain insight into God's heart when He shows concern for orphans. 2) God's concern for orphans, in a unique way, confirms all the other beats of His divine heart. Those two thoughts outline the final section of this book.

The juxtaposition of *"religion"* and *"pure and undefiled"* may have jolted the first readers of *James 1* just as it should startle us. Religion often tends to be external, with actions such as church attendance and worship rituals veiling what is actually at work in a human heart. However, religion that is pure and undefiled suggests that the external actions accurately reflect the inner soul of that person.

At the beginning we noted the rough division in theological thinking between the external and internal qualities of God. God is creator, almighty, holy, and ubiquitous. The study of those aspects of God are integral

> **"Pure and undefiled" suggests that the external actions accurately reflect the inner soul.**

to understanding the Christian faith, but our focus has been to press for the more internal qualities of God, to seek out His heart. The writer of *Psalm 68* obviously has the same extremes in mind when, in the midst of long descriptions of God's visible power and deeds, he focuses on God's tending to those who are alone. The image of the powerful and almighty God caring for the needs of orphans and widows may jolt us when we first hear of it, but further reflection on God's attention to the vulnerable reveals critical details about the heart of the powerful and almighty God.

There are orphaned children all over the contemporary world. There are several hundred thousand children in the United States who are wards of the various states. These children live in residential care facilities, in foster care, in adoptive families, or with their biological parents under the watchful eye of a supervising agency. Substantially more children in Africa live without at least one parent as the result of violence, AIDS, and other calamities. Natural disasters in undeveloped nations have left many children without parents in these poverty-strick-

> **This general survey only begins to explore the crisis of today's orphaned children.**

en countries. While in Ukraine, I visited numerous orphanages where children lived in institutional care, many of them victims of the Chernobyl nuclear power plant disaster in 1986. This general survey only begins to explore the crisis of today's orphaned children. The whole picture is beyond my full comprehension. I can identify with the little baby for which my fellow faculty member and his wife provide foster care. I remember the smell and the smile of a little orphan boy that I held in my arms in central China. I can still see the Ukrainian orphans in their institutional beds. But the immensity of the world's orphan population is beyond me.

God, as I understand His heart from Scripture, has abilities beyond my own, more compassion and concern deeper than any human I have ever known, and this God, whose heartbeat we have sought to hear, knows every one of these orphaned children. He is father to each one of them. He is *baba* to that little Chinese boy, *papa* to the Ukrainian girl, *mzazi* to the African child whose parents died of AIDS, and *tatay* to the youngster in the Philippines. I do not mean to sentimentalize God. This study does not aim to reduce our thinking about God into a formless emotional response, but rather to help us to see deeply into His heart through His concern for a group of children that still dot our human landscape. By telling us He is Father to the fatherless, God reveals a significant part of His inner being, gives us access to His heart, allows us to know Him at an intimate level.

In a sense, God as the father of the fatherless gives us a more concrete expression of the God who reveals Himself through concepts such as steadfast love, justice, and righteousness. In fact, God's concern for the orphan is the exact heart we would expect from a God whose inner qualities have been discussed in this book.

> **God knows and is father to each of these orphaned children.**

CONCLUSION

God does not act the way we often want Him to act, nor do we necessarily find in His heart the qualities we expect. God is not a

Santa Claus who brings us all we desire, nor is He a dispassionate force unable to hear our cries. God desires to be known by us but does not fully reveal Himself. We must never mistakenly conclude that we fully understand Him. I believe every aspect of God explored in this book finds a focus in fatherless children. There might be other ways to summarize the heart of God, but all of the divine passions we have explored in this book fall somewhere on the spectrum between the image of God as Father of the fatherless and the call for the practice of *"religion that is pure and undefiled before God, the Father"* (*Jas 1:27*). That does not make this a book about orphans, but it does suggest that biblically we cannot speak of God's heart and all that makes Him smile without talking about the world's most vulnerable people.

We have symbolically pressed our spiritual ears against God's chest to listen to His heartbeat. In seeking to know His heart, we have learned of His special concern for the world's orphaned children. He is their Father. He had

> **We cannot speak of God's heart without talking about the world's most vulnerable people.**

the writers of Scripture from every era of biblical history stress His concern for those who are isolated from networks of human concern. James gathers all that revelation into one simple sentence: Concern for these is pure and undefiled religion in the heart of God.

The presence of millions of orphaned children in the world initially prompts us to wonder why there are so many and why they are in such desperate situations if God has taken the role as their Father. We may think He is not being a very good Father to these children He has adopted. Yet what we see of God's work with orphans parallels His activity in *Genesis*. At times God's work is obvious; at other times He does not seem to be around. Human evil seems to triumph. Yet in the end, God takes that evil human intent and turns it into good. Orphans often seem to suffer as the result of human evil. Despite that evil intent, God works good. For years, nobody could see how God was working good in Joseph's life, but He was and He did. Nobody can see how God is working good in the lives of these orphans, but He is and He will. It may not be the way we wish God worked, but God works in providential ways we often do not see.

Human sin does not go unnoticed by God. It grieves Him to His heart. Despite His regular commands and reminders to the human race to take care of the widows and orphans, humans often do neither. Wars produce more orphans. Some humans hoard resources that could feed others who are starving. Such behavior at one time caused God to grieve to the extent that He destroyed a world full of sinners by a flood, but it did not change the human race. Sin, even sin against vulnerable children, continues to spread, noticed and grieved over by God, who now takes other measures to combat this evil.

> **God works in providential ways we often do not see.**

Among those measures is God's promise to be with us. In the most unexpected ways, God pulls alongside people who seek Him and orphans who need Him. The God who repeatedly promises to be with His people gives that promise concrete form in His claim to be Father of the fatherless. In ways that even our biological fathers cannot parent us, God parents these parentless children.

God's promise to be with us prompts Him to come to us. He comes with might and tenderness, as *Isaiah 40* teaches, but then comes as a baby, as Jesus, as the crucified Son of God, as Immanuel, giving up heaven to move into our neighborhood. Jesus taught us that the kingdom He leads is made up of children and those who are like children. Perhaps an unrecognized expression of God with us is His role as parent of parentless children. God is Father to each of the world's orphaned children, being with them in a unique and special way.

God's intent is to bless the world. His first words to the first humans invoked the blessing. His promise to Abraham promised blessing through Abraham's children. Blessing is the unique theological term that speaks especially to children. Jesus offered the little children His blessing. God's substantial blessing to the parentless child is to step in as the surrogate Father, being present for them in place of the ones who brought that child into the world. God expresses solidarity and blessing to the world's orphaned children by being their father.

The claims for God's heart would be audacious if it were not for His claim to be unique. There is no one like Him who is what He is and who does what He does. His concerns, demands, and power arise out of His distinctiveness. God expresses this part of who He is by taking the name Jealous. In a world that increasingly values pluralism, God demands adherence to a narrower set of beliefs and values. Among those qualities is God's sensitivity to the brokenhearted in the world, among whom are the orphans. The orphans are singled out as an expression of God's heart. God loves the entire world, but pays special attention to the brokenhearted. God hears the cries of the brokenhearted, especially those who are orphans.

God's self-disclosure in *Exodus 34:5-7* and the statement of His delight in *Jeremiah 9:24* reveal elements of His inner nature. Many of these elements are relationship-oriented: He reveals His name, operates with mercy, grace, steadfast love, and faithfulness. He delights in a righteousness that champions justice with steadfast love. When those with whom He seeks relationship fail, His anger is slow in coming and does not last long. Often He delays discipline for several generations. Given a God with this kind of heart, it comes as no surprise that He hears the cries of the broken and acts on them, that He parents the parentless and consistently calls attention to their plight.

> **God loves the entire world, but pays special attention to the brokenhearted.**

The world's orphans bring the injustice and unfairness of life into plain focus. Clearly lacking in any responsibility for their difficulties, parentless children are weak, vulnerable, and dependent. Human evil and wickedness often cause their plight and regularly intensify their predicament. The injustice of this situation must be addressed. Knowing the heart of God, we can say with certainty that these injustices will be addressed, clearly and finally.

Jesus' story in *Luke 15* depicts a father waiting for his wayward child to come home. When the returning son comes into view, the father springs into action. He runs. He embraces. He kisses. He calls for a celebration. The father represents God who shows compassion and welcomes the son home.

We join that son in the moment when he understands, as never before, the heart of his father. We join him in listening to the father's heartbeat. When we do, we know that we have come home.

WHAT DO YOU SAY?

1 Isaiah gives four positions one can take with regard to the fatherless:

a. Defend the fatherless

b. Oppress orphans

c. Despise orphans

d. Have nothing to do with the fatherless

Does one of these positions describe your present thinking about orphans? If not, how would you describe the position you take with orphans? Is this position biblical?

2. Make a list of fatherless children you know. Spend time praying for each child.

3. Make a list of people or agencies that are caring for "at-risk children." Spend time in prayer for these caretakers.

4. God has always cared for the widow and orphan. How did God show care and concern for these: Ishmael, Hagar, Naomi, Ruth, Lot, Esther?

5. How can we better practice *James 1:27* concerning pure and undefiled religion in:

a. our families

b. our churches

c. our community

d. our world

AFTERWORD

A few short strides take me back to the curtain,
And crossing that mortal line, I descend
From Sinai's peak. No wonder Moses wore a veil
After speaking with the Lord; no wonder I am wrapped
In a shroud that sheds divinity.

—Nathan Shank

The words above are from the perspective of the high priest as he returns from an encounter with God on the Day of Atonement. The priest's experience mirrors that of Moses when he comes down from the wondrous *Exodus 34* experience with God. Both men grasp something new about God; both now see their Lord in a different, brighter light. Hopefully this book has helped you, the reader, see God in a new way.

This book has helped us, the proofreaders and sounding boards for this book, see God in a different way. For starters, the two of us have had the wonderful opportunity to spend a lot of time with this material. We read the early drafts and gave feedback on what did and did not fit. We "growled" over each chapter and text and considered how each one helps us listen to God's heartbeat. We have been able to contribute our own thoughts to the book, which has let us express how we have heard God's heartbeat in our own lives. In the process of searching for misplaced commas and unclear sentences, we have been on our own quest of knowing what is in God's heart.

Now that the proofreading is finished and the dust is settling, we think it is appropriate to share what we have learned from our time

> **It's hard to deny that people now are overwhelmingly interested in the relational aspect of God.**

of pondering over both this book and God's Word. One question we both had coming into the writing project was how this book would speak to our generation. At the time of this writing, we are both in our early twenties, members of what many people have called the "postmodern" generation. Whether or not you believe that the world has moved into a postmodern mind-set, it's hard to deny that people at the moment are overwhelmingly interested in the relational aspect of God. While that interest may be an inherent part of human nature, it has certainly been brought to the forefront in recent years. This book speaks to that interest—indeed that *need*—of knowing God personally and relationally.

One aspect of God both of us have come to appreciate is how *relational* He is. He is not a God who sits on His throne across the street and pays no attention to His creation. He is a God who sits on our couch and is there for us when we need Him. He is a God who is delighted when we act like Him, who is heartbroken when we act selfishly. This is a God who is "with us," who comes to us on our own terms. This is a God who cares about people—more than that, He cares about getting to know people.

Another aspect of God we find relevant for our generation is that He is *multifaceted*. In this book there are many personal stories that reveal facets of the author's life. All the stories, though coming from different ages and perspectives, emotional contexts and social settings, describe one person. Just as the author's stories show he has depth and diversity to his makeup, God's stories reveal that He has many sides: He is both compassionate and punitive, forgiving and jealous, slow to anger but fearsome when provoked. At the same time, these many sides describe the same Person. Humans are complex because they reflect the multifaceted nature of their Creator. The fact that God has such a diverse personality makes Him that much more appealing to a generation that values relationships.

Finally, we see in a new light the *stories* about Him. Stories are powerful, and one of the best ways people in our generation relate to one another is through stories. We both have heard Bible stories since we were children, but those stories take on new meaning in light of studying God's heart. As children we may have known the story of Jesus in the manger, but we could not have comprehended the depth of the name Immanuel or the significance of calling God "Father." As teens we may have been bored and confused by Micah and Jeremiah, but as we've grown older have begun to realize the magnitude of righteousness and justice. People of our generation can appreciate the depth of the Bible's stories; people older than us can continue to read the Bible in ways that are fresh and new. Although age does not guarantee wisdom or maturity, we have found that the older we become, the richer and broader the Bible's stories can become. We hope the same is true for readers of this book, regardless of their age.

> **May all of us yearn to listen to God's heartbeat, and want to know Him more and more.**

Ultimately, we hope this book helps *you* see God in a different light. Just as the high priest and Moses saw God's glory and were forever changed by the experience, and just as our study has helped the two of us see Him in a brighter, more vivid light, we hope that you have caught a glimpse of the glory and the relational nature of God's heart. Our generation needs light in this world; may they find it in who God is. May all of us yearn to listen to God's heartbeat, and may we want to know Him more and more.

Peter Cariaga and Nathan Shank
Oklahoma City, Oklahoma
September 5, 2008

WHAT OTHER AUTHORS SAY

Allen, C. Leonard. *The Cruciform Church*. Abilene: ACU Press, 1990.

Anderson, B.W. "Old Testament View of God." In *The Interpreter's Dictionary of the Bible*, pp. 417-430. Edited by George A. Buttrick. Nashville: Abingdon, 1962.

Anderson, Lynn. *The Shepherd's Song: Finding the Heart to Go On*. West Monroe, LA: Howard, 1996.

Ball, David Mark. *'I Am' in John's Gospel: Literary Function, Background and Theological Implications*. Edited by Stanley E. Porter. Journal for the Study of the New Testament Supplement Series 12. Sheffield: Sheffield Academic Press, 1996.

Birch, Bruce C. "Divine Character and the Formation of Moral Community in the Book of Exodus." *The Bible in Ethics: the Second Sheffield Colloquium*, pp. 119-135. The Library of Hebrew Bible/Old Testament Studies. Sheffield: Sheffield Academic Press, 1995.

Bosch, David J. *Transforming Mission: Paradigm Shifts in Theology of Mission*. Maryknoll, NY: Orbis, 1991.

Bosman, J.P. "The Paradoxical Presence of Exodus 34:6-7 in the Book of the Twelve." *Scriptura* 87 (2004): 233-243.

Breuer, Mordecai. "Dividing the Decalogue into Verses and Commandments." In *The Ten Commandments in History and Tradition*, pp. 291-330. Edited by Ben-Zion Segal. Jerusalem: Magnes Press, 1996.

Bright, John. *A History of Israel*. 4th ed. Philadelphia: Westminster Press, 2000.

Brown, Steve. *Approaching God: Accepting the Invitation to Stand in the Presence of God*. New York: Howard, 2008.

Brueggemann, Walter. *The Book of Exodus: Introduction, Commentary, and Reflections*. The New Interpreter's Bible. Nashville: Abingdon, 1994.

_____. "**Crisis-evoked**, Crisis-resolving Speech." *Biblical Theology Bulletin* 24 (1994): 95-105.

_____. *Deuteronomy.* Abingdon Old Testament Commentaries. Nashville: Abingdon, 2001.

_____. "The Epistemological Crisis of Israel's Two Histories (Jer 9:22-23)." *Israelite Wisdom: Samuel Terrien Festschrift,* pp. 85-105. Missoula, MT: Scholars Press, 1978.

_____. *Genesis.* Interpretation. Atlanta: John Knox, 1982.

_____. "'**Impossibility**' and Epistemology in the Faith Tradition of Abraham and Sarah (Gen 18:1-15)." *Zeitschrift für die alttestamentliche Wissenschaft* 94 (1982): 615-634.

_____. *The Message of the Psalms: A Theological Commentary.* Minneapolis: Augsburg, 1984.

_____. "**Trajectories** in Old Testament Literature and the Sociology of Ancient Israel." *Journal of Biblical Literature* 98 (1979): 161-185.

Camp, Lee. *Mere Discipleship: Radical Christianity in a Rebellious World.* 2nd ed. Grand Rapids: Brazos Press, 2008.

Cassuto, Umberto. *A Commentary on the Book of Exodus.* Jerusalem: Magnes Press, 1959.

Clines, David. *The Theme of the Pentateuch.* Journal for the Study of the Old Testament Supplement Series. 2nd ed. Sheffield: Sheffield Academic Press, 1999.

Cohn, Robert. "Narrative Structure and Canonical Perspective in Genesis." *Journal for the Study of the Old Testament* 25 (1983): 3-16.

Cotham, Perry C. *One World, Many Neighbors: A Christian Perspective on Worldviews.* Abilene, TX: Leafwood, 2008.

Crick, F.H.C. *What a Mad Pursuit: A Personal View of Scientific Discovery.* New York: Basic Books, 1988.

Dahlberg, B.T. "Anger." In *The Interpreter's Dictionary of the Bible,* pp. 135-137. Edited by George A. Buttrick. Nashville: Abingdon, 1962.

Denton, Robert C. "The Literary Affinities of Exodus XXXIV 6f." *Vetus Testamentum* 13 (1963): 34-51.

Diamond, A.R. Pete, and Kathleen M. O'Connor. "Unfaithful Passions: Coding Women Coding Men in Jeremiah 2-3 (4.2)." In *Troubling Jeremiah,* pp. 123-145. Journal for the Study of the Old Testament Supplement Series 260. Edited by A.R. Pete Diamond, Kathleen M. O'Connor, and Louis Stulman. Sheffield: Sheffield Academic Press, 1999.

Dyrness, William A. *Themes in Old Testament Theology*. Downers Grove, IL: InterVarsity, 1977.

Fretheim, Terrence. *Exodus*. Interpretation. Philadelphia: Westminster John Knox Press, 1991.

_____. *The Suffering of God*. Overtures to Biblical Theology. Philadelphia: Fortress, 1998.

Gardner, Lynn. *Where Is God When We Suffer? What the Bible Says about Suffering*. Joplin, MO: College Press, 2007.

Gericke, J.W. "Sounds of Silence: An Anti-realistic Perspective on YHWH's *ipsissima verba* in the Old Testament." *Old Testament Essays* 18 (2005): 61-81.

Glueck, Nelson. *Hesed in the Bible*. New York: Hebrew Union College Press, 1975.

Hanson, Anthony. "John I.14-18 and Exodus XXXIV." *New Testament Studies* 23 (1976): 90-101.

Hawkins, Ralph K. *While I Was Praying: Finding Insights about God in Old Testament Prayers*. Macon, GA: Smyth and Helwys, 2006.

Hays, Richard. *The Moral Vision of the New Testament: A Contemporary Introduction to New Testament Ethics*. New York: HarperCollins, 1996.

Helyes, Larry. "The Separation of Abraham and Lot." *Journal for the Study of the Old Testament* 26 (1983): 77-88.

House, Paul. *Old Testament Theology*. Downers Grove, IL: InterVarsity, 1998.

Jackson, Timothy P., ed. *The Morality of Adoption: Social-Psychological, Theological, and Legal Perspectives*. Grand Rapids: Eerdmans, 2005.

Jacobs, Louis. *The Jewish Religion: A Companion*. New York : Oxford University Press, 1995.

Kaiser, Walter. *Hard Sayings of the Old Testament*. Downers Grove, IL: InterVarsity, 1988.

Keller, Timothy J. *The Prodigal God: Recovering the Heart of the Christian Faith*. New York: Penguin Group/Dutton, 2008.

_____. *The Reason for God: Belief in an Age of Skepticism*. New York: Dutton, 2008.

Laney, J. Carl. "God's Self-Revelation in Exodus 34:6-8." *Bibliotheca Sacra* 158 (2001): 36-51.

Levenson, Jon D. *Creation and the Persistence of Evil*. Princeton: Princeton University Press, 1994.

Lewis, C.S. *Mere Christianity*. New York: Macmillan, 1943.

Mackay, John L. *Exodus*. Mentor Commentary Series. Fearn, Scotland: Christian Focus, 2001.

Martin, Catherine. *Trusting in the Names of God: Drawing Strength from Knowing Who He Is*. Eugene, OR: Harvest House, 2008.

McCann, J. Clinton. "'Abounding in Steadfast Love and Faithfulness': The Old Testament as a Source for Christology." In *In Essentials Unity: Reflections on the Nature and Purpose of the Church: In Honor of Frederick R. Trost*, pp. 206-211. Edited by Frederick R. Trost, M. Douglas Meeks, Robert D. Mutton. Minneapolis: Kirk House, 2001.

McConville, J.G. *God and Earthly Power: An Old Testament Political Theology—Genesis–Kings*. Library of Hebrew Bible/Old Testament Studies 454. New York: T & T Clark, 2006.

McCord, Hugo. *Getting Acquainted with God*. Murfreesboro, TN: DeHoff, 1965.

McKenzie, Steven L. *King David: A Biography*. New York: Oxford, 2000.

Meredith, J.L. *Meredith's Book of Bible Lists*. Minneapolis: Bethany House, 1980.

Mettinger, Tryggve N.D. *In Search of God: The Meaning and Message of the Everlasting Names*. Philadelphia: Fortress, 1988.

Miller, Patrick D. "The Way of Torah." *Princeton Seminary Bulletin* 8 (1987): 22-23.

Mills, Mary. *Images of God in the Old Testament*. Collegeville, MN: Liturgical Press, 1998.

Moberly. R.W.L. *At the **Mountain of God**: Story and Theology in Ex 32–34*. Sheffield: JSOT, 1983.

_____. "How May We **Speak of God**? A Reconsideration of the Biblical Theology." *Tyndale Bulletin* 53 (2002): 177-202.

_____. *The Old Testament of the Old Testament: **Patriarchal Narratives** and Mosaic Yahwism*. Minneapolis: Fortress Press, 1992.

Niditch, Susan. *War in the Hebrew Bible: A Study in the Ethics of Violence*. New York: Oxford, 1993.

Nouwen, Henri J.M. *The Return of the Prodigal Son*. New York: Doubleday, 1992.

Olson, Dennis T. *Deuteronomy and the Death of Moses*. Overtures to Biblical Theology. Minneapolis: Fortress, 1994.

Packer, J.I. *Knowing God*. London: Inter-varsity, 1973.

Parry, Robin. "Ideological Criticism." *Dictionary for Theological Interpretation of the Bible*, pp. 314-316. Edited by Kevin J. Vanhoozer. Grand Rapids: Baker, 2005.

Peterson, Eugene. *Eat This Book: A Conversation in the Art of Spiritual Reading*. Grand Rapids: Eerdmans, 2004.

_____. *The Message*. Colorado Springs: NavPress, 2002.

Preuss, Horst Dietrich. *Old Testament Theology*. Vol 1. Louisville, KY: Westminster John Knox, 1995.

Raitt, Thomas M. "Why Does God Forgive?" *Horizons in Biblical Theology* 13 (1991): 38-58.

Sakenfeld, Katharine Doob. *The Meàning of Hesed in the Hebrew Bible*. Chico, CA: Scholars Press, 1978.

Schwarz, Gerold. "The Legacy of Karl Hartenstein." *International Bulletin of Missionary Research* 8 (1984): 125-131.

Shank, Harold. *Children Mean the World to God*. Nashville: 21st Century Christian, 2001.

_____. "**Justice and Righteousness**: Foundations for Ministry." In *A Handbook on Leadership*, pp. 44-51. Edited by David Duncan. Chickasha, OK: Yeomen Press, 2005.

_____. *Minor Prophets*. The College Press NIV Commentary. Joplin, MO: College Press, 2001.

_____. "The **Six Other Days**—Worship and Ethics." In *In Search of Wonder: A Call to Worship Renewal*, pp. 95-118. Edited by Lynn Anderson. West Monroe, LA: Howard, 1995.

Sheldon, Charles. *In His Steps*. Peabody, MA: Hendrickson, 2004.

Shelly, Rubel. *The Names of Jesus*. West Monroe, LA: Howard, 1999.

Spangler, Ann. *Praying the Names of God—A Daily Guide*. Grand Rapids: Zondervan, 2004.

Swindoll, Charles R. *David: A Man of Passion and Destiny*. Great Lives from God's Word Series. Nashville: Nelson, 1997.

Trible, Phyllis, *God and the Rhetoric of Sexuality*. Overtures to Biblical Theology. Philadelphia: Fortress, 1978.

VanGemeren, W.A. *Interpreting the Prophetic Word*. Grand Rapids: Zondervan, 1990.

Van Leeuwen, Raymond C. "Scribal Wisdom and Theodicy in the Book of the Twelve." In *In Search of Wisdom: Essays in Memory of John G. Gammie*, pp. 31-49. Edited by Leo G. Perdue and Bernard Brandon Scott. Louisville, KY: Westminster John Knox Press, 1993.

Von Rad, Gerhard. *Genesis*. Old Testament Library. Philadelphia: Westminster, 1972.

_____. *Theology of the Old Testament*. New York: Harper and Row, 1962.

Watts, John D.W. *Isaiah 34–66*. Word Biblical Commentary. Waco, TX: Word Books, 1987.

Weinfeld, Moshe. *Deuteronomy 1–11: A New Translation with Introduction and Commentary*. Anchor Bible. Vol. 5. New York: Doubleday, 1991.

Westermann, Claus. *Blessing in the Bible and the Life of the Church*. Overtures to Biblical Theology. Philadelphia: Fortress, 1978.

_____. *The Promises to the Fathers*. Philadelphia: Fortress, 1976.

_____. *Prophetic Oracles of Salvation*. Louisville, KY: Westminster/ John Knox, 1991.

_____. *What Does the Old Testament Say about God?* Atlanta: John Knox Press, 1979.

Wong, Amy Ng. *Guide to God*. Uhrichsville, OH: Humble Creek, 2002.

Wright, Christopher J.H. *Knowing God the Father*. Downers Grove, IL: IVP Academic, 2007.

Yamauchi, Edwin. "Chanan." In *Theological Workbook of the Old Testament*, p. 302. Edited by Gleason Archer, R. Laird Harris, and Bruce Waltke. Chicago: Moody, 2003.

Scripture Index

Scripture Index

329

PROVERBS

ECCLESIASTES

ISAIAH

JEREMIAH

Subject Index

What the Bible
Says Series

What the Bible Says about Worship:
His Story, Our Response (Item #963)
Written by: Dinelle Frankland

It is the only story worthy of such an all-encompassing response. The Response described within these pages are biblical; they offer a glimpse into worship that pleases God, enabling us to discover appropriate and meaningful responses to God who never changes.

What the Bible Says about Suffering:
Where Is God When We Suffer? (Item #719)
Written by: Lynn Gardner

Where Is God When We Suffer? addresses the topic from various perspectives. It begins with Lynn's own personal story of loss and suffering. Dr. Gardner then guides us through a study of both OT & NT examples of suffering. He also describes scriptural principles that offer help and hope for those going through hard times and for the family and friends trying to help them.

What the Bible Says about the Holy Spirit:
Power from On High (Item #517)
Written by: Jack Cottrell

Dr. Jack Cottrell with his "leave no stone unturned" approach to studying Scripture, has completed the research for us as he examines the many concepts and characteristics of the Holy Spirit.